The Right to Learn

Purpose, Professionalism and
Accountability in State Education

Edited by

Caroline Cox and John Marks

Centre for Policy Studies

First published in 1982
by Centre for Policy Studies
8 Wilfred Street, London SW1 E 6PL

Typeset and printed by
Princo B.V., Culemborg, The Netherlands

ISBN 0 905880 39 0

This paper is one of a series of contributions to debate on current economic, social
and political issues. The Centre does not seek to express a corporate view through
its publications, the authors of which are chosen for their independence and
intellectual vigour.

Contents

Change and Obstacles to Change

Evaluating and Monitoring Change in Education: The Role of Research

Education, Society and Culture

The political and economic climate of the 1980s is very different from the brave new dawn of the early 1970s. Many people – especially the young – are avid for a new direction. In education there is widespread and growing anxiety about many of our schools and some of our colleges, as old and young alike become increasingly disillusioned with the left-wing educational "wisdom" of recent years.

The aim of members of the Centre for Policy Studies' Education Study Group is to analyse what has gone wrong and to develop new ideas and policies. For too long, educational "experts" of the left have had the initiative; we are committed to challenging their ideas and turning what is seen as politically unthinkable today into the everyday common sense wisdom of tomorrow. Such re-thinking is vital if we are to preserve and enhance what is best in our educational and cultural heritage and to meet the challenges of the next decade.

These essays mark the beginning of this ambitious, but realistic, programme. The contributors come from a wide variety of social and intellectual backgrounds and draw on firsthand experience in many different educational settings – schools, polytechnics, universities and a college of education. We are united in a common concern for the future of education and in a commitment to certain principles.

Where we stand

We share certain beliefs and values which stem from a coherent intellectual and political position. We believe, for example, that there should be more freedom and more choice in our education system. Over the last fifteen years, education policy has been dominated by an emphasis on equality, including equality of outcome, which has been at the cost of freedom and the development of different abilities and interests of individuals. The result has been the growth of socialist policies which have led to a drastic reduction in freedom of choice and, especially in many secondary schools and some colleges, a levelling down or homogenization in the quality of education.

Alternatives, and freedom to choose between them, are nowadays only available to a very small minority of children – the 5 per cent or so whose parents can choose schools in the private sector. The vast majority have virtually no choice whatsoever. Our commitment to a number of policies designed to increase freedom of choice has far-reaching implications. For example, freedom is spurious if there are no alternatives from which to choose, and "blind" if parents and pupils do not have adequate knowledge with which to make an informed choice. We believe, therefore, that there should be a greater variety of types of school, and we advocate the provision of more information – locally and nationally. Locally, so that parents can choose schools most appropriate for their children's interests and aptitudes and nationally, so that education policies can be based on knowledge rather than prejudice, and policies can be judged by a well informed public.

We share anxieties and worries about recent developments, suspecting, for example, that wholesale comprehensivization has often been harmful, and that such policies as mixed ability teaching may have very undesirable effects, not only for more able children, but also for those who learn more slowly. Most worrying of all, we believe the children most likely to suffer from such changes are not middle class children, whose parents can "work the system" by moving house or by "going private" but working class children who have no alternative but to attend their neighbourhood school.

The quality of much educational research worries us, especially as it has often been used to justify the cherished nostrums of politicians and policymakers. Naturally, we appreciate the need for research. But it must be sound research which gives the public a clear and accurate account of what is going on in our schools and colleges. We therefore recommend that all publicly funded educational research should be subject to stringent scrutiny and that researchers should be required to make relevant information available to the public in a clear and straightforward way.

We believe that our three central commitments – more information, more diversity and more choice – are entirely compatible with the values and ideals of a free society, but are in direct opposition to the values, ideals and policies of the socialist alternative which has been so influential during the past fifteen years. During this time our state education system has been characterized by secrecy and the imposition of an increasingly monolithic structure. We give two examples. The ethos of secrecy is illustrated by the case of a parent governor of a large comprehensive school who cannot obtain information about the examination results of the school of which he is a governor. We believe that this is shocking. For although we all recognize that there is much more to education than examinations, we also know that examination results are important. They are important for pupils, as they provide the basic qualifications with which they enter the world of work. They are important for the public as they give some indication of a school's ,academic attainments – and of how they change over time. We therefore believe that this information should be available together with any other information which the school or the local authority think it would be helpful to provide. This would reduce the danger of the publication of a crude "League Table" of schools. Therefore, we strongly support the present government's policies on this matter and we argue that the withholding of information from those with a legitimate interest is indefensible.

However, we suspect that the educational establishment may have good reasons for withholding details of exam results. For example, we know of one large comprehensive school which did not obtain a single O-level pass in Chemistry and only a handful in Physics – thus eliminating an adequate intake to a science sixth form.

Our second example is the growth of the increasingly monolithic system of secondary education brought about by the enforced imposition of comprehensive schooling, often in the face of strong resistance from parents and teachers. In 1966, less than 10 per cent of our country's schoolchildren were in comprehensive schools; now, over 85 per cent are. Although there are some very good comprehensives, we should be up in arms about the forcible imposition of a monolithic system and the resulting restriction of variety and choice. We know that the previous system had many faults and that for many children it failed to offer alternatives. However, we believe that for many children the remedy is worse than the problem. We are deeply worried about the way the comprehensive system is developing. We therefore argue that it is urgent to restore both more choice and more accountability. How can this be done?

Our Proposals

Clearly, we cannot discuss all the aspects of education in one book, nor can we deal in detail with many which we do consider. However, we believe that our proposals for change are much more radical and progressive than the alternative policies put forward by those on the left. They would go a long way towards making our education system more accountable to the people of our country, more responsible to the needs of society, and more compatible with the ideals of democracy.

i. The purposes and framework of education

Our aim is to provide more freedom in education with a wider variety of schools so as to meet the interests and aptitudes of pupils and to serve the needs of society. We propose, therefore, the establishment *within the state system* of a number of schools in our major cities as "centres of excellence" specializing in particular subject areas. Such specialization could make more efficient use of scarce teaching resources and provide educational opportunities of a higher quality than can be provided in the vast majority of inner city comprehensives. We envisage, for example, specialist schools in languages, mathematics and sciences, technical subjects, arts and humanities, music and drama, and physical education. These schools would also teach the basic "core curriculum", just as the existing specialist music schools do. In this way, children from all backgrounds could have access to opportunities for educational excellence without having to leave the state sector. We are not ashamed of the concept of excellence. In his essay "Educational Fundamentals: The Four Es", Antony Flew explains why and shows that, if we accept the concept of excellence – as we surely must – then this necessarily implies the existence of elites and is incompatible with any educational philosophy which aims at equality of outcome as one of its goals. The article also shows that belief in the necessity for external examinations is a touchstone for distinguishing those who take teaching and learning to be the primary purposes of education, compared with those who would downgrade – or even do away with – these purposes.

We also believe that the education system should be more accountable both to parents in particular and to society in general. In the chapter "Accountability and the Purposes of Education", John Marks and Caroline Cox analyse the purposes of education – both in school and post-school – and relate them to suggestions for changes such as the introduction of student loans, and a reconsideration of the concept of tenure, especially for staff in some overblown departments in polytechnics. They also urge readers to see the present "cuts" in context by pointing out the massive increases in educational expenditure over the past fifteen years and they ask whether, as a nation, we have really received value for money.

ii. The content of education: standards, curricula and examinations

A graphic account of life in two different kinds of school is given in the chapter "The Two Nations in Education" by Elizabeth Cottrell who has taught in both a comprehensive and a girls' grammar school in the same neighbourhood. She describes vividly the contrast in attitudes, ethos and educational provision between them and shows, among other things, that the quality of education is not a simple result of the lavishness of resources. The grammar school did not compare favourably on material resources but, in terms of order and educational opportunities, it appeared a much better and happier place.

An article published by the Institute of Mathematics, reprinted here, demonstrates serious cause for anxiety about standards of attainment in mathematics in recent years. This must be a matter of national concern, as basic mathematical skills are so important for everyone in contemporary society, and the training of mathematically inclined pupils in the more advanced skills is crucial for a nation which depends on technology for its economic survival. The acute shortage of mathematics and science teachers in our schools may partly explain the problems in helping pupils attain a grasp of these subjects[1] and is an additional argument in favour of using well qualified teachers more economically – for example in specialist schools, so that pupils in the state system can have the benefits of being taught by experienced teachers.

However, in another subject area, there is not a shortage but an excess. We refer to the explosion of students and courses in the social sciences in the 1960s which left a legacy of large numbers of graduates in subjects such as sociology, many of whom have moved into jobs such as social work. Many others were appointed to academic posts in universities and polytechnics during the period of expansion in the late 1960s and early 1970s. They are still there, despite falling student numbers; the high salaries and favourable conditions of work provide little incentive to move. Hence the discussions which characterize some faculty board meetings about developing courses solely in order to retain staff in post – discussions which smack far more of self-interest than of the nation's needs. One outcome of this situation is that there are now many sociologists hungry for new fields to conquer.

This phenomenon of sociological imperialism has coincided with a recognition by practitioners in fields such as medicine and nursing of the desirability of introducing their students to the social factors which influence health, illness and the provision of health care. It has also coincided with a growth of courses for students of science and technology which are designed to help them understand the social context of science and the social responsibilities of scientists. Our concern is that many of the sociologists appointed during the 1960s were, like much of sociology itself, very young and academically immature. Many were, and still are, ideologically committed to political positions of the far left in ways which preclude their commitment to traditional academic values.[2] This contaminates their teaching and, we suggest, makes it less than useful for practitioners of medicine, nursing and science. In the chapter "What has Athens to do with Jerusalem?" Caroline Cox and John Marks try to show how sociology, appropriately taught, can make a valuable contribution to these courses, but warn those responsible for organizing them that they should be careful to ensure that the sociology taught is academically reputable and professionally relevant.

   Examinations, so often decried by self-styled radicals and progressives, are not the be-all and end-all of education. However, they are important as indices of attainment for individuals, for schools and colleges, and for society. Any proposals, therefore, to change the system of public examinations need careful scrutiny if we are not to lose our bases of assessment and comparison of standards. The chapter by Alan Grant, "Quality or Equality – Educational Standards and the Examination System", looks at the present system and at recent proposals to change the arrangements for 16+ examinations and to introduce new examinations for those staying at school in the sixth form. He traces the origins and development of these proposals for change and makes significant criticisms of the work of the Schools Council and of the Waddell and Keohane committees. He is particularly critical of attempts by teachers' organizations both to control public examinations and to extend the use of Mode III examinations in which teachers assess their own pupils' work.

iii. Change and obstacles to change

We believe that the present system is so entrenched, and so upheld by vested interests, that we need to put forward some radical proposals for public discussion and debate. In this way those responsible for policy decisions can benefit from the public's reactions to suggestions for alternative ways of organizing our education.

   One of the greatest flaws of the "Great Debate" on education was that it ruled certain issues out of court from the start. The main object seemed to be to give the appearance that something was being done to meet public anxieties, all the while ensuring that no fundamental changes would be contemplated in the policies dear to Labour Party militants. Our proposals are radical in that they change the financial basis of our education system.

   The first, discussed by Marjorie Seldon in her chapter "Education Vouchers", would give parents the right to spend their own money on schools of their choice – money which is at present spent on their behalf by local education authorities. We believe that such a policy would do more to make schools accountable to the interests of parents and pupils than any other single piece of legislation. It would also make it much easier to set up new types of school, such as the new Yarm School in Cleveland, because parents would not be paying twice over for any education outside that already provided by local authorities. This change could be a very creative and educationally valuable way of encouraging a greater diversity of school and would do something to bridge the chasm that now exists between the state and independent sectors. LEAs would, of course, retain a crucial role in providing special schools for pupils such as the physically and mentally handicapped – the sort of community role on which local authorities should, in future, primarily concentrate. Those schools with persistent problems could be helped by local education authorities devoting resources to them on the basis of positive discrimination. Initial administrative and other difficulties – which there could well be – should not be allowed to rule out an educational policy which is in the interests of our children's future.

   Marjorie Seldon also discusses the voucher plan in Spain which allows parents using private schools a grant equal to pupil cost in the state sector and mentions

"Bill 33" in British Columbia, which funds private school pupils up to one-third of their fees. She speculates on the possibility of a financial break-even point, after which the taxpayers' contribution to state education would decline – an interesting, not to say magnificent, possible outcome for vouchers in Britain!

In our second proposal, we make the case for student loans which are mentioned in a number of articles. Such schemes for funding higher education are widespread in many other countries ranging from social democratic Sweden to Japan and West Germany. In fact, Britain is the odd one out in its present overwhelming commitment to giving students parentally means-tested grants. We believe that it is now time to abolish the anomalies of these grants, which often cause real hardship to students whose parents cannot or will not provide the assumed parental contribution. We need to treat students who are receiving the privileges of higher education more as adults and to realize that the education they receive will still be heavily subsidized. The objections to loans raised by bodies such as the National Union of Students are based on arguments which do not stand up.[3] For example, exemption clauses can be designed to take account of situations such as graduates who are unable to pay back their loans because they choose relatively low-paid but worthwhile jobs – such as nursing. Other arguments such as the "negative dowry" effect or the deterrent effect on working class students have been shown to be irrelevant in countries such as Sweden which has a higher proportion of women students than the UK and where loans do not deter students from a wide range of social backgrounds. We do not advocate student loans primarily for economic reasons, although over the long term they would probably represent financial savings, but because they would do more to change the ethos of higher education than any other single measure. Loans would open up opportunities for higher education to a wider range of students of all ages; their introduction would link the "right" to higher education with the responsibilities associated with its benefits.

We are not naive; we recognize that really radical proposals will meet fierce opposition. The strongest and most vociferous sources will probably be from those with deep vested interests – such as the leadership of the National Union of Teachers. We offer an account of this organization in the chapter by Fred Naylor and John Marks "The National Union of Teachers – Professional Association or Trade Union or ...?" so that readers may have a greater understanding of its membership, the ways in which it works, the kind of causes it has espoused, and the political tenor of its influence.

However, there are other, more intangible, aspects of the educational establishment which make it unresponsive to change. In his chapter "Knowledge, Debate and Choice in Education" Digby Anderson describes some of these. For example, he refers to the limitations of the so-called "Education Debate", showing how it is inherently inconclusive – more a sop to democratic consultation than a sincere attempt to take the public's concerns seriously – and how all too often, debaters have their own vested interests. The author argues that too much time is taken up teaching would-be teachers a flimsy subject "education" and not nearly enough to seeing that new and old teachers teach well in schools. Teaching could take a leaf out of nursing's book and ground its preparation of practitioners in a more firmly rooted aprenticeship system, rather than in an increase in relatively vacuous subjects like the sociology of education. We would be on our guard against any attempt to increase the length of teacher training and would prefer an increase in professional monitoring and in-service education. We should also insist that all teachers know their subject as well as their teaching technique, and that they are up-dated in it. Lastly, teacher education and assessment must be given teeth. Bad teachers must be sacked, bad students failed and bad lecturers retired.

Finally, Stanislav Andreski, in his chapter "Distortions of Education by the Vested Interests of the Bureaucracy", identifies a bureaucratic-educational complex as a major obstacle to change. He shows that many seemingly incomprehensible features of the present situation in education can be explained in terms of the vested interests of this complex. Under the smokescreen of ultra-egalitarian phraseology, the bureaucratic-educational complex pursues its own interests with an almost total disregard for the long-term interests of those whom state education is supposed to serve. He concludes that unless Britain makes much better use of its available brainpower, 'it will quickly sink to the level of a cold Haiti when the oil runs out'.

iv. Evaluating and monitoring change in education: the role of research

Educational research is a flourishing industry. Bodies such as the National Foundation for Educational Research (NFER) have been handsomely funded to study aspects of our education system such as mixed ability teaching or sixth form provision. However, they have often assiduously avoided critical appraisal of some of the most profound changes in the education system: for example, the imposition of comprehensive schooling – misleadingly called "the comprehensive experiment". We say "misleadingly" because this "experiment" has been virtually immune from evaluation by systematic research. In the words of Guy Neave:

> The advent of the comprehensive education system – albeit incomplete as yet – stands as one of the most significant developments in secondary education since 1902, that is, from the time when the State first supported secondary education. Yet, either by irony or by paradox, this event has remained virtually unaccompanied by any sustained research of an empirical variety. To be sure, we have had £100.000 worth of bromide from the NFER. But that ceased in 1972 after the appearance of three reports remarkable only for the virtuosity with which they avoided the major issues.

Neave surmises that this is due to the "political sensitivity" of the issue and asks:

> 'But does political sensitivity in any way justify failure to monitor the most important reform in secondary education since 1902?' The answer – empirically and morally – must surely be 'no'. Empirically it remains unjustifiable because, without adequate up-to-date information we can only discuss the issue in terms of prejudice. Morally unjustifiable also because, without such enquiries and information, we are, in effect, asking parents to endorse our convictions, beliefs and prejudices either for or against comprehensive education, without the opportunity of making their own judgment on the development of a national education system.
> 'Puir, wee cow'ring tim'rous beastie
> O what fear's lurking i' thy breastie.'[4]

We share Guy Neave's concern over the absence of research enabling us to evaluate major educational changes. We also share his suspicions that the educational establishment is reluctant to hear about findings which are uncomfortably challenging to current policy. However, we need to remember that educational research has been very influential and that politicians are keen to use it as a basis for policy when it suits their predilections. Fred Naylor in "Educational

Myths and Research" exposes faults and fallacies in a number of research studies which feature widely on reading lists for teacher training courses, for many popular "Sociology in Education" courses, and for Open University courses in education. They have, therefore, been very powerful in shaping attitudes of teachers and others concerned with education. Many of the studies on which Fred Naylor turns his critical searchlight are shown to have serious flaws or defects – a shaky foundation on which to base policy in an area where so much is at stake.

The Department of Education and Science (DES) also spends large sums of public money on research. One recent study goes some way, in principle, to meeting Guy Neave's criticism about the lack of any attempt to evaluate the comprehensive system of secondary schooling. The DES awarded £36,000 to the National Children's Bureau (NCB) for a research project intended to evaluate "Progress in Secondary Schools" by studying those children in the National Child Development Study sample who had spent their school years between the ages of 11 and 16 in comprehensive, grammar or secondary modern schools. The NCB reported their findings in a large report published in July 1980 and in a booklet *Concern*, sent free to over 5000 members of the NCB. Guy Neave spoke of "bromides". That would be too mild a term for the impression created by this research and the publicity which it generated. Its effects were more like those caused by the drug known in medical circles as "mist euphoria"! The press widely reported the NCB research as 'A success story for the comprehensives' and gave them "Full marks". Politicians like Shirley Williams and Neil Kinnock seized on their findings, claiming credit for the success of comprehensives and appealing to this research as a justification for pushing forward with even more compulsory comprehensivization. Alas! A cool look at the report itself reveals a cause for "Real Concern". The research methods are open to criticism and the picture conveyed is deeply disturbing. For example, on important issues such as educational attainment in reading and mathematics, truancy, behaviour in school and parental satisfaction, the comprehensives do badly in comparison with the grammar and secondary schools which they replaced. Even more worrying, the longer the schools have been comprehensive, the worse they are. Thus, the outlook for the 85 per cent of our nation's secondary schoolchildren now in the comprehensive system is pretty bleak. However, the overwhelming impression created by the report was one of reassurance: the researcher herself summed it up: 'My message to the 85 per cent of children now in comprehensives is that they need not be downhearted' (*Daily Telegraph*, 16 July 1980) – a comment which does not seem to be warranted by her own data. In an attempt to put the record straight, we wrote a critical appraisal "Real Concern: an appraisal of the National Children's Bureau report on 'Progress in Secondary Schools' ". A summary is included here together with an account of subsequent developments.

It is worth noting in this context the severe criticisms made by H.M. Inspectors on London's comprehensive schools.[5] Despite extremely generous financial provision and very favourable pupil/teacher ratios, the academic achievements of many of the comprehensive schools pioneered by the ILEA are disastrous. In the HMI's own words:

...too many secondary schools expect too little from their pupils at all levels ... where schools choose to group their pupils without reference to individual abilities and achievements, teachers often fail to adjust their own approaches accordingly and pupils suffer ... some schools view O-level as an inappropriate target ... for any of their pupils. There is therefore a considerable tendency for many pupils of all abilities ... to achieve less than they are capable of ... Much A-level work is slow, narrow and unchallenging, with a considerable minority of pupils taking three years to prepare for the examinations and then performing poorly.

Overall the ILEA public examination results are well below the national average and '... make it clear that many pupils in ILEA secondary schools are under-achieving'. Is this vicious circle of low teacher expectation and low pupil attainment being repeated in comprehensive schools all over the country? Until more information is made publicly available, the question will remain.

v. Education, society and culture

We cannot understand changes in our education system without looking beyond it to the surrounding society. Prevailing ideas and values will inevitably influence teachers, parents, pupils and policy makers. The past fifteen years have seen the results in education of the beliefs and commitments of those who formed the "progressive egalitarian consensus". As the name implies, they espouse "progressive" ideas about bringing up children and organizing schools which emphasize their overriding concern with equality. Mixed ability teaching and comprehensivization are some of the fruits of these ideas. The people who have espoused them tend to be predominantly middle class, many of them younger "radicals" and members of the intelligentsia. However, the pigeons are coming home to roost. Some of these now not-so-young middle class "progressives" have children who are coming to the age when they are eligible for comprehensive schooling. Many of them are as deeply worried now as other parents have been all along – the system which they engineered for other peoples' children looks less appealing for their own. Some, therefore, move house to a catchment area of a good comprehensive school or one of the few remaining selective schools; others opt into the private sector – following the example of many Labour MPs. Yet others accept from a comprehensive school an education for their children which they find desperately worrying and try to remedy its deficiencies by providing such compensations as private coaching. But these options are not so readily available for the great majority of the population – the working class in whose interests the more egalitarian system was supposed to be established.

We suggest that some of our proposals would go a long way towards remedying the pernicious results of the educational policies of these progressive egalitarians and would help all groups within our society to gain access to the type of education they want.

Some former progressive egalitarians are now becoming aware of the results of their beliefs and are rethinking their position. This involves a reassessment, not only of policies of schooling, but of education in its broadest sense. By this we mean the induction of children into our cultural heritage and into the adult world through which this heritage is transmitted. Patricia Morgan, in "What's the Free New World doing to the Children?" discusses some of the broader implications of progressive education and its close relation, child-centredness. If we fail to meet our responsibilities as parents and educators, she suggests, we shall be in danger of creating "the last generation". She argues that progressive child rearing is fundamentally incompatible with humanity, and spells out the implications of her analysis for the family, the school and the world of work.

Arthur Pollard emphasizes the importance of a vigorous and healthy culture, rooted in the past, in the final chapter "Conservatives, Culture and Education". He warns that we need to be constantly aware of the reality of evil, and that we should, therefore, be moderate and tentative in any attempt to change society. Like Hayek, he alerts us to the dangers of the 'synoptic delusion' and points to the disastrous consequences of utopianism.

This conclusion sums up our position. Our proposals for choice and freedom are the antithesis of the socialist alternatives. Whereas socialists believe in their right and ability to draw up and impose a blueprint upon society, we believe that humanity and society are too complex to be constrained in this way and that attempts to do so lead inevitably to totalitarianism. Socialists in this country and in all the numerous socialist countries abroad have shown themselves averse to critical evaluation of their policies. They have actively prevented public dissemination of information about what is happening in matters of direct public interest – such as education. By contrast, we believe that the public has a right to know, and that the education system should be accountable to the public. Also, because the socialists have, over many years, sacrificed numerous freedoms in order to enforce their overriding ideals of equality, we believe that there is an urgent need to restore more freedom in the interests of the individual and of society.

And so we bring the wheel full circle, reaffirming our common values and our commitment to more freedom, more choice, and more information on which to base that choice. Time is short. Unless we can achieve some radical reversals of present trends, the socialists will press their policies forward until they achieve their aim: irreversible social change creating a monolithic system which allows no alternatives and from which there is no escape. If that occurs, the freedoms which we have enjoyed will be denied to the next generation, and it will be too late to resurrect them. We will then, indeed, have been guilty of creating "the last generation" to experience freedom and culture as we have been privileged to know them.

Caroline Cox and John Marks   December 1980

Notes

1. *Aspects of Secondary Education in England – a survey by HM Inspectors of Schools*, HMSO, 1979.
2. *The Attack on Higher Education*, J. Gould, Institute for the Study of Conflict, 1977.
3. "Student Loans and the NUS", M. Blaug, *Journal of Economic Affairs*, Vol. 1, No. 1, October 1980.
4. "Sense and Sensitivity: the Case of Comprehensive Education", G. Neave, *Quantitative Sociology Newsletter*, No. 21, 1979.
5. *Educational Provision by the Inner London Education Authority*, report by HM Inspectors, DES, November 1980.

The Purposes of Education and the Framework for Education

1

Educational Fundamentals: the Four Es

Antony Flew

*Professor of Philosophy at Reading University since 1973,
previously (since 1954) at Keele. Numerous visiting appointments, mainly in the USA but also in Canada, Australia and
Malawi. Founder member of the Council of the Freedom
Association, a Vice-President of the Rationalist Press Association, and sometime (1976-9) Chairman of the Voluntary Eutha-
nasia Society, now Exit. His books include* Hume's Philosophy
of Belief, An Introduction to Western Philosophy, Crime or
Disease?, A Rational Animal, *a one-man volume of philosophical "Black Papers"* Sociology, Equality and Education, Thinking About Thinking, *and* The Politics of Procrustes – *philosophical essays on equality and socialism.*

*The four Es are education and examinations, excellence and
elites; and the purpose of the present paper is to bring out that
these important ideas are necessarily and essentially connected. The three fundamental truths about their connection
are all conceptual: their truth, that is to say, arises from and
depends upon the very meaning of the terms involved. So they
ought perhaps to be perfectly obvious and trite. Yet they are
today widely and influentially denied. People have been –
indeed they still are – advocating and implementing policies
which, even when they do not reject unwelcome truisms
outright, ignore them.*

Introduction

X The Four Es are education and examinations, excellence and elites. The purpose of this paper is to bring out that these important ideas are necessarily and essentially connected. The three fundamental truths about their connection are all conceptual; their truth arises from, and depends upon, the very meaning of the terms involved. So they ought, perhaps, to be perfectly obvious and trite. Yet they are today widely and influentially denied. People have been – indeed still are – advocating and implementing policies which, even when they do not reject unwelcome truisms outright, ignore them.

Teaching and Learning

The first bread and margarine fundamental is that education is – and any proper educational policy ought to be – concerned with, and directed at, teaching and learning. Surely, someone will protest, that at least must be too obvious to everyone to be worth anyone's saying? (It is in general a good test of whether something is worth saying – though not, of course, the only test – to find what people, and how many people, offended by the utterance of that proposition, would wish to dismiss it as false or otherwise unacceptable.)

Consider, first, the title of a recent article by Mrs Jean Floud, the Principal of Newnham College in the University of Cambridge and one of our most respected social engineers. It is, quite simply, "Making Adults more Equal: the Scope and Limitations of Educational Policy",[1] from which it would appear that for Mrs Floud educational policy – or a policy for education – has nothing to do with teaching and learning.

It just is a policy for enforcing Procrustean ideals of equalization or, insofar as it does have anything to do with teaching or learning, the concern is to subordinate these to that quite different and non-educational – if not anti-educational – objective. 'To obtain the maximum equalizing effect' she says, '... distribution must be not only independent of, but negatively related to, the distribution of inherited inequalities of fortune, including genetic make-up' (p. 50). It is clear that she herself goes along with the conclusion attributed to the distinguished American egalitarian, Christopher Jencks: '... we must see to it that ... the link between vocational success and living standards is effectively broken' (p. 38). It remains for us only to remark that these are policies guaranteed to produce an equality of misery for all – or for all except members of the new class of official equalizers and their recognized social scientific advisers.

Secondly, consider the significant "Foreword" by Mr Tyrrell Burgess to the British edition of that distinguished book *Inequality* by Christopher Jencks and other Harvard colleagues. Burgess writes:

> This book has infuriated a great many people in the US and promises to infuriate people here. It does so by stating the liberal and radical assumptions about education and then testing them against the evidence. The assumptions are found wanting. Take the effect of education on later life-chances, particularly on income. There is nearly as much income variation among men from similar families, with similar educational credentials and with similar IQ scores, as among men in general ... The conclusion seems inescapable: reforming the schools will not bring about social change, because even huge changes have quite small social effects.

Having drawn some of what he sees as the more particular morals for Britain, Burgess continues: 'If reformers are not to be permanently frivolous they must be interested in whether their policies are failing. At least Jencks and his colleagues provide a convenient check list. To almost any proposal for education we can now ask "did it survive the Jencks test ..." '. Finally, Burgess speaks of 'the experience of the schools. Their failure as engines of social change may derive from two connected circumstances'. These are, first, that the schools are just not very effective and, secondly, that 'the schools themselves seldom have, explicitly or implicitly, the objectives which society assumes them to have'.[2]

Two incidentals deserve a moment of our attention before we come to the present main point. In the first place, even those who repudiate the Procrustean ideal – apparently shared by both Burgess and those whom he is here addressing – cannot but commend the sincerity of purpose and the rationality shown in his insistence that research should be done to monitor the success or failure of public policies, and that those policies must be amended or, if need be, reversed in the light of the findings of that research.

We are bound favourably to contrast his attitude here with that of Edward Short, when Minister of Education in the late 1960s, and of his successor, Shirley Williams, in the late 1970s. Mr Short, it may be remembered, launched a programme of officially sponsored research only after he had undertaken, on behalf of the party and the government, an absolute and irreversible commitment to universal and compulsory comprehensivization. Mrs Williams, in her turn – as those who speak of her flexibility and moderation must not be allowed to forget – loyally insisted that the "Great Debate", touched off by Prime Minister Callaghan's speech at Ruskin College, must not on any account be allowed to threaten that sacred cow. No criticisms or investigations would be acceptable if they showed that it was not delivering enough of the milk of teaching and learning; or suggested that educational production might be improved by preserving and extending some measure of selection.

The second incidental is the notion of life-chances, one of the less abstruse technicalities of contemporary sociology. Its orthodox definition is given in Mrs Floud's aforementioned article: 'people's economic and social opportunities' (p. 37). Nevertheless, four pages later, in a manner altogether typical of sociological investigators, she simply equates 'differences in people's life-chance(s)' with 'the variation in individual incomes'. Burgess, similarly, in the first of the passages quoted, identifies life-chances with lives led. For 'the effect of education on later life-chances, particularly on income' just is, for him, the effect on later income.

This almost universal confusion has a strong appeal to socialist social scientists. First, it facilitates the identification of the widely popular and economically dynamic ideal of equality of opportunity with the much less attractive contemporary passion to impose equality of outcome. Secondly, the same muddle conceals and sanctifies the professing social scientist's understandable but inexcusable professional reluctance to take account of the obstreperous facts of individual human diversity – diversity from the moment of birth as well as in and as a result of choices made later. A parallel confusion is endemic in the proliferating sociology of the relations between access to educational opportunities and vocational outcomes as well as, less surprisingly, in the politically motivated abuse of its findings. To misconstrue evidence of inter-group inequalities of achievement as by itself proving exactly correspondent inequalities of opportunity seems to be the norm rather than the exception.[3]

These two incidentals are both independently important. We shall have occasion to return to them. But the central contention here and now is that Burgess – well-publicized as an acceptably progressive British educationist – is, like Floud, taking it absolutely for granted – and taking it absolutely for granted that his readers, too, will take it for granted – that educational policy is a policy for equalization. It has nothing, apparently, to do with teaching or learning. The failure of the schools, if they have failed, is a failure to implement the Procrustean purposes of socialist educationalists and socialist social engineers. And, as Burgess remarks in conclusion, their supposed failure in this main object is in part to be attributed to the fact that too many schools do not have 'the objectives which society assumes them to have'. (For "society" read "socialist intellectuals", and then pause to be thankful that so many schools are, it appears, still concerned to teach subjects rather than to realize anyone's vision of a *Brave New World*.)

Those so old-fashioned, not to say reactionary, as to hold fast to the truism that education and educational policy must be essentially concerned with and for teaching and learning need, today, to be ever aware that there are many others, and most influential, for whom the name of the game is either some form of equality, or class struggle, or almost anything else but education. When, but only when, this deep gulf is recognized shall we be able to understand why so many people appear indifferent to what we ourselves see as the basic question – whether or not our comprehensively reorganized schools are getting more pupils up to higher levels of educational attainment.

Monitoring Progress

Our second fundamental is perhaps a shade more exciting – bread and jam, perhaps, rather than bread and margarine. It, too, and its immediate implications are far too often ignored or denied. The truism – but the truth – is that anyone sincerely either trying to teach or to learn anything must be concerned to monitor progress. Hence, some sort of reliable testing, though not any particular form of examination, is essential to, and no sort of excrescence upon or irrelevant interruption of, the business of education.

We have here the educational special case of an absolutely general truth. It is a condition of sincerity in the pursuit of any purpose whatsoever that the purposer should be constantly concerned to monitor success or failure in pursuing whatever aim it is which he professes to pursue. Suppose that the aim is – dare we admit to such a thing? – to run a business at a profit; then our sincere and rational would-be profit maker will most certainly keep accounts to show him what parts of his business are and are not paying their way. Suppose the aim is to win a cricket match; then our players will certainly not be indifferent to the question of whether anyone is keeping score.

So, by the same token, those who are sincerely trying either to teach or to learn must be disposed to monitor their progress, or their lack of it, by some form of testing or examination – although not, of course, by an equal necessity any particular form. Readers of Ernest Bramah's delightful Kai Lung stories will at this point recall a wise warning: 'It is a mark of insincerity of purpose to seek the Sacred Emperor in low class teashops'.

It is similarly a mark of insincerity of purpose to ask to be employed as a teacher while proudly proclaiming – as one of the staff of the University of Edmonton did while I was in Calgary – that one has a conscientious objection to all assessment or grading. That statement should have been accepted as an announcement of resignation; but no one will be surprised to learn, in the spineless and unprincipled darkness of these times, that it was not. Had it been, it might usefully have been indicated to the unintending resigner that others more genuinely conscientious are inclined always to suspect any ostensibly moral intuitions pointing to such personally congenial conclusions. For our moral hero was among university teachers of the great majority in having to confess 'I hate examining'.[4]

Once this conceptual truism has been clearly and forcefully expounded it must, surely, be admitted as being undeniably true. Equally undeniable, and no less neglected, is the more particular corollary that if anyone, in any field, is sincerely trying to improve levels of achievement then he must be concerned to test whether or not – and if so, how far – he is succeeding. Yet I have found many who have heard, and sometimes with some impatience said that they accepted, these points, who are unable or unwilling to maintain their grasp through the heat of the day. Instead, they stand ready to overlook the neglect of them by others, while themselves sympathetically sighing for the unexamined life. (It was the gadfly Socrates who maintained, albeit not exactly in the present context, that 'the unexamined life is not to be endured'!) Two or three current applications should ram the charges home further, and reveal their quite formidable explosive power.

The 1975 Bullock Report[5]

Many reviewers exulted in what they took to be the implications in the Report that there was no clear evidence of any general decline in basic literacy and, in particular, in reading skills. Such a conclusion must, they thought, confound those notorious evil-intenders and double plus ungood crimethinkers – the writers of the *Black Papers*.[6]

The correct interpretation is utterly opposite and an occasion for alarm. In the first place, had the DES, the local education authorities and the schools really been aching to raise levels of achievement there would have been clear and decisive evidence. After all, as no great practical or theoretical difficulties arise in testing basic literacy or reading skills, it would not be hard to determine where and how far these had improved, deteriorated or remained the same. Had all those concerned really been directing their efforts at this modest but vital objective of improving basic literacy, they might still have been unsuccessful. But we can be quite certain that there would not now be any doubt or question how far they had succeeded or failed. (If and inasmuch as it really is impossible to determine whether some objective has or has not been attained, then the whole project of pursuing that impossibly elusive end must become no more sensible than *The Hunting of the Snark*.)

In the second place, in a period during which the proportion of the national income spent on public education has increased, the question we ought to be in a position to ask and to answer is not whether, and by how much, and where, standards have declined, but by how much and where they have already improved and are now set fair towards still further improvement. What we have a right to expect – both as heavy taxpayers and as victims of the inflation and of the relative and absolute national impoverishment caused by miserable productivity and inordinate government expenditure – is clear and decisive evidence that more children are reaching higher levels of educational achievement – and sooner!

The 1977 Institute of Mathematics Survey[7]

As a one-off exercise, this survey could, obviously, not throw any direct light on whether, in this particular, things were on the up-and-up, or whether – as seems more likely – they were proceeding more or less rapidly towards – in Mr Muntalini's characteristic phrase – 'the demnition bow wows'. Nevertheless, there are two points for us to take.

First, and very much by the way, these spot tests just happened to reveal an average 18 per cent absenteeism, with the highest figure, 28 per cent, in the Inner London Education Authority's schools – on which, just to twist the knife in the wound, *per capita* spending is considerably higher than under other authorities. (It becomes obvious that true truancy figures would all be much higher – those officially given are based only on registers called at the beginning of each day.)

Secondly, in the light now of what has been said about criteria for sincerity of educational purpose, we cannot but harbour black thoughts towards all authorities, from the DES down, which have never had, and do not now propose to start, any leaving examinations. These could be the most immediate and effective way to discover what, if anything, has been taught to and learnt by those under their charge. Leaving examinations would also provide a useful incentive to learn, especially if those achieving a tolerable all-round minimum were permitted, as their reward, to leave school a little before serving out the usual full sentence.

Let us also ponder the existence and performance of the Inspector of Mathematics of the ILEA, and of his no doubt generously staffed office. Presumably everyone in that office knew, as indeed they were paid to know, how bad the situation has been and is; and presumably they were, as also was and is their duty, constantly drawing the attention of their political masters to the seriousness of the situation. Why, then, was none of the information gathered in and by that office made available to the parents of the children in those schools and to the rate payers who are forced to pay out such enormous sums for such miserable results? Why was it left to the private enterprise of a body running on the proverbial shoestring of privately provided money to make all this alarming information available to the public?

Examinations – Year against Year Comparisons

A-level examinations are, as we all know, conducted annually. But the results published are for purposes of direct year against year comparisons vitiated by one, none too frankly acknowledged, practice. The examiners allot annually to each of the different grades distinguished roughly the same percentage of candidates. This lamentable procedure was, it appears, originally introduced in 1960 under the direction of the old Secondary Schools Examination Council. It has been followed ever since, always with the support of the successor Schools Council, itself strongly influenced if not always fully controlled by the leadership of the National Union of Teachers.[8]

It is a curious practice to find sponsored by people for whom "competition" is so bad and "fairness" so good a word. For it must tend to make the higher grades places for which the examinees compete among themselves, rather than markers of some level of achievement which – without regard to the performance of others – any, or even every, candidate might possibly attain. It is also bound to generate unfairness as between candidates entering in strong and weak years. Sibling Alpha in a weak year may get an A on a performance no better and no worse than that for which, in a strong year, sibling Omega is put down with a B.

So what can we do but infer that these normally deplored disadvantages of the established practice are, in the eyes of its supporters, more than compensated by advantages? My own suspicion is that what the NUT treasures as an overriding merit is precisely what I, and others straightforwardly concerned for educational advance, see as a gross fault – namely that it makes direct year against year comparisons impossible. Certainly we shall not even be aiming for educational advance, much less knowing that it is in truth being achieved, until and unless not only these but all our other major examinations are so designed and conducted as to make such direct year against year comparisons both valid and easy.[9]

Excellence and Elites or Equality of Condition?

The third and most disturbing of our three fundamentals relates excellence and elites both to one another and to what is to many today the supreme good – equality of condition. To achieve excellence in any sphere is to become a member of an elite; as such one is no longer, in whatever may be the relevant respect, equal to those who have not achieved this particular form of, or perhaps any, excellence. A moment's thought is sufficient to show that these three ideas are, indeed, related in this way. But, as A.E. Housman so mordantly wrote, in the Introduction to his edition of *The Satires of Juvenal*, 'Three minutes thought would suffice to find this out; but thought is irksome, and a moment is a long time'.

One immediate consequence of this third simple and fundamental truth is that we are bound to feel uneasy and untrusting when we hear professions of educational commitment from those for whom, in the name of their own Procrustean ideal of an equality of condition, both "excellence" and "elite" have become obscenities. Consider, for instance, the caution issued in the offical NUT weekly *The Teacher* of 26 June 1970 to Mrs Thatcher, then newly appointed Minister of Education. *The Teacher* warned against 'those who preach the importance of excellence' and told her sharply not to be tempted by 'arguments defending an elite in education'. They probably realize now that, with Mrs Thatcher, they might as well have saved both their breath and their ink!

Compare with those chilling schoolmasterly rebukes two equally sinister statements from the NUT document *Examining at 16+: the Case for a Common System*. Issued in November 1978, it confidently proclaims; 'In maintaining two quite separate examinations, designed for pupils of different ability ranges, the present system is as divisive, and hence educationally indefensible, as the coexistence of grammar and secondary modern schools'. In the all-in nightmare world of the NUT Executive there would be 'no artificial division between "pass" and "fail" ' and hence, happily, no pupils would ever 'again feel that they have "failed" '. (The quotation marks are as inserted by the NUT.)

It appears that these Canutes would have not merely the laws of nature but even the laws of logic roll back at their command. For it is of the essential nature of any examination system, which in any sphere measures attainment in any dimension, distinguishing the better from the worse, that it is in this respect inherently divisive. And where no logical room is provided for the possibility of failure, there can be no space for any conception of success either. Again, wherever and whenever anything at all is done outstandingly well, necessarily and inescapably there is excellence. If, furthermore, in any sphere of human activity or sensibility – whether educational, or industrial, or sporting, or aesthetic, or whatever else – there is indeed excellence; then, by an inexorable compulsion, there has to be an elite united by the possession of that excellence. (Very likely, of course, it will be united by that alone.)

So, if the NUT and others sharing this self-image of progressive comprehension really do want a world in which no one is ever to be aware of having failed, then they will have to abolish, among other things, all true tests and examinations of whatever kind. Goodbye, therefore, to all educational endeavour. Come this revolution, the authentic Jacobins of universal mediocrity must insist that no one ever be allowed to do anything outstandingly well – much less encouraged in such elitist and divisive ways by competent and conscientious teachers.

Most of the educationists, union officials and education bureaucrats who execrate examinations, excellence and elites – and still more of those who silently consent to their seductions – fail to see the logical connections between the Four Es or to foresee the ultimate consequences of pursuing pernicious policies. (Indeed, if everything was already clear to everyone there could be little point in publishing papers such as this.)

Yet, one thing which all left-thinking persons can be relied upon to oppose to the bitterest end is any move to promote excellence by reintroducing some element of academic selection into the state secondary system. It is nevertheless entirely obvious that far too few of our children will reach the higher standards which they are able and willing to attain, especially in the harder and/or shortage subjects, if we continue to refuse, in the name of undivisive comprehension, to crowd the willing and talented into the classrooms of those now deplorably few teachers able to offer modestly advanced instruction. If we really do want both to get the trained abilities which the country needs and ensure that all our children achieve the maximum of which they are capable, then selection cannot be avoided.

It is high time – and long over time – to appreciate what many of these enemies of excellence know very well, and that is that any education involving other subjects which not everyone will take, or going further in any subject than everyone else will go, is to that extent essentially and inherently divisive. So, if this unspeakable divisiveness is altogether unacceptable, there is nothing for us but 'cognitive equality'[10] and then, in very short order, headlong economic and non-economic decline.

When we hear university Vice Chancellors and the like explaining that, while of course not being elitist, they do nevertheless rather think that some standards of academic quality ought to be maintained, we cannot interpret them as being in flat-out opposition to any and every achievement of excellence. But there is a question which needs to be pressed against such persons. They accept the world "elitist" as properly a term of abuse, yet do not really want to force everyone and everything down to the same dim level of mediocrity. So what is it which makes some forms of selection for quality elitist and bad, whereas others – like getting a winning sports team by picking and training the best available players – are innocuous or even admirable?

At the beginning of one recent academic year I told all my first year philosophy students that while, of course, they should denounce in their essays whatever they believed that they had good reason to denounce, if they were going to denounce Plato or anyone else as elitist, would they please first explain what they meant. I have to report that in the year that followed there was no response either in essays or examinations. Nor did I have to read any denunciations of elitism. That, at least, was pure gain.

I will now go further. I propose a meaning which if accepted would make elitism for me, it not for many who now employ it as an undefined term of abuse, a very bad word indeed. From this day forward let it be used to describe any doctrine or practice which demands or supports government by supposed experts, experts neither responsible to nor ejectable by the governed, experts prescribing altogeth-er without reference to what those subjects themselves may happen actually to want, what they are to be taken to need. Plato's Guardians –the philosopher kings of *The Republic* – are the original paradigm case of such an absolute and irresponsible ruling elite; while as the advocate of such a system Plato must be scored correspondingly as the philosophical founding father of all elitism.

In our own time, of course, by far the most important absolute elites are the ruling Communist parties; the most numerous and powerful elitists are members and fellow-travellers of such parties. Suppose, therefore, that we do give a sense of this sort to the words "elitist" and "elitism". Then we must recognize that a great many of those presently most loud in their denunciations will have, in honesty, either to be silent or else to reconstrue these words as words of praise. Certainly we cannot but notice how many of the loudest of the denouncers of elitism are associated, if not with some form of Marxism-Leninism, then at least with that "democracy of the committed" nowadays favoured by the apparatniks of both the Labour Party and trade union left.

Alternatively, if we are to go on describing, and abusing as elitist, any kind of discrimination and selection for quality, then we all need to recognize what we are doing. We are – in the name of the strange, false god of equality of outcome – repudiating all standards of excellence in every field of human achievement. If this repudiation is not itself very soon repudiated, then our whole country will be in irreversible decline to become a squalid totalitarian slum, a slum in which every person, every product, and every activity would be shoddy, shifty, shabby and through and through third rate.

Notes

1. The article is in P.R. Cox, H.B. Miles, and J. Peel (Eds) *Equalities and Inequalities in Education* (Academic Press 1975), pp. 37-51.

2. Christopher Jencks and others *Inequality* (Allen Lane 1972), pp. 1-2.
3. For a consideration of some remarkable examples from three different countries see Chapter II of my *The Politics of Procrustes* (Temple Smith, 1981). Procrustes, by the way, was a legendary Greek innkeeper. Determined to accommodate all comers in the one and only bed to be provided in his inn, he cut the tall down and racked the short out longer, all to the approved uniform size.
4. In D. Rubinstein and C. Stoneman (Eds) *Education for Democracy* (Penguin Education, Second Edition 1972) Raymond Williams writes with a shade more suspicion of his own natural inclinations to self-indulgence "... it is not only because I hate examining ... that I believe its radical reform is necessary" (p. 217).
5. *A Language for Life: A Report of the Committee Appointed by the Secretary of State for Education and Science under the Chairmanship of Sir Alan Bullock* (HMSO 1975).
6. See G. Orwell *1984* (Secker and Warburg 1949), especially the Appendix on Newspeak. Perhaps I should take this chance of confessing that I am not, strictly speaking, a member of that honourable company. My solicited contribution to *Black Paper 1975* (Dent 1975) was indeed accepted by the Editors: '... delighted with your article. It is most forceful and exactly what we want'. But before the typescript reached the printers my contribution was, against editorial protests, removed by the publishers: '... it was inappropriate in the context of other Black Paper articles.' Happily publishing in Britain is still pluralistic and competitive rather than, as socialists would have it, a trade union or state monopoly. So that blacked black paper, its forcefulness undiminished, appears in my *Sociology, Equality and Education* (Macmillan, 1976).
7. The report itself appeared first in the *Bulletin of the Institute of Mathematics and its Applications*, Vol. 14, No. 4, April 1978, pp. 83-6; and is reprinted as Chapter 4, below.
8. See, for instance, C.B. Cox and R. Boyson (Eds.) *Black Paper 1977* (Temple Smith 1977), p. 6; and compare C.B. Box and R. Boyson (Eds), *Black Paper 1975* (Dent, 1975), p. 38.
9. That the need for such reforms is urgent may be suggested, though not shown, by one or two statistics: both of the declining popularity of the harder subjects in our own country; and of the rising numbers and proportions of students achieving given levels of attainment among our closest Continental competitors.
    See, for instance, Max Wilkinson *Lessons from Europe* (Centre for Policy Studies, 1977), especially pp. 6-7 and 79-82. Or, more recent, compare *The Economist* for 27/IX/80: 'Although 9 out of 10 British pupils begin learning a foreign language ... only 3% finish with an A-level... Among the choice of subjects for A-level, modern languages ... became increasingly unpopular during the 1970s.' Then again: 'Of the total number of boys entered for A-level French in 1977, some 34% came from the private sector. For German the proportion was 36%... The schools from which these ... candidates were drawn take in only five-and-a-half percent of the total secondary school population.'
10. Christopher Jencks and others *Inequality* (Allen Lane 1972), Chapter III.

II
Accountability and the Purposes of Education

John Marks and Caroline Cox

Caroline Cox is Director of the Nursing Education Research Unit, Chelsea College, University of London, and was formerly Head of the Sociology Department at the Polytechnic of North London. Qualified as a nurse at the London Hospital and later studied part-time at the Central London Polytechnic, gaining a B.Sc. (Sociology) and an M.Sc. (Economics) from London University. She has been co-director of a major Department of Education and Science research project in Higher Education, and has been a tutor with the Open University for eight years. Publications include People in Polytechnics *(co-author), and* A Sociology of Medical Practice *(co-editor). She has three children, all of whom attended a comprehensive school.*

John Marks is Senior Lecturer in the Physics Department of the Polytechnic of North London and is responsible for a course "Science and the Making of The Modern World" taken by all science students at the Polytechnic. He took a B.A. (Natural Science) and a Post-graduate Certificate in Education at Cambridge University, and a Ph.D. (Nuclear Physics) at London University. He has taught at a direct grant school and has been a university lecturer at London University and in Sweden. He has been a tutor with the Open University since its inception. His publications include Relativity. *He has three children, two of whom attend a comprehensive school of which he is an elected Parent Governor.*

Caroline Cox and John Marks are co-authors of Student Representation in Polytechnics, Education and Freedom – the Roots of Diversity, *and, with Keith Jacka,* Rape of Reason, *and* Marxism, Knowledge and the Academies *(in* Black Paper 1977).

The British education system needs to be more accountable both to individual parents, pupils and students and to society. This chapter discusses the purposes of education, both in schools and in higher education, and relates these purposes to practical proposals for increasing accountability, such as reassessment of tenure and changes in the methods of financing and organizing education. Specific proposals include the introduction of loans and state scholarships in higher education and of educational allowances or vouchers for schools. The aim is to ensure more direct accountability, more adaptability and responsiveness to change, more effective use of scarce resources and more democratic involvement without *jeopardizing teaching and learning – the essential purposes of education.*

"Cuts" in Context

The present hue and cry about "cuts" completely ignores the fact that in the last 30 years expenditure on education has increased from less than 3 per cent to about 6 per cent of GNP,[1] reaching a total of £8,800 million in 1978-79. Since GNP in real terms has itself nearly doubled over this period, this corresponds to an increase in expenditure of about 300 per cent. The amount spent per child per annum has increased from £470 to £770 since 1960 at constant (1977) prices while the average pupil-teacher ratio has decreased from 30.4 to 23.8 in primary schools, and from 21.1 to 17.0 in secondary schools since 1950.

There has been an even more dramatic rise in the resources devoted to higher education. Student numbers rose from about 137,000 in 1956-57 to about 514,000 in 1976-77 – a fourfold increase – while expenditure, at 1979 survey prices, rose from £795 million in 1966-67 to £1,240 million in 1976-77.[2]

It is clear that the nation made a massive increase in its investment in education.[3] Has this investment improved the quality of education? How account-able are those who run our schools and colleges for the resources they receive?

Accountability

Given such high levels of spending, it is timely to see whether the present mechanisms for accountability are adequate. It may also be timely to discuss the principles which ought to underlie any change in policy designed to increase this accountability.

To do this we need to ask a number of further questions. To whom should teachers, academics and administrators be accountable? How far should such accountability be to individuals or to society? Or, to put it another way, to what extent is education a private good – to be financed and provided by individuals, or a public good – to be financed and provided by the state.

The answers to these questions are inevitably bound up with the purposes of education, since different purposes may require very different types of account-ability.

Purposes of Education

We take a traditional view of the purposes of education – a view which until fairly recently was generally accepted by most academics, teachers and members of the public. A kind of unwritten contract existed which governed the practice of education. More recently the terms of this contract have become confused as other purposes have emerged and started to compete with traditional ones. There is much to be gained by restating these traditional purposes and thus trying to spell out that unwritten contract; and by identifying those other purposes which are incompatible with that contract.

Higher Education – Purposes and Accountability

Traditionally, higher education has two purposes, the preservation, advancement and transmission of knowledge, and the training of individuals in the advanced skills needed by society.

For the *preservation and advancement* of knowledge, academics are responsible directly to the academic community in their individual subjects. It is essential for the healthy functioning of the academic community that all the key academic decisions – appointments, admissions, assessments and choice of research topics – should be made by academics. This is the core of academic freedom which must be respected by society *provided that* the academics only use academic criteria in making these key decisions.

For the *transmission* of knowledge, academics are responsible to students and to other members of society, such as future employers, as well as to the academic community.

For the *training* of students in advanced skills, academics are primarily responsible to students and to the professional organizations which supervise the qualified practitioners of the advanced skills.

In higher education there are thus two primary channels of accountability – to the academic community with respect to the preservation and advancement of knowledge, and to students and other members of society with respect to the transmission of knowledge and training in advanced skills. And while these two responsibilities are in some ways complementary, a certain tension exists between them which ought to be reflected in the pattern of accountability in higher education – and in the related questions of tenure, finance and methods of organization.

Schools – Purposes and Accountability

Traditionally education in schools has three purposes:
(i) providing children with access to accepted bodies of knowledge;
(ii) giving them a range of essential intellectual and practical skills;
(iii) encouraging commitment to some of the values of our cultural heritage.
The bodies of knowledge are many and various – knowledge of mathematics and the sciences, of geography and history, of languages and literatures, of music and the arts and of engineering and technical skills. And children must acquire many intellectual and practical skills if they are to have access to all these bodies of knowledge. Perhaps the most important of these skills are basic literacy and numeracy – the essential tools needed for any future citizen of a modern industrial society. And, although the idea of "our cultural heritage" may be despised by so many "radicals", the majority of parents would surely wish their children to appreciate that heritage and to show a preference for rational discussion as opposed to more or less violent demonstrations. These are the fundamental purposes of education in our schools.

In all these areas of basic education the direct responsibility of teachers is to parents and pupils. And, as with higher education, this responsibility should be reflected in the pattern of accountability – and in the related questions of tenure, finance and organization.

Note that for teachers in schools there is nothing corresponding to the primary responsibility of academics in higher education for the advancement of knowledge through research. Teachers depend on the academic community for authoritative judgments concerning the bodies of knowledge they teach; which is why it is entirely appropriate for the academic community to control examinations in higher education and also to have a major say in formal school examinations. Because teachers in schools are transmitting knowledge which they themselves do *not* generate, it is inappropriate for them to set and mark their own public examinations. This raises the principle of "externality". In schools, as staff are teaching knowledge which they have obtained from the wider academic community, they should be accountable to that community for the standard of their work. Hence the need for university representation on examination boards and for external examiners. This also avoids the dilemmas of internally set public examinations where invidious pressures arise for teachers to tell pupils "the answers". Moreover, the principle of externality also holds in higher education, both to maintain academic standards and to ensure that academic justice can be seen to be done.

What Education is Not

The traditional purposes of education – teaching and learning – have long formed the basis of the unwritten contract between academics, teachers and society. On this view education is not a tool for explicit social engineering (as Caroline Wedgwood Benn would have it – more keen on uniformity and social equality than on education[4]). Nor should it aim at equality of outcome for all regardless of their talents or abilities (although even the OECD has come out in favour of equality of outcome as a goal[5]). Even less should it be a medium of indoctrination or a seedbed of revolution (as described, for example, in *Rape of Reason*[6] or the Gould Report[7]). Finally educational institutions should not be regarded as independent city-states of the young – run by and for the pupils and students (for all sorts of non-educational purposes as described by John Searle[8]).

Although these purposes are in serious conflict with the traditional purposes of education, they have all had their advocates in recent years among both academics and teachers who, we suggest, are in breach of their unwritten contracts with society. Any discussion of accountability should spell out means of redress for parents and students who are being given one of these substitutes for education.

Accountability in Practice – Principles and Mechanisms

The present system of accountability does not follow the principles discussed above, either in higher education or in schools. For example, there is the bogus Wedgbenn "accountability" which comes when matters are put under the control of people who are supposed to be speaking for some collective public. Witness the despotic behaviour of a Local Education Authority which imposes policies against the wishes of school Governing Bodies.[9]

Let us also consider the deliberate suppression of information on standards which would have been of real public interest. For example, when the Assessment of Performance Unit found that pupils in independent primary schools consistently performed better in mathematics than those in state schools, this information did not appear in the published report.[10] And when, for their recent report on secondary schools,[11] HM Inspectors collected data on GCE and CSE examination results, including grades, for all the schools in the survey, they *did not publish any of it*. They made lengthy comments on the influence of external examinations on schools, but in all the report's 313 pages, they made no attempt to relate examination results to any of the multitude of other factors they documented and discussed. Thus a rare opportunity was missed to publish information on the academic performance of 10 percent of the country's secondary schools – with whatever qualification and comment as seemed appropriate. This information must still be available in the DES and *should be published forthwith as an appendix to the report*. The public has a right to know what is happening – especially in matters concerning academic standards which are vital to the future of our children and our country.

So what changes can we suggest which would bring principles and practice more into alignment? We will first discuss the role of the professionals – the academics and the teachers. Then we will look at the structures of education – institutions and methods of finance and organization. All the time we will try to relate the discussion to what is practicable and to the principles and purposes which we believe are fundamental to sound educational policy.

Academics and Teachers – Accountability and Tenure

Higher Education

Let us consider first the responsibility of higher education for the preservation and extension of knowledge. It is by no means obvious that we need forty-five universities, thirty polytechnics and a growing number of colleges of higher education to serve this purpose. What *is* necessary is that the various branches of the academic community should carry out their traditional function of maintaining and enhancing academic standards. In doing this their primary responsibility is to decide who are to become full members of the academic community, which raises questions of academic freedom and of tenure. Academic freedom is a privilege granted by society to the academic community. It is a freedom which needs to be exercised responsibly in the context of the subtle constraints imposed by the academic community itself – the need to submit all claims to knowledge to the public scrutiny of other academics who will judge it according to well-established academic criteria. But unless the members of the community are both properly qualified and relatively free from external pressures, these constraints will not operate. So the need arises for some form of tenure – to be granted to the leading members of each academic discipline after an appropriate period of apprentice-ship and probation. However, tenure should not be automatic, and problems arise because the size of the tenured academic community needed to preserve and extend knowledge is not easy to determine. What is certain is that its optimum size is significantly less than the present numbers of academic staff employed in our institutions of higher education.

This brings us to the other purposes of higher education – the transmission of knowledge and the training of students in advanced skills. It is for these purposes that higher education has expanded so rapidly in recent years, not least in the expensive matter of paying the salaries of many more academic staff. As we argued earlier, for these purposes academics are responsible to students, professional organizations and the wider society as well as to the academic community. Tenure is only applicable if *all* these responsibilities are being satisfied. So we need to devise mechanisms which enable these functions of higher education to be performed in a way which is more accountable both to the needs of individuals and of society *and* which is therefore capable of adaptation as these needs change.

Schools

As we argued earlier, the main direct responsibility of teachers is to parents and pupils. If teachers are satisfactorily introducing pupils to worthwhile bodies of knowledge and providing them with the practical and intellectual skills they need, then they are fulfilling their responsibilities. But if they are not fulfilling these responsibilities, because they are not able or willing to do so, they should not expect tenure or be surprised if they are asked to leave their posts.

Or, if changes in the population (such as a falling birth-rate) and other social factors affect the demand for teachers' services, they should not expect indefinite tenure. How does one justify a job which provides such tenure regardless of the demand for services provided? As needs change, our education system must adapt so as to serve those needs.

Organization and Finance – Accountability, Diversity and Choice

For many years to come, we believe that the state will continue to provide the major part of expenditure on education. What we need to do is to devise mechanisms which both safeguard the essential purposes of education and improve accountability. If at the same time these mechanisms can enhance choice and increase people's autonomy in the way in which they spend their resources, so much the better.

Higher Education

Once again, the preservation and extension of knowledge needs to be considered separately from teaching functions. For these purposes there is much to be said for buffer organizations such as the University Grants Committee and the Research Councils which partly insulate the academic community from direct political and economic pressures. However, it would still be preferable if institutions of higher education were to derive a larger proportion of their research income from sources other than central government. An increase in private endowments or income from foundations would be a welcome diversification which would help to maintain academic freedoms in the harsher financial climate of the 1980s.

For the transmission of knowledge and training in advanced skills, the situation is different. It is necessary that the academic community retains responsibility for curricula, admissions, assessments and appointments, provided that those responsibilities are exercised with due recognition of the legitimate interests of students, the professions and other members of society. But present arrangements provide little incentive for academics to give due weight to these other interests. And let us remember that such incentives are necessary. As Adam Smith wrote of the moribund Oxford of his time, 'The discipline of colleges and universities is in general contrived, not for the benefit of the students, but for the interest, or more properly speaking, for the ease of the masters'. He also wrote that '... the endowments of schools and colleges have necessarily diminished more or less the necessity of application in the teachers. Their subsistence, so far as it arises from their salaries, is evidently derived from a fund altogether independent of their success and reputation in their particular professions'[12]. There are many ways in which Adam Smith's analysis applies today whether it be in the departments hit by falling student demand so that there are nearly as many staff as students, or in places where staff have subverted the purposes of education trying, for example, to turn schools or colleges into seedbeds of revolution.[13]

The remedy that Smith proposed may still have something to teach us today. It was that a greater proportion of the income of universities be derived from fees.

We propose that institutions of higher education should charge fees which reflect a significant proportion of their teaching costs, something nearer 80 percent than the current 20 percent or so. This in itself would be valuable since it would stimulate a greater awareness – in the minds of academics, students and the public – of the true costs of higher education. However, if fees and other costs continue to be borne primarily by the State then there is little incentive for students to make responsible decisions when they embark on costly advanced courses. This is why most of students' maintenance costs and possibly a proportion of their fees should be met by loans rather than by automatic grants. In order not to discriminate against students on high cost courses in subjects such as science, engineering or medicine, we suggest that the full cost of an arts or library-based course should be used as a basis for calculation of student contributions for all students, while the extra fees for laboratory-based courses should be met by the state; similar allowances should also be made for courses which last longer than the "normal" three year degree course. Student loans would not only test students' motivation and induce them to expect and seek out a higher standard of teaching; they would also be more equitable since graduates can expect significantly greater career rewards than non-graduates. The *right* to such a loan – tenable also for courses in further education – could help to ensure the availability of post-school education for anyone who genuinely wants it.

Loans for students are completely practicable – at least seventeen countries now use them.[14] The most extensive systems exist in Sweden and other parts of Scandinavia where they were introduced by Social Democratic governments and have been in operation for more than thirty years.[15] Moreover, a recent survey in Britain[16] showed that a scheme involving loans was supported by a majority of the general public (in a national survey) and by a substantial minority of students and their parents (38 percent of students and 46 percent of parents in a survey at Bath and Exeter Universities). One significant argument in favour of a loan scheme is that it would treat the student as an adult – independent of his parents – and thus eliminate the thorny problem of the parental contribution and the anomalies associated with it.

In addition to student loans, a significant number of state scholarships – which cover the full costs of higher education – should be introduced. This would make it possible for individuals, if sufficiently talented, to seek entry to any of the country's educational institutions and also enable the government to decide the overall numbers of students they wished to finance in full; more scholarships could be given in subjects which were considered to be of greater national importance.

We believe these proposals – in combination – would lead to greater account-ability in higher education without sacrificing essential standards. They would also lessen the present excessive dependence on the state. And, if they led to more initiatives like the Independent University at Buckingham, we would be delighted.

Schools

In schools, one of the most worrying developments in recent years has been the growing gulf between independent and state schools. The Direct Grant schools used to serve a "bridging" function, offering a third kind of school with excellent educational opportunities for many children whose parents could not afford the fees of the other independent schools. Since these schools were abolished by the Labour government in 1976, we have moved rapidly towards "Two Nations" in education, each being very different in its culture, values and attitudes.

There are indications that many would like to consider sending their children to some kind of independent school. However, there are two major deterrents. The first is financial. Few can afford the fees, although a recent survey[17] has shown that a majority of all parents, including nearly one half of working class parents, would be prepared to pay a significant proportion of the cost of secondary education if the state provided the rest. The same survey showed that 81 percent of the population, and 75 percent of Labour voters, thought that parents 'who want to should be allowed to pay extra to send their children to fee-paying schools.'

The second deterrent is political – the Labour Party's vociferous opposition to the existence of private schools despite the fact that many Labour politicians send their children to such schools. This doublethink is seen, for example, in the way Kevin McNamara, the left-wing Labour MP for Kingston-upon-Hull Central, supported the closure of private schools while choosing to send two of his sons to a public school. Thus, while exercising freedom of choice for his own family, he was diminishing freedom of choice for others. An even more drastic element in Labour thinking has been the policy proposal, backed by Neil Kinnock, the Labour Front Bench spokesman on education, that pupils from private schools should pay much higher fees at universities than pupils from state schools. This discriminatory policy was proposed by a group containing Caroline Benn, Jack Straw, former President of the National Union of Students, and Christopher Price, Chairman of the House of Commons Select Committee on Education, Science and the Arts.

The significance of the chasm between state and independent for those who cannot afford fee-paying schools is greatly increased because choice within the state system is so severely restricted. As Adam Hopkins puts it: 'For most people in Britain, apart from the 6 percent with enough money to opt for private education, there is at present no real freedom of choice of secondary school. In rural areas there is generally only one school which a child can reasonably attend. In most cities, schools are either strictly zoned or "fed" from certain specified primary schools'.[18] And this situation is positively welcomed in some quarters; again in Hopkins' words: '... the egalitarian wing of the Labour Party believe that choice of *any* kind destroys the principle of neighbourhood schools and were not prepared to countenance this'.[19]

The National Union of Teachers (NUT) also favour restricting parental choice. A 1970 policy statement says:

> By comprehensive education ... we mean the absence of selection procedures which either directly or indirectly prevent each school from having a representative cross-section of the full ability range ... if legislation is to have more force than a pious hope, it is necessary to limit parents' choice of

school. It was for this reason among others that we suggested ... that parental choice should not be exercised contrary to public policy.[20]

Moreover, some local authorities are now trying to restrict parental choice even when places are available at popular schools. For example, the Labour Council in the London Borough of Brent proposed cutting the intake of some popular schools by as much as 20 percent (the maximum allowed under the 1980 Education Act without issuing public notices) in order to try to force parents to send their children to unpopular schools. And the following statement by the Director of Education implies that, if it were not for the existence of a Conservative government at Westminster, the local authority might adopt an even more forceful policy: 'It seems unlikely that attitudes at Westminster would change sufficiently to allow the direction of pupils that this would imply'.[21]

We hope that 'attitudes at Westminster' will never allow such 'direction of pupils' but, with the current hostility to parental choice shown by the Labour Party and the NUT, we cannot be sure. And the organized left clearly regards parental choice as undesirable and something to be destroyed. Witness Professor Brian Simon, Professor of Education at the University of Leicester, who has recently called for 'the extirpation of covert systems of selection through the operation of "parental choice" '.[22]

By contrast, we believe that an increase in genuine parental choice could be the single most important factor both in making schools more accountable and in enhancing their standards of attainment. As the school population declines over the next few years, it will be much more possible than ever before to offer parents greater choice within the state system, especially in urban areas. Of course, for choice to be genuine it will be necessary for schools to publish much more information about their aims and achievements – including their public exami- nation results. Without adequate information, the freedom to choose is a spurious freedom. But this would surely be very desirable in an open society which values its traditional and hard won freedoms such as freedom of speech and information.

Such an increase in parental choice would, over time, encourage schools to be more responsive to the expectations of parents and thus increase their account- ability. Remember it was parents, voting with their feet, who finally brought the scandal of William Tyndale School to public attention. But this accountability would be much more direct and effective if it could be backed by financial incentives too.

We therefore advocate the introduction of a scheme for financing education which would give financial resources – in the form of an educational allowance – to every family for their children of school age. These allowances or vouchers could then be "cashed" at schools chosen by parents. They would be sufficient in value to meet the full costs of state education; if a family wanted to send a child to a fee- paying school, it could use the voucher to help to defray the cost and the school would receive the money. In this way, parents could vote for the type of education they want, both inside and outside the state system – not only with their voices but also with financial backing. Schools which were seen to be desirable and which stimulated high demand, could benefit from the resources they would attract; less popular schools would have additional incentives to respond to the community's wishes. Thus, democratic freedom of choice would be enhanced and financially endorsed. Of course, choice would not be unlimited – it never is in the real world.

Nor would schools be required to accept all applicants. But nevertheless choice would be considerably greater than under the present system.

We believe that a policy which is so consistent with the principles of freedom should be given a chance. And it is worth noting that this policy would encourage different types of innovation. For example, if enough parents wanted to organize an entirely new type of school (say, some kind of "free" school, a religious school, or even a political school – such as a communist school), they could obtain the resources to do so. Since our education system already has schools representing different religious beliefs, the opportunity to establish other schools reflecting different aspects of our pluralist society or even different fundamental aims for education should be entirely compatible with our values of diversity and tolerance.

It is worth emphasizing that a system involving public funding of private schools has operated successfully in the Netherlands since 1917. There, private schools are in the majority, and 65 percent of government education expenditure goes on private schooling.[23] As Max Wilkinson puts it in his book *Lessons from Europe*:

> The dichotomy between the need for state control and the pressure for local initiative in education has been solved in a unique way in Holland. Any group of parents or citizens may found a private school which will, automatically, qualify for state subsidy under certain conditions ... the constitutional amendment in 1917 which put public and private schools on an equal financial footing has since been extended to other types of school, with the result that the majority of Dutch schools are in private ownership... the consequence of stressing the importance of private initiative in the founding of schools has been a proliferation of specialised secondary institutions. Parents have a choice of ten different types of secondary education...[24]

These range from general schools to specific kinds of technical and vocational training.

This experience shows that it is perfectly possible to combine public funding with a considerable degree of parental choice and the provision of private schools. However, we should perhaps recognize that the Dutch system has been associated with a fairly high proportion of GNP being devoted to education. But if a voucher scheme were based on current unit costs per pupil, it could well prove a more economical way of encouraging diversity and choice in Britain. It would also help to close the socially divisive gap between state and independent schools which the policies of the last few years have done so much to widen. And it would do this in a way which brings the possiblility of choice to *all* parents and not just a few as is the case with the assisted places scheme.

However, a voucher scheme would be sure to encounter predictable and vehement opposition – from the administrators, the local education authorities and from teacher unions. Why? The administrators and the local education authorities would oppose it primarily because it would reduce their power – although they might argue that it would be administratively complex, which could well be true during the transitional stage. And unions such as the National Union of Teachers would oppose it because they are against freedom of choice for parents.[25] When the Kent County Council carried out a feasibility study[26] on a voucher scheme, the National Union of Teachers combined with the National Association of Schoolmasters/Union of Women Teachers to advise their members to reject a voucher scheme and to state that they would not be prepared to teach in a voucher school. They even supplied their members with suggested reasons for opposition! And the NUT have since published a leaflet[27] attacking the Kent proposals primarily because they would not give parents *unlimited* choice of school. They ignore the fact that choice would be significantly greater than under the present system and they give little weight to the opinions of parents, two-thirds of whom thought that their present choice of school was too restricted.

Thus there is likely to be enough grass-roots support for a voucher scheme to counterbalance the predictable opposition of those with vested interests in the present system.

Conclusion

Our proposals, if implemented, would shift the emphasis in the organization of education away from the University Grants Committee, the Department of Education and Science and local educational authorities and towards individual universities, colleges and schools. In our view this would be a welcome change since it would involve many more people in educational decisions and would make our education system much more directly accountable than it is at present because the professionals – academics and teachers – would have a direct incentive to be more professional. The state would still have a major role to play since it would continue to provide most of the financial resources. But they would be spent in ways which were much more under the control of individual citizens. In our view education is neither wholly a public nor a private good, and the blend we propose of public finance and individual control would thus be entirely appropriate. The result would be a much more equal partnership between the state, the professional academics and teachers, and parents, students and pupils.

As a nation we choose to devote enormous resources to education. It is entirely appropriate in a democratic and open society that there should be more direct accountability, more adaptability and responsiveness to change and more democratic involvement in education. The problem is how to achieve these desirable ends without jeopardizing teaching and learning – the essential purposes of education.

We think that our proposals, taken together, would both improve the way in which we use scarce educational resources and help to enhance the educational effectiveness of our schools and colleges.

Notes

1. Compare the proportion spent on defence: in 1960 the ratio of defence to education spending was 1.75 but by 1974 education had overtaken defence and the ratio had fallen to 0.87. `
2. All these figures are taken from DES statistics.
3. Level funding or even a small decrease in real terms as proposed in the 1980 White Paper on expenditure makes virtually no difference to this statement.
4. Wedgwood Benn, C. *We Must Choose Which We Want* (National Union of Teachers and the Campaign for Comprehensive Education, 1974).
5. OECD Conference on Policies for Educational Growth, Paris, 1970.
6. Jacka, K., Cox, C. and Marks, J., *Rape of Reason – The Corruption of the Polytechnic of North London* (Churchill Press 1975).

7. Gould, J., *The Attack on Higher Education: Marxist and Radical Penetration* (Institute for the Study of Conflict 1977).
8. Searle, J., *The Campus War* (Pelican 1972).
9. The Labour controlled Local Education Authority in Brent imposed policies concerning pupil governors and corporal punishment against the explicit recommendation of a school Governing Body.
10. Reported at a conference of the National Council for Educational Standards, September 1979.
11. *Aspects of Secondary Education in England – A Survey by HM Inspectors of Schools* (HMSO 1979).
12. Smith, A., *The Wealth of Nations,* on pp. 249 and 246 of the 1977 Everyman Edition (J.M. Dent 1979).
13. See references 6 and 7 above.
14. Evidence to House of Commons Select Committee on Education, Science and the Arts, May 1980.
15. Woodhall, M., *Student Loans* (Harrap 1970).
16. Lewis, A., Sandford, C. and Thomson, N., *Grants or Loans* (Institute of Economic Affairs 1980).
17. Harris, R. and Seldon, A., *Over-ruled on Welfare* (Institute of Economic Affairs 1979).
18. Hopkins, A., *The School Debate* (Penguin 1978), quoted in Cox, C. and Marks, J., *Education and Freedom – The Roots of Diversity* (National Council for Educational Standards 1980).
19. Hopkins, A., op. cit.
20. National Union of Teachers, Annual Conference, 1970.
21. *Secondary Education in the 1980s – a Consultative Document* (London Borough of Brent 1980).
22. Simon, B., *Education and the Right Offensive,* in the February 1980 edition of *Marxism Today,* a journal published by the British Communist Party. Professor Simon is a member of the Communist Party's Theory and Ideology Committee.
23. France, too, has a significant private sector – 17% of children there are in private schools, many of which are subsidized by the state. For example, more than 80% of teachers in private schools have their salaries paid by the state.
24. Wilkinson, M., *Lessons from Europe* (Centre for Policy Studies 1976).
25. See reference 20 above.
26. *Education Vouchers in Kent* (Kent County Council Education Department 1978).
27. *The case against Education Vouchers,* Fightback Series No. 3 (NUT 1978).

The Content of Education:
Standards, Curricula and Examinations

III
The Two Nations in Education

Elizabeth Cottrell

Head of Research at the Centre for Policy Studies. Educated at grammar school and the universities of Cambridge (M.A.) and Nottingham (Ph.D.), she is a qualified teacher and has taught in every type of secondary school and also in adult education. She is an Examiner and Moderator for GCE O- and A-levels. She resigned from the civil service in 1976 on being adopted as Prospective Parliamentary Candidate for Redcar, which she fought for the Conservatives in the 1979 General Election.

Through carelessness and ignorance we have divided our children of secondary school age into two nations. These are illustrated by the two schools, a state comprehensive and an independent grammar school, which are discussed in this chapter. The schools are compared in terms of physical equipment, curricula, streaming, staffing, discipline; attitude to Assemblies and Religious Education and to the socio-economic backgrounds of the pupils.

The independent school represented order and harmony, the comprehensive chaos. The assumption that parents want these chaotic schools is challenged with evidence from various surveys and from the schools which parents have founded, especially the new Yarm school in Cleveland.

It is argued that parents have the right to information about schools and especially the right to choice. This is the only way to eradicate these chaotic schools. The problem is urgent, because an alien generation is being created. Only an enlightened Conservative Party can remedy this. It should do so speedily.

'I was told that the Privileged and the People formed Two Nations' (Disraeli, *Sibyl*, Book IV, Chapter 8, 1845).

Disraeli's two nations were the rich and poor of industrial Victorian England, separated by barriers which were largely the result of economic forces. In the latter half of the twentieth century we have divided our secondary school children into two nations. These are the "Privileged" whose parents can choose their schooling because they can afford to pay for it, and the "People" who have no choice except the state comprehensive neighbourhood school because their parents cannot afford to pay. There are variations within these two broad divisions, such as the children who attend the few remaining grammar schools, but this is how the majority of the nation's children are divided.

This tragic division is not the result of economic forces, but of a small amount of strong left-wing political will, assisted by a vast amount of ignorance and carelessness. Politicians, especially local councillors, have been led astray by educational theories which are largely unproved or proved only in limited contexts.[1] They have even been used as tools by those, sometimes in positions of power in the local or national educational establishment, whose ultimate aim is the destruction of the free society.

As a Conservative, it distresses me when Conservative politicians allow themselves to be so used. In its approach to education during the last twenty years, the Conservative party has exhibited some of its worst features. It has shown its lack of political will, its concern for opportunism rather than principle, its often abysmal ignorance of the state education system and the feelings and aspirations of those who use that system. There are honourable exceptions who speak with both knowledge and conviction – a notable example is Dr Rhodes Boyson – but many members of the party have allowed one of the finest educational systems in the world to disappear by default.

I am not saying that all state schools – or, at least, all comprehensive schools – are bad and all independent schools good. I am saying that many features common to many comprehensive schools are deprivations to their pupils. There must be some good comprehensive schools.

Similarly one assumes that there are bad independent schools. These are rarely heard of because no parent would waste money for long on a school which turned out illiterate, untrained, ill-disciplined, uncultured pupils. Any fee-paying school which produced such results would soon lose its customers and therefore its existence. The parents in the state system cannot so withdraw their custom. Bold would be the man who refused to pay his rates because he felt his child's schooling to be inadequate (although over 50 per cent of his rates are spent on education).

There *are* good comprehensive schools. There are certainly some whose pupils achieve distinguished A-level results and Oxbridge entrances. But I am concerned with the "average" comprehensive school and the education, in every sense of the word, which the "average" pupil receives there. Academic results, although important, are only one measure of a school's achievement.

I want to record my views because I believe that too little is written about schools by those who have taught in them. The basis for the opinions expressed here is my own recent teaching experience. To this are added views which I have gathered from others, mostly parents, in my capacity as a Conservative parliamentary candidate in a traditionally Labour area, and as a speaker to various groups and organizations throughout the country. The evidence I present is, therefore, largely personal and anecdotal and has the validity of personal experience.[2] Much of the evidence about schools is based on research surveys in which pictures of real schools are often lost in a mass of data. As an experienced headmaster said of the recent survey by the National Children's Bureau,[3] 'The ordinary parent wants to know what happens at the school down the road'.[4]

My instinctive care and concern is for the state schools and those educated in them, especially bright working-class children. My brothers and I were such, educated in local authority grammar schools. These are the children I believe to be now the most deprived. I say this to show that I have no original personal bias towards the fee-paying sector of education. I *want* to be able to say that state schools are the best schools and am only sorry that I cannot.

In this essay I compare two schools in which I taught in succeeding terms some three years ago. They were in the same area, about ten miles apart, but mentally and spiritually they were in different worlds – illustrating the Two Nations. School A was an 11-16 state comprehensive school, School B an 11-18 selective independent school. School A was fully comprehensive in years 1 and 2, years 3 to 5 were still secondary modern school children. School B was a former direct grant grammar school, taking in a wider band of pupils than under the 11-plus system. Both were day schools. School A had 1250 girls and boys, School B some 600 girls.

While it is difficult to make generalizations from two schools, I was assured by local authority representatives that School A was an "average" school, not one of their "problem" establishments. School B was very "minor" in independent school terms. Thus the comparison is not between the William Tyndale School and Eton; moreover, I could draw very similar contrasts between other comprehensive and independent schools in which I have taught.

As far as physical equipment was concerned, School A was certainly the superior. The first thing one noticed was the newness of most of the desks. Yet their purpose was obscure as they were used purely as tables. It seemed that if they were used for storage the contents were invariably stolen.[5] This meant that the children struggled round school with great shopping-bags or haversacks full of their possessions, a seemingly unnecessary complication in their lives. School B had little dark-stained old-fashioned desks – often too small for their occupants. But each girl had a desk of her own for her possessions – a private base at school.

School A had some fine sets of almost new text-books and other resource material. One was asked to order more of these if possible before the end of the summer term or the allowance for them in the following year might be cut. Yet, except for those used by a few O-level pupils, these books were normally handed out at the beginning of a lesson and collected in at the end – a waste of ten minutes' teaching time. It was said that the children could not be trusted with them – if taken home they would be lost or defaced. And they would only have added more weight to the shopping bags. Dare one misquote 'Unto whom little is given, of him is little expected.'

In School B the textbooks, although not out of date, were old. The girls vied with one another for the book which had had the greatest number of owners or had been used by an older sister or friend. Each girl had a textbook of her own for each subject, and the first homework of the autumn term was to cover these books with brown paper.

School A had three television sets – one had to be up very early to book one of them. I believe that there was a television set in School B, but I never heard of anyone using it.

To have good modern equipment is not reprehensible if it enables one to teach better lessons and produce better results. But what School A did suggest was that state schools are in no way deprived of this modern equipment; attempts by some of them to blame their inadequacies on their lack of it seem, at best, muddle-headed and, at worst, downright dishonest. In terms of physical equipment the average state school would seem to be far better off than the average independent school.

At first sight there was little difference between the curricula of the two schools. School A, with its wider ability range, offered more opportunity for practical work. Technology and Home Economics were important departments. Latin was not taught[6] but French and Spanish were. In School B Latin, French and German were taught, and Greek was available as an option after the third year. All sciences were taught in both schools. School A taught Social Studies: in the lower school this was a fairly harmless mixture of history and geography often with a local flavour. In the fourth and fifth years it became Social Education and occupied 70 minutes a week in an attempt to honour the compulsory Religious Instruction lesson demanded by the 1944 Education Act.[7] I shall say more of this later. The school provided Commerce as an optional subject in years 4 and 5. In the third, fourth and fifth years, 70 minutes a week were spent on Careers lessons; third year careers work was 'based on self-assessment; the importance of understanding strengths and weaknesses in physical, intellectual and personality makeup'.[8] Fourth year careers work included 'job simulation tasks in the classroom'.[9] Parents might be forgiven for wondering whether 70 minutes a week could not have been better spent on more practice in those basic skills (reading, writing and arithmetic), without which no job is attainable.

Yet with these few exceptions any School A parent looking at his child's timetable would have seen a range of traditional subjects. Here one realizes the danger of not knowing the curriculum content, not knowing what may masquerade under an innocently traditional title. It is not enough for governments to insist that so much time must be allotted to certain subjects, such as English or Religious Education, without also discovering how that time is spent and what that subject covers.

Let us take English as an example. The foundation of education must surely be the use of one's own language. Many children in secondary modern schools took English Language as their only and/or most important O-level subject. Yet in School A, not only did the majority take a CSE English Language course, they took a CSE Mode III.[10] The head of the English department informed the third-year parents that 'A Mode III exam, in fact, contains no exam at all'.[11] He felt that it, therefore, eliminated the possibility of the apparently reprehensible "once-for-all" test situation. It also eliminates any of these pupils from getting a job which asked for English Language O-level – unless a gullible employer would accept a Mode III Grade I. It seems particularly unfair to the pupils to give them this kind of examination in a subject as important as English. There were surely few secondary modern schools which did not give at least their top stream the opportunity to take English Language at O-level.

English Literature was also offered as an optional subject after the third year. The head of English thought it as well to warn pupils what they were undertaking: 'Students plumping for this option should be keen readers if not actual book-worms... Much of the course, in fact, will be taken up by reading'.[12] *Mirabile dictu.* The more able pupils were given the opportunity to study for O-level English Literature – although they were warned that this would mean some extra lessons out of school time. O-level English Literature could not be fitted onto the "normal" school timetable. Might it not usefully have replaced some of the time spent on Careers or on Social Education? Again, the head of English felt that pupils must be warned of the limitations of the O-level course:

> The course is totally different from English Language CSE ... There will be little or no opportunity to write your own stories and poems in this option. Your time will be taken up in studying works of merit by great English and American writers.[13]

Perhaps it was not surprising that none of the fourth year had chosen to study English Literature and had thus cut themselves off at the age of 14 from regular guided contact with one of the mainsprings of their cultural inheritance.

In School B, all pupils – however limited, and stream 3 were secondary modern school children – took O-level English Language and English Literature as a matter of course. The fact that the vast majority of these achieved pass grades suggests that many secondary modern school children, well-taught and well-motivated, can do this, as, indeed, they did in the secondary modern schools.

Let us now consider Religious Education – which certainly sounds conventional and traditional, and is another subject which the present government intends to include in its core curriculum. Here are some of the questions from a CSE Mode III paper called "Religious Studies" which had been set in School A.

> – What changes have taken place in the field of contraceptive facilities and sex education in the last 20 years or so?
> – What difference has (*sic*) (a) contraceptives, (b) sex education made to the lives of young, single people?

The compulsory Religious Education (Social Education) syllabi for the fourth and fifth years included such subjects as "Sweating", "Masturbation", "Self and Authority", "World Problems seen through the eyes of individuals", "People who are different". Nowhere in the syllabus is any reference made to considering these problems in the light of religious traditions – whether Christian or any other. So, even if children of 14 - 16 are capable of studying these matters, even if there are teachers capable of teaching them, even if they should be taught under the blanket of RE, the children were being deprived of access to their Christian cultural heritage – they would leave school largely ignorant of their own or, indeed, any other great world religious tradition. The CSE RE option did include some Bible study, as did first and second year work, but the child's contact with the Bible at school would be minimal – another severance from a mainspring of his cultural inheritance.

At School B, RE teaching was based on the Bible and the Christian tradition.

At the end of the third year, the pupils at School A chose their options for the remaining two years of their school lives and, therefore, their O-level or CSE subjects. Apart from English Language and Mathematics which were compulsory, six optional subjects were to be chosen, although not all of these were examination subjects. Pupils were advised to choose a balanced programme and most did so. The noticeable omissions were English Literature, as mentioned above, and the scarcity of work in foreign languages. Of 240 fourth-year pupils, only sixty (25 per cent) were studying a foreign language; of these eighteen were following a new European Studies course whose linguistic content was considerably less than that of the traditional CSE language courses. Fourteen were studying both French and Spanish. So 75 per cent of pupils received no instruction in any European language after the age of 14. Is this not cultural deprivation?

In fairness, it must be said that these statistics might well improve when the intake of children at School A is fully comprehensive. But many secondary modern schools allowed for more language teaching than this. There was no classical studies' course at School A, so that there was little contact with the cultures of Greece and Rome.

In School B every girl studied a language until she was 16. A very popular classical studies course was provided for the non-Latinists, so that all pupils encountered Graeco-Roman culture at some stage in their school career.

O-level options at School B ensured that every pupil took English Language, English Literature and Mathematics, a language, a science and about four other optional subjects which gave them a well-balanced certificate. All girls took the O-level examination. At School A, O-level was available as an option in some subjects, but CSE seemed to be more encouraged. Not even the *top groups* normally took O-level but only a few of the top pupils. In Mathematics, for example, Course A, the "top" course, was 'A course for the most able, leading to a CSE Mode I examination in Fifth Year. Any boy or girl showing particular aptitude will have the opportunity to enter for the GCE O-level examination'.[14] No O-level courses were provided in Art, Needlework, Spanish, Music, Woodwork, Metalwork or Technical Drawing. We have already seen the comments of the head of the English department, which seem to disparage the O-level examination.[15] The general comments in the Information Booklet included the following rather strange statement: 'GCE O-level is a pass-or-fail examination' (is that not the definition of an examination?), 'but the results of the CSE are expressed as a range of grades from I down to 5, all of which are of value to a pupil as a qualification for life after school.' Is a GCE grade then not of value? What *is* the meaning behind this statement? It is not even accurate as, sadly, O-level itself is no longer a pass-or-fail examination, since the introduction of Grades A-E in 1975, none of which was meant to be "failing".[16]

Apart from Maths and a few minority subjects in the fourth and fifth years, all subjects in School A were taught in what their Booklet called 'the mixed-ability situation'. There are many comprehensive schools where this is not so – where pupils are streamed or at least taught in bands or sets. Yet some educational theorists would argue that a school cannot be truly comprehensive if the pupils are streamed[17] and that School A is, therefore, the best type of comprehensive school. I believe that mixed-ability teaching benefits none of the pupils. To whom should the lessons be directed – the potential University entrant or the remedial reader? If both are in the same set one or other will be deprived. And if the teaching is directed at the pupils in the middle-ability range then both the most bright and the least bright will be deprived. Perhaps an exceptionally able teacher could cope, but most teachers are inevitably average teachers. Perhaps it would be possible to teach small groups in this way, but the mixed-ability groups that I taught for CSE contained as many as 27 pupils. With such large groups there was virtually no opportunity for the "individualized learning" concept – the teaching of individual children separately – which constitutes much of what is called mixed-ability teaching. Not that this has a great deal to commend it: it is absurdly uneconomical and no one gets very much teaching so that the bright children, particularly, become very bored. It needs very small numbers and very able teachers.

There may be social arguments for mixed-ability teaching, although the "individualized learning" concept is positively anti-social. The educational arguments, such as that the presence of bright children in a class stimulates and challenges the rest, rarely work in practice because, like so much modern educational theory, they ignore human nature. The high flyers are much more likely to be held down by the lack of the stimulus of comparably able fellow class members and to be content with a mediocre performance. Mixed-ability teaching, therefore, contains the seeds of national economic disaster because it fails to realize the full potential of both the brightest children and the least bright. It penalizes those who should contribute most to national wellbeing and makes the less adequate even less adequate.

School B was totally streamed in all years except the first.

Comparison of the examination results of the two schools would not be fair given their very different histories. Suffice it to say that about 0.5 per cent left School B with no academic qualifications whereas judging from the fourth-year work which I received at School A, some pupils leaving there must have had a reading age of less than nine.

Academic prowess is only one part of a school's achievement. What of general behaviour, appearance, discipline in the two schools?

Both had a uniform. In School A, the girls generally wore it, the boys – especially fourth and fifth years – less so. There seemed little attempt to enforce it or to point out that the denims favoured instead were probably far more expensive, and were ugly and slovenly. It might have been difficult to make this point when several of the staff (of both sexes) came to school in denim jeans, sometimes frayed and worn. In School B, uniform was worn by all the girls. Female staff were asked not to wear trousers.

One of the curious features of School A was that the girls always walked round school wearing their coats. They claimed that, if left in the cloakroom, they were "nicked". This situation was accepted, the only stipulation being that coats should be removed during lessons – another waste of teaching time. But the "nicking" was apparently accepted as inevitable.

As far as the general discipline of School A was concerned individual teachers exercised it in their own classrooms, but behaviour in the general parts of the school was shocking. At 4 pm any short and/or slight female teachers were well advised to cower quietly in their classrooms until the stampeding mob had gone.

This mob could be quelled by large men with large voices, but no one else stood a chance. Many of School A's pupils, particularly the less intelligent, were totally confused by the apparent lack of common standards among the staff. If some teachers let them sit with their feet on the desks, they argued quite reasonably, why should others object? Some staff allowed swearing and chewing, others did not. At least one teacher encouraged pupils to call him by his Christian name – why did not all the staff do this, asked some? Others, wiser in their generation, found this disturbing and obviously craved for the disciplined order of former times. One of the wildest spirits told me that he had preferred his primary school 'because you knew where you were, if you were bad you got hit.' The pupils did not even know if they were supposed to say 'good morning', some teachers did, others did not. There were prefects, but they were mainly message carriers and wielded little authority.

One expected School B to be less noisy, because there were fewer pupils and no boys, but there was here a great sense of order. In a much smaller building with far less space, girls moved quietly and quickly. Classes rose cheerfully to greet their teachers. There were common standards of behaviour, stemming largely from a common standard set by the staff. Some teachers were certainly stricter than others but all inculcated and expected the same basic standards of behaviour. An unspoken code of consideration for others prevailed. A class could be left with a prefect as safely as with a member of staff. There was a cheerful symmetry about the place, only achieved in School A in odd corners like the library.

It was, perhaps, in the staff that the two schools were most different. It is difficult to comment upon the quality of teachers because it is so true as to be almost platitudinous that their excellence or otherwise has little to do with their paper qualifications. Yet these are one of the few bench marks by which we can judge them. In School A, twelve of the sixty-two staff were graduates. A further thirteen were specialist Home Economics, Physical Education or Technology teachers some of whom would have qualified before it was possible to get a degree in these subjects.[18] It seemed curious that so few of the young teachers, appointed after the school became fully comprehensive and at a time when competition for teaching jobs was presumably fierce, were graduates; only two of the twelve were under thirty. While no one claims that a degree necessarily makes a good teacher, there was a scarcity of university experience for the teaching of children, a fair percentage of whom must have been of university potential. There was a scarcity of people who had studied their own subject in the depth necessary to achieve a degree; some people who had themselves been incapable of studying to Advanced level were teaching children who would be well able to do so. This was less serious than it would have been in a comprehensive school with a sixth form. Examples certainly exist of A-level subjects being *taught* by those who were themselves incapable of studying them. At least that was not the case here.

In more general terms, there was a scarcity of that breadth of vision and culture which many people, though by no means all, imbibe from a university education. It seemed strange that of the four teachers who constituted the senior management team, only one had a degree and that had been achieved on a year's secondment course, so none of them had had a conventional university education.

About 12 per cent of the staff of School A had qualified for teaching as mature students, many of them in the "teacher-training bulge" of the 1960s. Like many people, I had always paid lip-service to these late entrants to the teaching profession, arguing that they would bring a wider experience into the narrow world of school and, therefore, broaden the outlook of their pupils. That may be true but the reality has disadvantages too. First, the entry standard of these older trainee teachers was often very low, much lower than that of the school-leaver trainee teacher, and the pass rate at the end of their courses was frighteningly high.[19] Secondly, having "succeeded" themselves without a conventional academic education they cannot always see why it is necessary for others. These older people are often more articulate than the young teachers straight from college and, therefore, exert an influence disproportionate to their numbers on both staff room and pupils. Their "training" has not necessarily included those cultural foundations which most teachers imbided in their own schooling. Some few of them, especially among the men, entered teaching because they were not very successful in their previous jobs. This is particularly true of those who came out of industry. They, therefore, help to perpetuate that feeling of opposition to industry which is one of the banes of British schools. Some of these teachers came from heavily unionized jobs and have brought these attitudes into teaching, which is probably one of the reasons why the profession has been so much more union-minded in the last twenty years. I do not say that all or any of those teachers at School A who had been trained in maturity had all or any of these characteristics, but the law of averages would suggest that some of them had some of these characteristics.

School B had about thirty-nine members of staff, including six who taught only in the junior school. Of these, six were non-graduates and a further four were non-graduates teaching PE and Home Economics. The vast majority of the staff were professional teachers who had entered the profession in their early twenties and saw it as their life's career. This may have given some of them a narrowness of vision but this is surely a danger present in every profession. No one ever suggests that doctors or lawyers are dangerously narrow because they have been practising the same trade since their twenties, yet their jobs may be just as narrowing as teaching.

The teachers in School B shared the same educational and cultural background. They had widely differing views, on politics and religion for example, but common standards and values. They thought it important to be clean and tidy, well-spoken and courteous. Their views are often contemptuously dismissed as "middle class" values, but when analysed they are, in essence, the values of all decent people, regardless of so-called class. At least they gave their pupils a standard to emulate or to reject. The social pattern of School A, where like the ancient Israelites everyone "did what was right in his own eyes", must have been most confusing to the pupils, as some of them freely admitted.

This lack of a common "ethos" in School A was seen most forcibly in its Assemblies. Incidentally, I was amazed to find that comprehensive schools can break the law, apparently with impunity. Section 25 of the 1944 Education Act stipulates that

> the school day in every county school and in every voluntary school shall begin with *collective worship* on the part of *all* pupils in attendance.

Yet, at School A, the third, fourth and fifth years had school assembly only three times a week and house assembly once. The reason for this was never clear since the school hall held all the upper school. Apart from any other consideration this flouting of the law surely set a very bad example to the pupils.

The content of the Assemblies was also puzzling. Only once, at the end of term, was a hymn sung, although the school had an excellent piano and some good musicians. Prayers there were, and often the Lord's Prayer. But the main part of the Assembly was usually a reading and a chat by a member of staff. The Bible was rarely read. Most of the literature chosen was commonplace and ephemeral. So, again, these children were starved of the Bible which, all spiritual considerations apart, is superb literature, and of other fine literature which they might have imbibed from this period. They were cut off from that Judaeo/Christian tradition which is the basis of our way of life. And I believe that their parents were cheated too, for many parents, totally uncaring about their own religious life, do want their children to receive religious teaching and assume that the school is providing it.[20] The talks by the staff were vaguely moral and often based on personal experience. United with a living religious tradition they might have been useful. There were notable exceptions – I failed to see how one teacher's explanation of why he was an atheist could possibly qualify as "collective worship". Even less relevant, though possibly less harmful, was the same young man's description of his American holiday which was the subject of one house assembly.

These Assemblies had no pattern or order and they gave none to the day. Their format was presumably based on the idea that children dislike conventional Assemblies. N.G. Quine's research suggests the opposite. In the schools which he investigated the pupils '... accepted assemblies – their only criticism being that there was too little emphasis on hymns and prayers'.[21] Even if the majority of children do not listen in an Assembly, impressions are registered on their subconscious minds. Surely it is better for these to be of great literature and religious tradition than of ephemeral "chat". It is no exaggeration to say that these children were greatly deprived in their Assemblies. It seemed particularly unfortunate that the traditional assembly was abandoned in the third year, at the age of 13, a notoriously unsettled age. Were the children to accept the implication that at that age one put away childish things – like religion?

School B, which as an independent school had no legal obligation to hold a religious Assembly, held one every day. It was very traditional, consisting of a hymn, a Bible reading, and a prayer. There was, indeed, room for some modernization. Nevertheless, it promulgated traditional Christian faith and Judaeo-Christian culture. It was orderly and dignified. It left one calmed and refreshed for the day's work.

Yet it was School A which, while depriving its children in practice, paid most lip-service to the development of the whole personality of the pupil. One of the main ways in which it sought to achieve this development was through a strong system of pastoral care, using form and house tutors, heads of year and heads of house. What were the apparent results of this?

I found in School A an almost obsessive interest in the socio-economic background and circumstances of the children. A child's deficiencies were almost automatically attributed to his background; 'What can you expect – they're a one-parent family' or, even stranger, 'What can you expect, he's one of eight (or nine or ten) children.'

One thought of that great scholar, Sir Ernest Barker, eldest of seven children of a farm labourer, of Aneurin Bevan, politician and orator extraordinary, one of the ten children of a Welsh miner; and of the thousands of ordinary people who had found their large families a blessing, not a curse. I thought of my own father, one of the twelve children of a Welsh collier. He would have laughed heartily at the idea that he was "deprived". And what of one-parent families? One thought of Ramsay MacDonald, first Labour Prime Minister of Great Britain and product of a "one-parent" family. Or what of Ernest Bevin, that great Foreign Secretary? The illegitimate son of a village midwife who had separated from her husband some years before his birth and called herself a widow, the youngest of six sons, orphaned at 8 and brought up by a half-sister, never knowing who is father was – would he not have been a prime target for pastoral care? But he was only one of the thousands of men and women, successful in small ways and in great, who have sprung from such families. Are the children of today so much less capable?

No one would deny that there are circumstances in which it is important for a school to know of an individual child's home background but a knowledge of his socio-economic group is largely irrelevant and leads to those rash generalizations I mentioned earlier. While a caring teacher must be aware of the possible problems which may arise from a child's background, if a child is to overcome these they should surely be forgotten for all practical purposes in day-to-day life, lest they become a permanent crutch or excuse. The greatest gift that one can give a child is the opportunity to leave the problems and complexities of its background at the school door. School should provide an escape into a world of order and sanity.

Such an escape was provided in School B. The children there had their problems. The current phenomenon of one-parent families knows no "class" or income barriers, nor do parental promiscuity or alcoholism. But School B provided an ordered society for its pupils and gave those who had little security at home at least one secure base in their lives.

Much of the pastoral concern in School A sprang from the best of motives but, like all charity, it could be heavy-handed. In cases where a child had great difficulties the house/year head or form/house tutor was encouraged to visit the home. What was the reaction of the parents to these – surely, to them – interlopers? What was the effect on working-class pride, a pride which I know from personal experience? I found it very hard to believe that these people were so sunk in failure that they had lost all pride.

A combination of factors, including this interest in pastoral care, resulted in an inordinate amount of attention being given to the *few* who were the greatest trouble-makers, the most inadequate, not necessarily academically, but socially and spiritually. These few, and few they were, had far more attention from the staff than any potential Oxbridge scholar in any grammar school of my acquaintance. Meanwhile, the *good* majority were often ignored, surely a temptation to any child seeking a little attention to join the troublemakers? This is a serious phenomenon in a school. It sows the seeds of the great attention paid to these nuisances in later life, by trade unions or social services, for example. Of course, they are important, as all people are, but far more important for our national future, both economic and spiritual, are the *good* children who will become the *good* citizens. Why should they be neglected?

School B produced few notorious troublemakers. The most obvious reason for this was that it could always ask such pupils to leave. School A had no such ultimate deterrent. Suspension, a favourite punishment, was regarded as a holiday; expulsion only meant transfer to another school. There will be no answer to this problem until a national decision is taken to let these unschoolable children go free and remain unschooled. We could then devote our expensive educational resources to the vast majority who will appreciate them.[22] Meanwhile, our School As should pay far less attention to this minority of troublesome children.

I have tried to draw a picture of two schools, based on my own experience. The picture is subjective and incomplete, but I believe that it is the one that any ordinary person, accustomed to normal society and its accepted moral and behavioural standards, would have drawn. I believe these two schools to be representative of many others.

The word I would use for School A is *chaotic*. Given that there are many schools in this land today that share many features of School A, why have they been allowed to develop in this way?

Many educational theorists tell us that these are the schools that people want. They say that parents do not want their children to be taught old-fashioned subjects, they do not want them to be made elitist by a streaming system, they do not want out-moded religion thrust down their throats nor alien middle-class standards of speech and behaviour forced upon them. Why, then, are such theorists so passionately opposed to educational vouchers or to any other means of increasing parental choice, a choice which would presumably vindicate their views? I ask them for their evidence for these supposed parental preferences. There may well be some research somewhere that provides it. But those of us who deal with the Mrs Joneses of this world know that they do not want chaos, academic or social, for their children. Nor is it fair to say, as some educationalists do, that they had similar chaos in the secondary modern schools. The secondary modern school in which I taught ten years ago was far more like School B than School A. There has been no popular outcry for the quality of education which I found in School A and no election manifesto of any party has ever promised it.

Least of all do so-called "ordinary" people desire this kind of education. Socialism, with its desire to destroy conventional standards, appeals mainly to middle-class intellectuals. The "working classes" may vote Labour (although a majority of them do not even do that), but they passionately believe in the old-fashioned virtues which socialism mocks. They are practical people and want their children to be equipped to get a job. They also want them to be well-turned-out and well-behaved, and are disappointed when a school does not teach them any of these things.

Public concern with education is far greater than most educational experts or politicians realize. As a parliamentary candidate I found that education was the most popular subject on the doorstep, at meetings and in private conversations. Much of the concern came from women, but some from men too. They worried about poor examination results, poor teachers, about choice of subjects and especially about the lack of discipline. Some, whose children would almost certainly not have passed the 11-plus, regretted the passing of the old system with its smaller schools and, in their view, more dedicated staff. Many parents resented the neighbourhood school concept and their lack of choice of school. When one pointed out that the old system had offered only a limited choice, the common reply was 'but at least there was the chance of the grammar school.' But it was not so much comprehensivization that worried these people, but *what went on in a particular school*. One could have quoted surveys on the blessings of comprehensivization to them *ad nauseam* but their children still had to go to a specific school and *they saw the evidence before them*.

Nor were these people by any means all Conservative voters. That would have been difficult in a constituency with a Labour majority of over 10,000 and a (then) Tory vote of only 12,000. A large proportion were in social classes C, D and E.[23] Many might be said to be "Conservative" only on education policy.

I find a similar concern for education among all the groups, throughout the country, to whom I speak in my political capacity. Try as I will to direct their discussion into other channels, it inevitably comes back to education. They are concerned for academic standards but above all for discipline and the inculcation of moral values and standards in schools. It was in prosperous Surrey, an area of "good" state schools, that a lady said: 'What point is there in politicians giving parents a choice of school? What choice do we have when state schools are so uniformly bad and private schools so expensive?'

In County Durham, an old farmer told how he would pause in his ploughing, look around and declaim:

> Breathes there a man with soul so dead
> Who never to himself hath said
> This is my own, my native land.

'They don't seem to teach children that sort of thing in school nowadays', he commented. Sentimental, perhaps, but apposite.

As all this evidence is anecdotal, I sought some documentary evidence which might possibly support it. I compiled a very rudimentary questionnaire[24] and asked it of forty-eight sets of parents, all of social classes C, D and E, in the general area of Schools A and B. This was a very small sample, but the answers were reasonably consistent.

Of those questioned, 75 per cent would have liked a choice of secondary school[25] and would have been willing to pay extra costs such as bus fares to enable a child to reach a chosen school. A third of the parents wanted daily Acts of Worship, and half wanted at least one a week. All parents thought the provision of teachers and books the top priority for a school, both more important than audio-visual equipment, and teachers twice as important as new desks. The parents were almost universal in considering training to get a job as the most important thing a school could give their child, closely and naturally followed by good O-level results. The teaching of good manners and good speech they felt to be primarily the duty of home, not school. Only a sixth did not want their children punished at all, and a third wanted corporal punishment. Two-thirds approved of school uniform. A quarter would have liked the choice of a single-sex school.[26] The reasons 42 per cent gave for saying that they would consider an independent school if they could have afforded it were most interesting. They included: dissatisfaction with the area's state schools and especially with the lack of choice; belief that independent schools provided "a better education – the right curriculum, better academically qualified staff and more individual tuition". Remember that these comments all came from parents for whom School A made so many excuses and on whom they blamed so many of their children's faults. It suggests to me that these parents, of average and lower than average social and economic status, know what makes a good school and would use an educational choice system wisely. Many middle-class people, including perhaps some councillors, seem to find this hard to believe.

It is interesting to see that the conclusions of my questionnaire are largely borne out by the very careful survey conducted by the Kent County Council on the subject of education vouchers.[27] Although Kent is generally regarded as prosperous and rich compared with Northern England, nearly 75 per cent of the parents interviewed were of class C and below, over 40 per cent being of class C2, skilled manual workers. This was one of the main conclusions of the Survey:

> The great majority of parents felt that they should be allowed to choose which school their child was to go to and 60 per cent thought that they did not have enough say in choice of school at the moment … 21 per cent of secondary school parents were willing to pay towards travel to the school of their choice.[28]

A larger proportion of parents in Classes C to E felt that they should have a choice of school regardless of cost, 58.4 per cent of Class D as against 46.3 per cent of Class B.[29] Strange decisions for "working class" parents who are said to neither know nor care about education.

When it came to judging a school 'It would seem that for the majority of parents the quality of teaching staff overrides all other considerations'.[30] Other important features were the school's academic record and firm discipline. Concern about school buildings came well down the list.

A survey conducted by Tyne-Tees Television in January 1980[31] also found interest and concern for education. In the area of Tyneside, Wearside and Teesside – which is also the area of Schools A and B – 93 per cent of those interviewed were using state schools for their children, yet 58 per cent declared themselves in favour of private education. Whereas 21 per cent of the state-school parents declared themselves dissatisfied with their children's education, *all* the private sector parents were satisfied with theirs. Opinions on comprehension were almost equally divided, 49 per cent thinking it was the best form of education, 47 per cent that it was not.

No information is given about the social class of the respondents in this survey but we can assume a large proportion of Cs to Es in this area, by no means acquiescing silently in a comprehensive upheaval.

In some instances, parents have shown their concern for their children's education by actually setting up schools. A notable example of this is Yarm School in the county of Cleveland where a group of parents and other well-wishers bought the old grammar school, abandoned by the local education authority as a result of its comprehensive reorganization and, in 1978, opened it as a new independent day grammar school for boys. To quote the School Prospectus:

> Many parents in the area felt that the total loss of schools based on an academic tradition was too high a price to pay.

As the school is largely funded by a Share Bond scheme, parents have a strong interest in its continuing success. According to the Headmaster, Mr R.N. Tate, parents are not interested only or even primarily in academic results. They are looking for educational values and the inculcation of old-fashioned virtues, like self-discipline, loyalty, courtesy, pride in their school. They feel that comprehensive schools, at least the ones they know, do not stress these things. Strong minorities of the parents welcome a single-sex school and a traditional attitude towards religion.

Mr Tate says that the Yarm parents could be roughly divided into three groups. There are the 25 per cent who come themselves from the independent school tradition; the majority, perhaps half, had received a state grammar school education themselves (at least one parent had), and wanted their sons to have the same style of education. The remainder had themselves attended secondary modern schools and did not like what they saw of the values of the comprehensive schools. Although it would be invidious to make detailed comments, the Yarm parents certainly include some in Classes C to E, people who are willing to make the sacrifice of putting sometimes 25 per cent of their income into school fees.

Yarm is possibly the best example of a school founded by parents. But there are others, such as the village school at Madingley near Cambridge which the local parents bought when the education authority proposed to close it.[32]

Given the great parental concern and interest shown by these various examples, why are so many subjected to the School As of this land? There seem to be two main reasons. First, the ignorance of many parents about what is really going on in these state schools. This is often deliberately fostered by teachers and their unions,[33] by the local education authorities and by the whole educational establishment. They argue that as parents are not professional educators, they have no right to intrude upon the professional precincts of the school.

The Conservative Party manifesto of 1979 promised that 'Schools will be required to publish prospectuses giving details of their examination and other results.'[34] This requirement is provided for in the Information Clauses of the Education Act 1980.[35] The clauses, themselves, are rather vague but the Consultative Document[36] which amplifies them spells out in more reassuring detail the information which the schools should publish. This is certainly an important step in the right direction. Examination results should be known and cannot be falsified.[37]

But, how will the prospectus quantify other important aspects of the school, such as staffing and staff turnover, curricula, methods of school organization, discipline and pastoral care? What external monitor can be provided for these, as the Examination Boards provide an external monitor for examination results. I believe that there is a strong case for all this information to be monitored by an outside body; perhaps this could become a function of a fully restored government inspectorate. The local education authority teachers need an independent commentary on their activities, not one supplied by an adviser employed by the same authority – 'How can Satan cast out Satan?'

Information about a product is valueless if one has to buy it willy-nilly. Information is useless unless there is a choice – the choice to buy elsewhere. Pundits are shocked when education is spoken of in this way, 'as if it were a commodity like bacon'. It is precisely because it is a commodity far more important than bacon that it is so appalling that the British subject has more choice when buying bacon than when selecting a school for his child. Those parents in areas which provide no choice of school[38] are as deprived as the nineteenth-century factory worker forced to buy all his food, of poor quality and high price, at his master's tommyshop.[39]

The Conservative Party has paid lipservice for some time now to the idea of parental choice. In the 1979 Manifesto it promised to 'place a clear duty on government and local authorities to take account of parents' wishes when allocating children to schools, with a local appeals system for those dissatisfied'.[40] This promise is honoured in Section 6 of the Education Act 1980, but there is a limiting clause (Section 6.3 (a)) which provides an escape route for the local authority. The parental preference may be overruled 'if compliance with the preference would prejudice the provision of efficient education or efficient use of resources'.

This clause seems to give the local authority the chance to block as much parental choice as it wishes. The parent certainly has the right of appeal – but this puts all the onus on him, making hard labour of what should be a fundamental right.[41] The government must find some way of making parental choice at least 99 per cent mandatory on a local authority.

Can a parent have any real choice of school until he is treated as a customer, not as a suppliant for the state handout of education? For state education is *not* free, as socialists and other muddled thinkers maintain: it is only free at point of reception and is, in fact, vastly expensive. This expense is borne mainly by local ratepayers and a large percentage of these are parents. Virtually every parent will be a ratepayer and will, therefore, be paying – albeit indirectly – for his child's education. That is why he has the right to choose. If he were paying directly he would be the honoured customer as he is in an independent school, not the humble suppliant. And, incidentally, the child whose education is paid for generally knows that his education is a privilege not a right, because it has to be bought for him. How many children educated by the state realize that? The parent's psychology would change too – he would not accept an inferior product if he was handing out real money for it, his interest in a school would be closer, and he could – and would – withdraw his custom if dissatisfied.

The obvious answer is a voucher system, which would transform the parent into a customer. Forget the 5 per cent of parents who would burn the voucher. Their children are the unschoolable who are already using up far too many of our educational resources. Marjorie Seldon argues the case for the voucher system forcibly later in this book, but it seems to me to be much the best way in which to eradicate the School As of this country.

The problem of these schools is urgent. For in them we are producing an alien generation of children who do not accept the common standards and customs of society and who are starved of its culture. They are the majority of our future citizens, and it is unfair to deprive them of their natural inheritance – unfair to them, and dangerous for the future of the common weal.

The majority of the Conservative Party never understood the grammar schools. They did not understand the tremendous cultural heritage which these schools gave to their pupils. So they did not understand what they were doing when they allowed that heritage to be removed. The removers knew full well – they wished to create an alien generation, a "proletariat" out of touch with all the higher springs of national life.

We now have a more enlightened Party, led by a woman who was herself educated at a grammar school. This revivified Party must realize the people's concern for education. They must hear the clamour for true reform which comes even from the rank-and-file of their own Party. Only the Conservative Party can restore this lost inheritance to the children of this land. That they should do so is a matter of national urgency.

Notes

1. Many of the successful early comprehensive schools were small schools in rural areas. See R. Pedley, *The Comprehensive School* (London 1970), p. 69.
2. This point seems worth stressing. The article is not based on academic research but on personal experience which, although necessarily limited, has a strong validity of its own. While the facts about both schools are correct, the interpretation is, of course, my own. They could be interpreted quite differently. My stance is unashamedly polemical. I am not seeking to make definitive statements about different types of education but presenting evidence from which I believe certain conclusions can be drawn. Nor do I seek to question the integrity or motivation of others. These may be very high while the directions in which they work are misguided or just plain wrong. I sought to support my conclusions by a small survey (see p. 53). Again in no way could this be definitive. It merely stands as part of a body of evidence all of which seems to point in the same direction.
3. Jane Steedman, *Progress in Secondary Schools,* National Children's Bureau (London 1980).
4. Peter Dawson, *Daily Telegraph*, 17 July 1980.
5. The word used in the school was "nicked", a very popular word there.
6. I believe that Latin was introduced in the following year, taught to a few pupils outside normal school hours.
7. Education Act (HMSO 1944), Section 25.
8. Booklet of Information for Third Year Parents, 1977.
9. Ibid.
10. This is a CSE examination where the syllabus is written by the staff at the school and the examination set and marked by them. An external moderator from the CSE Board assists in awarding the final grade – the only external monitoring received. A Mode III is, therefore, open to criticism because so much responsibility for it rests within the school and it is likely to be much more subjective in content and assessment than a Mode I examination. It lacks the authority of a true external examination and provides no guarantee that the student has acquired a recognized common core of knowledge in a particular subject. A large proportion of the marks is awarded for coursework done by the pupils and, sometimes, as in the Mode III English described here, there is no examination at all, the grade being based wholly on coursework.
11. Booklet of Information for Third Year Parents, 1977.
12. Ibid.
13. Ibid.
14. Ibid.
15. See pp. 44-5.
16. Although only Grades A-C are recognized as representing what used to be pass grades.
17. See Pedley, op. cit., pp. 102ff.
18. All references to degrees include B.Ed. degrees.

19. Even as recently as 1975/76, of all students accepted for teacher training 41 per cent had not been able to pass O-level Mathematics, 25 per cent had only reached GCE O-level standard, and nearly 9 per cent had only the minimum of five O-levels *(Annual Report Central Register and Clearing House Limited – Autumn 1975 Entry)*.

20. See p. 53 for parents' views on Assemblies.

21. See N.G. Quine, "Polarised Culture in Comprehensive Schools", *Research in Education*, No. 12, November 1974.

22. This is a radical idea which obviously needs more explanation than is possible here. It is discussed more fully by Peter Dawson in the *Weekly Educational Review*, 18 June 1980.

23. 75.4 per cent were classes C, D and E compared with a national average of these classes in England and Wales of 56.3 per cent. (Figures from the 1971 Census.) C, D and E are the lowest three of the five socio-economic classes used by the Office of Population Censuses and Surveys. The Crowther Report showed that the grammar school academic sixth forms contained about 45 per cent of pupils from these classes (*Crowther Report*, Volume 1, p. 230).

24. See Note 2.

25. In this area no choice is *offered* to parents. They may achieve one by applying to the local education authority and possibly invoking Section 76 of the 1944 Education Act.

26. A choice not available under this local education authority.

27. *Education Vouchers in Kent*. A feasibility Study for the Education Department of Kent County Council. Kent County Council Education Department, 1978.

28. Ibid, pp. 177-180.

29. Ibid, p. 185.

30. Ibid, pp. 184-85.

31. *Attitude Monitoring Report on Education*, prepared for Tyne-Tees Television, Marketing Consultancy Services Ltd, Newcastle-upon-Tyne, January 1980.

32. Another recent example is the new Wakefield Independent School.

33. A recent good example of this is the 'total opposition' of all the public sector teachers' unions to even Mark Carlisle's very modest proposals for publicizing examination results.

34. *The Conservative Manifesto*, 1979, p. 25.

35. *Education Act*, HMSO, 1980, Section 8.

36. *Education Act*, HMSO, 1980, Section 8. Consultative Document on the Content of Regulations about Information for Parents.

37. Although full explanations on grading systems etc. should be provided.

38. I hardly count Section 76 of the 1944 Education Act.

39. See Disraeli, *Sybil*, Book III, Chapter III.

40. *The Conservative Manifesto*, 1979, p. 25.

41. Recognized as such by the United Nations Covenant on Human Rights, Clause 26, Part 3, and by Article 2 of Protocol 1 of the European Human Rights Conference.

IV
A Pilot Test of Basic Numeracy of Fourth- and Fifth-Year Secondary School Pupils

Survey undertaken by the Institute of Mathematics

In November 1977 more than 8,000 fifth-year secondary school-children sat a mathematics test devised by the Institute of Mathematics. The test was concerned with only the most basic skills and was designed so that virtually every pupil ought to be able to answer all the questions correctly. Results were very poor, with less than 30% of the pupils gaining 90% or more; large differences existed between the results of schools in different areas. The results all give strong support to the concern which has been expressed in recent years about the numeracy of school leavers.

The following report was published in the Bulletin of the Institute of Mathematics and its Applications, vol. 14, No. 4, April 1978, pp. 83-6.

1. In November 1977 more than 8,000 pupils in maintained secondary schools in England and Wales sat a test of basic numeracy devised and arranged by the IMA. This report gives the results of that test. The purpose of the test was to provide some quantitative evidence on the level of attainment in simple mathematical skills of pupils eligible to leave school in the summer of 1978.

2. The test paper, shown in Appendix I, was devised by a small committee of experienced school teachers of mathematics. The skills demanded are in no sense those which the committee would regard as the final objective of a school education in mathematics. They are simply those which should be in the possession of virtually all children who, after 11 years of compulsory education, are about to enter the adult world where they will need to earn a living and to become responsible citizens. The first six questions, each of two parts, involve only the simplest of arithmetic, with which most pupils would have been familiar before leaving primary school. The remaining questions have been framed so as to apply simple arithmetical skills to everyday situations.* The maximum time allowed for the test was 40 minutes.

3. It is important to appreciate that this test paper is concerned only with the most basic skills. Hence it is not one on which a pass mark of say, 40 or 50 per cent (as might apply in examinations for O-level GCE or CSE) would be appropriate.

In a document issued in October, 1976, the Council of the Institute emphasised its long-standing concern about the inadequate level of mathematical knowledge possessed by school leavers and advocated the establishment of a national test of basic mathematical, mainly arithmetical, skills. It stated that 'Everyday life, the requirements of citizenship and the average job need certain basic skills in arithmetic, geometry and statistics, and schools should equip the great majority of pupils with these skills,' and 'It is inherent in the proposal that the result of the test is pass or fail, and that the pass mark is extremely high by conventional standards – say 95 per cent.'

The basis of the present test is that virtually every pupil on reaching the end of compulsory education ought to be able to handle the kind of simple problem included in this paper.

4. Six local education authorities were invited to take part and the Institute is grateful for their ready cooperation. They were chosen so as to cover different parts of England and Wales, with some attempt at balance between urban and rural schools and between industrial, suburban and agricultural areas. The authorities taking part were Buckinghamshire, Cleveland, Dyfed, Essex, Inner London and Leeds. Each authority was asked to nominate up to ten schools that would give a reasonable cross-section of the children in its area. One authority nominated more than ten schools and the selection was made by the Institute with the aim of giving the best geographical distribution within that area. It is therefore reasonable to assume that for all the six authorities the samples are representative groups of

---

*A comment should be made on the marking of one question on the paper. This is Question 11, on the difference in the annual rental of two flats. It was thought that some pupils would be competent enough to make an approximate calculation by multiplying the approximate difference in the weekly rent by 52. Some pupils did this. However, the great majority worked out £19.8 × 52 and £12.7 × 52, then subtracted one product from the other. Many who did this got the wrong answer but, in view of the statement in the question that an answer correct to within £20 would be acceptable, the answer was marked right if it fell within those limits. The results for this question are therefore more favourable than they would have been had the part of the question in brackets not been included.

pupils from those areas*. However, any figures relating to the overall performance of the whole sample of pupils examined could be only a rough approximation to the likely performance of a sample representative of the country as a whole. The groups are not proportional in size to the total numbers of pupils within each authority. The selection of authorities themselves cannot be better than a very rough approximation to the distribution of pupils in different types of environment throughout the country. The results are therefore presented separately for each authority.

5. Although education authorities and schools were informed that the test should be taken by every pupil present who was in his or her last year of compulsory education (fifth-year pupils), the Cleveland Authority eventually found that as the pupils in its schools would be taking mock O-level examinations close to the date of the test, it could only arrange for fourth-year pupils to take it. The results for Cleveland should therefore be read with this point in mind. These results are not included in overall totals.

6. Each authority and each school taking part in the test will be provided with detailed results of the performance of its own pupils on each question, together with appropriate comparative figures. The purpose of the present report is to give a broad picture of the results; details of performance on a selection of the questions are therefore included.

Table I
Pupils Tested (being all the pupils present on the day of the test)

Authority	Boys	Girls	Total	Absentees (as percentage of no. on roll)
5th year				
Bucks.	502	477	979	11
Dyfed	611	606	1217	15
Essex	871	810	1681	14
Leeds	1081	808	1889	16
London (ILEA)	685	705	1390	28
Total 5th year	3750	3406	7156	18
4th year Cleveland	641	630	1271	17
Total pupils tested	4391	4036	8427	18

*In one authority the schools are not reorganised on a comprehensive basis. A check has, however, been made that the proportion of selective place pupils included in the sample is exactly the proportion on which selective entry is based.

Table II
Numbers and percentages of Pupils Scoring (a) 100 per cent on Whole Paper, (b) 100 per cent on Questions 1 to 6

	(a) Full marks on whole paper						(b) Questions 1 to 6 all correct					
	Boys		Girls		Total		Boys		Girls		Total	
Authority	No.	%	No.	%	No.	%	No.	%	No.	%	No.	%
Bucks.	69	13.7	58	12.1	127	13.0	233	46.6	245	51.4	478	48.8
Dyfed	46	7.5	20	3.3	66	5.4	264	43.2	261	43.0	525	43.1
Essex	98	11.3	47	5.8	145	8.6	335	38.5	356	43.9	691	41.1
Leeds	80	7.4	27	3.3	107	5.7	366	33.8	322	39.9	688	36.4
London (ILEA)	18	2.6	2	0.3	20	1.4	179	26.1	175	24.8	354	25.0
Total 5th year	311	8.3	154	4.5	465	6.5	1377	36.7	1359	39.9	2736	38.2
4th year Cleveland	14	2.2	17	2.7	31	2.4	172	26.8	169	26.9	341	26.8

Table III
Percentages of Pupils Scoring 90 per cent or Better, and 80 per cent or Better

	90 to 100 per cent		80 to 100 per cent	
	Boys per cent	Girls per cent	Boys per cent	Girls per cent
5th year				
Bucks.	40.3	34.7	61.4	54.6
Dyfed	26.4	19.0	45.4	36.7
Essex	33.0	26.9	51.5	45.7
Leeds	26.3	14.9	45.5	34.1
London (ILEA)	16.0	8.7	31.9	21.2
4th year Cleveland	12.0	12.6	26.3	21.8

7. The numbers of pupils taking the test are given in Table I. The total number of pupils on the roll of the schools concerned in the appropriate year is approximately 10,200.

8. It has been stressed above that the test is one which ought to be within the capability of almost all pupils about to complete compulsory education. Particularly is this so of the simple Questions 1 to 6. Table II gives the numbers and percentages of pupils who obtained full marks on the paper, and corresponding figures for those who obtained full marks on Questions 1 to 6. It will be seen that only 8.3 per cent of boys and 4.5 per cent of girls in their fifth year obtained full

marks. Only 36.7 per cent of boys and 39.9 per cent of girls could answer all the first six questions correctly.

9. It might be argued that everyone is liable to make the occasional slip in arithmetical working even though a problem is fully understood, and that some criteria other than a mark of 100 per cent should therefore be used in assessing the results. The committee of teachers weighted the questions according to their assessment of difficulty, giving a total of 40 marks for the 30 parts of questions. Table III gives the percentages of pupils scoring 90 per cent or better (including, of course, those which are already listed in Table II as having 100 per cent) and 80 per cent or better. A mark of 90 per cent would allow for "the occasional slip." A mark of 80 per cent is, in the opinion of the committee, well below an acceptable minimum standard.

None of the results shown in Tables II and III for any authority is satisfactory. They all give strong support to the concern that has been expressed for some years and in many quarters about the level of numeracy of school leavers.

10. It is of interest to examine the performance of the pupils on individual questions and Table IV gives the percentages of *wrong* answers to selected questions. Four of these questions are in the first 12 parts that deal only with the simplest arithmetical processes. Three questions, 7(b), 10 and 16(b), are simple problems on percentages. Newspapers and television news bulletins assume every day that their readers or viewers understand the meaning of, say, a 9.9 per cent rate of inflation or a 16 per cent wage claim and, equally, that they understand the results of opinion polls. The results of this test suggest that such an assumption may not be well founded.

Question 12 deals with an everyday requirement of putting into figures a written or spoken expression of a sum of money: the result is surprising.

Finally, Question 17 requires the interpretation of a simple railway timetable. Timetables may not be included in most examination syllabuses but they are of

Table IV
Percentages of Wrong Answers to Selected Questions

Question		Bucks. Boys	Girls	Dyfed Boys	Girls	Essex Boys	Girls	Leeds Boys	Girls	ILEA Boys	Girls	Cleveland Boys	Girls
3(b)	6 × 79	15	13	16	14	21	15	21	18	24	26	31	22
4(b)	243 ÷ 9	14	14	19	18	26	20	22	19	31	30	32	26
5(b)	79.3 − 8.1	18	22	22	23	24	18	25	23	29	30	33	26
6(b)	13.5 ÷ 5	23	24	27	29	40	28	30	26	41	43	41	35
7(b)	40% as a decimal	34	48	48	55	46	54	54	66	58	72	70	70
10	20% reduction on £15 jeans	31	39	43	51	36	44	39	49	54	57	61	63
11	Rent	16	44	46	60	49	50	49	55	60	71	66	69
12	Cheque	19	21	29	33	34	35	35	44	53	54	55	49
13	Shampoo	19	26	25	31	23	24	26	31	33	43	40	35
16(b)	Opinion poll	38	45	46	58	44	48	49	64	58	72	68	69
17	Timetable (a)	55	66	67	79	62	67	68	71	76	88	69	86
	(b)	42	46	58	64	47	52	52	62	64	74	74	71
	(c)	36	41	53	61	40	46	47	61	58	70	69	69

obvious relevance to everyday life. In every authority these simple problems caused great difficulty.

11. There is no need for the Institute to comment further on the results or to attempt to interpret them. The results speak powerfully for themselves.

12. The Institute records its thanks to the officers and teachers of the six authorities taking part, to the volunteers who have marked the scripts, and, of course, to the pupils themselves.

Norman Clarke
Secretary and Registrar

Appendix I

1. (a) $14 + 35 =$
   (b) $43 + 282 =$

2. (a) $77{-}53 =$
   (b) $911{-}102 =$

3. (a) $7{\times}8 =$
   (b) $6{\times}79 =$

4. (a) $24 \div 6 =$
   (b) $243 \div 9 =$

5. (a) $13.3 + 2.8 =$
   (b) $79.3{-}8.1 =$

6. (a) $3 \times 42.5 =$
   (b) $13.5 \div 5 =$

7. (a) Write ¼ as a percentage
   (b) Write 40% as a decimal

8.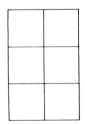

   (a) Shade in ⅔ of this diagram

   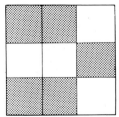

   (b) What fraction of this diagram is shaded?

9. Milk is 12p per pint. If I use two pints each day, what is my weekly milk bill?

10.

A reduction of 20% is given on sale items. What is the sale price of a pair of jeans marked at £15?

11. The rent of a large flat is £19.80 per week and that of a small flat is £12.70 per week. How much extra do I have to pay each year if I take the large flat rather than the small one? (You need not work this out exactly, an answer correct to within £20 will do.)

12. A cheque is made out for one hundred and forty nine pounds and nine pence. Write this amount in figures.

13.

How much do I save if I buy 2 large bottles of shampoo instead of taking the same quantity in small bottles?

14.

How many kgs excess baggage?

15. This chart shows the number of hours given to various types of programmes, in one week, on a radio channel

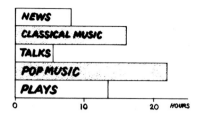

(a) How many hours are given to Classical Music?
(b) How many hours are given to Pop Music?
(c) To what type of programme is the least time devoted?

[*Note* The graph markings have been lost in this reproduction]

16. RESULTS OF OPINION POLL
      TASTING A NEW COFFEE

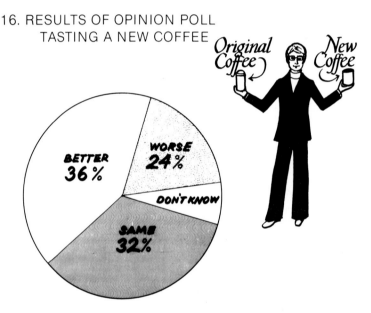

(a) In the opinion poll, what percentage said 'don't know'?
(b) If 250 people were consulted altogether, how many thought the quality of the coffee was just the same as before?

17. TRAIN TIMETABLE

Camtown	0712	0910	1312	1621	1907
Belford	—	0941	1342	1652	1937
Green Mill	0845	1055	—	1806	2020
Manchester	1023	1234	1602	1953	2200

(a) At what time does the fastest train of the day leave Camtown?
(b) If I have to travel to Manchester from Belford, what is the earliest I can arrive?
(c) If I cannot leave Camtown until 3 p.m. what is the earliest I can be in Manchester?

V
"What has Athens to do with Jerusalem?": Teaching Sociology to Students on Medical, Nursing, Education and Science Courses

Caroline Cox and John Marks

Sociology, if appropriately taught, can make a valuable contribution to the education of students on courses in medicine and nursing, in teaching and in science and technology. This chapter makes the case for including sociology and social studies in such courses but also warns against the dangers of allowing politicized sociology to be taught as religious dogma. Too often sociology can be a wolf in sheep's clothing – offering Marxism or ideologically bigoted socialism in academic dress. The professions should be wary of the sociological imperialism of many sociologists who were appointed, very young and academically immature, during the expansion of the 1960s, and with the current decline in sociology are looking for new fields to conquer. It is imperative to ensure that the sociology taught to students in professional courses is both academically reputable and professionally relevant.

Tertullian's notorious outburst at the end of the second century, 'What has Athens to do with Jerusalem?' is echoed in contemporary discussions on relationships between the pure, unsullied world of Academe and the hurly-burly world of social, ideological and political issues which comprise the stuff of everyday human life. Some problems of this relationship have been highlighted in recent years by developments in the teaching of sociology or social studies to students on courses in a wide range of other subjects.

For example, some academic sociologists believe that by providing "service" teaching on these courses they are prostituting themselves and their subject. Many of these are radicals who argue that to teach sociology to students on, say, professional courses, is merely helping budding professionals to prop up our rotten capitalist society. At the 1980 Annual Conference of the British Sociological Association one sociologist expressed their reservations: 'Whether professionals are either direct agents of capitalist control or merely servants of capitalism ... sociologists servicing the professions need to be aware of their role not only in legitimating the professions, but more widely in maintaining the *status quo*.'[1]

Other sociologists like the forthright Marxist Professor R. Frankenberg, assert that any attempt to impart sociology to professionals such as doctors is a lost cause; he implies that their vested interests are so strong and their practices so obnoxious that only a complete revolutionary change of our entire society will provide any effective remedy.[2]

Then there are those sociologists, also of the far Left, who take yet another view. They see the opportunity to teach sociology to students on other courses as a chance to spread their socialist gospel and they seize it accordingly – hence the large numbers of Marxist and other left-wing staff in influential posts in Higher and Further Education. That this has been a deliberate policy – and an intelligent move – is no secret. The well known American radical sociologist Alvin Gouldner is quite explicit: he describes it 'as a basis of financing the political efforts of those liberal-to-left ideologues who wanted to devote themselves to the transformation and réconstruction of the larger society'.[3]

These inhabitants of the city Athens believe that distinctions between Athens and Jerusalem should be broken down. They follow in the footsteps of the founding father of sociology, Auguste Comte, who saw sociologists as the new high priests of society. Believing themselves to be endowed with a vision of the Truth which they are entitled to impose on the world, these "academic" sociologists wish to use the Athens of the Academy as a means of bringing about a new Jerusalem – their Jerusalem – which in contemporary sociology means a socialist Utopia.

We take issue with all three positions. Academic sociology does have something of value to offer to students of other subjects – but it must meet the criteria embodied in the spirit of ancient Athens: a dispassionate search for truth and a respect for a plurality of views reflected in genuine open debate. This means that the dogmatism, the arrogance and the intellectual dishonesty which characterize so much that is written and taught in the name of sociology, and which we will be illustrating, are anathema. They must be exposed and rejected by the inhabitants of Athens and Jerusalem alike.

Therefore in this chapter we attempt:

(i) to present a case for teaching sociology to students training for careers in medicine, nursing, teaching, science and technology;

(ii) to demonstrate the dangers of allowing sociology to be taught as religious dogma; we will show how, in Britain today, it is too often a wolf in sheep's clothing – Marxism or ideologically bigoted socialism in academic dress;

(iii) to suggest some criteria for evaluating what is taught in the name of sociology and to offer some practical proposals.

The Case for Sociology (or Social Studies)

Sociology in medical and nursing training

Major advances in medical science, allied with significant improvements in standards of living, have brought about dramatic changes in the incidence and distribution of disease and in the causes of death. Revolutionary developments in medical therapeutics have virtually eliminated many diseases from our society, most notably the infectious diseases which were rampant killers only a few decades ago. Consequently, many more people live longer – and survive to suffer chronic illnesses and the infirmities of old age. Thus the medical and social success stories of one era herald the new pathologies of the next.

Current health care problems tend to have a significant social component. The management of chronic illness and infirmity poses challenges which are very different from those involved in the care of patients with acute infectious illness. Moreover, there has been a growing recognition of the importance of social factors in the causation of many diseases; in the variations in the incidence of different diseases between social classes; in patients' reactions to illness and in their willingness to seek medical help. These are some of the reasons why health care professionals have become increasingly aware of the importance of social factors in their work and why they have actively sought the inclusion of subjects such as sociology in the curricula of their professional training programmes. *The Report of the Royal Commission on Medical Education*[4] puts the case for the inclusion of behavioural science in medical training recommending: '... that all medical students should learn its elements in order to become aware of why patients and families behave as they do in situations of illness; of the social and cultural factors which influence patients' expectations and responses; of the problems for doctor, patient and family in the management of illness and handicap in the community; of the social, ethnic, occupational and psychological forces which can hinder prevention and treatment; and of the difficulties of communication, and other problems which arise from established expectations about the way a person in a defined situation will behave, particularly in hospital'.

D. Tuckett[5] amplifies the case:

At the present time most doctors in the NHS are excellent at saving lives, but few doctors are as good at minimizing the discomfort, inconvenience and physical or mental incapacity that are associated with the types of medical conditions (and their implications for the patients' activities and plans) that are now most frequently found in their surgeries and clinics. One aim of the application of sociology to medicine is to give doctors the ammunition, and the confidence, to deal as effectively with the patient's social and emotional needs as they now do with the physical ones.

Professor J. Wing of the Institute of Psychiatry[6] makes a similar point:

Scientific medicine has achieved its success by concentrating on more and more specific problems. Although, within these restricted limits, doctors can be fairly confident that medical actions will be beneficial, they cannot afford to ignore the wider psychological and social context, not only because so many complaints are couched in these terms, but also because rational treatment cannot be prescribed in an social vacuum.

The contribution of sociology to nursing is particularly important at the present time, for nursing is developing an identity as a profession complementary to, but distinct from, medicine, with its own unique contribution to the provision of health care. The Briggs Report in 1972[7] defined nursing as 'the major caring profession' and nurses are currently clarifying their role and responsibilities in ways which are maturing beyond the traditional medical "handmaiden" status. Obviously, a significant proportion of nursing will continue to consist of working with medical colleagues in the treatment of patients who are ill – in situations where medical staff have the primary responsibilities of diagnosis and treatment. But, for the growing proportion of our population suffering from chronic illness or disability, medicine has little to offer; what is needed is care, and this is the primary prerogative of nursing. Some of the implications of these developments were summed up at the Royal College of Nursing Annual Conference in 1978 by J. Clark[8] who argued that we should 'scrap the overwhelming dominance of medicine and the medical model of illness ... because it is ill suited to the problems which now confront us. To the degenerative problems of an ageing population, to the behavioural diseases such as obesity and alcoholism, to the care of the frail, elderly and the mentally and physically disabled, medicine has little to offer by way of a "cure". When what is curable has been cured and what is preventable has been prevented, there is still a good deal left. And what it needs is care'. Given this situation, nurses need to be adequately trained for the taxing demands which caring makes – which include an understanding not only of a patient's physical needs but also of his social and emotional condition. And here sociology does have a contribution. The wealth of sociological work which nurses find helpful in their clinical practice include studies of:

(i) social and cultural factors which influence people's perception of, and response to, pain and illness:

(ii) interpersonal relationships between professionals and their patients;

(iii) the organization, provision and uptake of health care;

(iv) particular kinds of patient care, such as the care of the chronic sick, the elderly or the dying. For a further discussion of the potential contribution of sociology to nursing, see C. Cox: "Who Cares? Nursing and Sociology: The Development of a Symbiotic Relationship", *Journal of Advanced Nursing*, May 1979.[9] The Council for the Education and Training of Health Visitors introduced a syllabus in 1965 which included a section "The Individual and the Group" comprising an introduction to basic sociological concepts. For the first time, all training schools included sociology as a core subject in the health visitor training course. In one of the basic textbooks on health visiting, G.Owen affirms its value: 'Although sociology leads to an understanding rather than practice, it is an understanding that can be recommended to people like social workers and nurses (and naturally to health visitors) ... As a means of communication ... it offers an understanding of groups and different cultures and therefore helps in establishing social contact. It may well also help to overcome any rigidity or authoritarianism ... and could be very important in helping to establish suitable attitudes and maturity and a readiness to question their own value systems where necessary ...'.[10]

It thus seems that sociology has "arrived" and is accepted in principle in medicine, health visiting and nursing, although there is considerable variation in the extent to which it is taught.

Sociology in Teacher Training

Education is essentially a social enterprise. Thus it is not surprising that teacher training courses have relatively large components of sociology, with particular emphasis on the Sociology of Education. The Sociology of Education is a large area within sociology which has blossomed since World War II, generating prolific studies – many of which have been influential in shaping educational policy. For example, some of the famous studies which compared the social class backgrounds of grammar school pupils with those in secondary modern schools showed a statistical over-representation of middle class children in the grammar school, and provided the comprehensive school lobby with some of its most powerful ammunition. Smaller scale studies which examined the dynamics of personal relationships within the classroom, such as the effects of streaming, were highly significant in shaping attitudes to policies concerning selection and were used to underpin arguments for mixed ability teaching.[11] Findings of studies such as these were often accepted uncritically by those who acted on them – despite their manifest limitations in terms of research methodology (see "Educational Myths and Research" by F. Naylor, p. 167).

Because sociology is so well established as part of the curriculum for teacher training, it is not necessary to labour the point in making a case for it. What is more problematic, and will be discussed later, is the nature of some of what is published and taught under the rubric of the Sociology of Education.

Social Studies in Science and Technology Courses

Until recently, the Council for National Academic Awards (CNAA) required all colleges offering CNAA degrees in these subject areas to include some teaching which would enable science and technology students to see their subject in a wider social, political, economic and cultural context. The precise wording of the CNAA's requirement was that students should be given 'an informed awareness of the significance of scientific, technological, economic and cultural factors in modern society, and of the contribution they can make in improving the quality of life, and in widening man's imaginative horizons and his understanding of his culture and environment'.[12] This regulation has subsequently been modified, but the principles underlying it are retained in a more general statement. Although the actual body of knowledge studied by science students is entirely independent of sociology, in a way that the study of education is not, there is a value in encouraging students to appreciate the influence of social factors in the organization of the social institutions concerned with science, and in the ways in which different societies generate and respond to scientific knowledge. It is also desirable to give them some account of how science has developed and how it has come to play such a central role in all our lives. Such background knowledge is essential if students are to think more deeply about their own roles and responsibilities as scientists or technologists and if they are to make an informed and intelligent contribution to contemporary debates on the interactions between science, technology and society.

The Dangers of Teaching Bad Sociology

It is because we sincerely believe that sociology can make a valuable contribution to the education of medical practitioners, nurses, teachers and scientists that we are concerned when we discern a number of ways in which some sociologists discredit the discipline either by the ways in which they teach it, or by the academically shoddy quality of their published work.

Intellectual Dishonesty and Bad Faith

This characterizes much sociology and can be illustrated first by certain brands of Marxist analysis of illness and medical care – a form of "tunnel vision" which conveniently focuses exclusively on the problems of illness and medical care in capitalist societies and never examines any of the problems of socialist societies. The result is a sleight of mind: capitalism is associated with disease and exploitation – therefore capitalism causes disease and exploitation. The elementary rule that one should never interpret correlation as cause is forgotten. An example of a book written in this vein is *The Political Economy of Health* by Doyal with Pennell[13], whose major thesis is that 'ill health in both developed and underdeveloped countries is largely a product of the social and economic organisation of society'. They advocate the development of a 'Marxist epidemiology' and reduce the role of medical practice and research in western societies to 'maintaining a healthy labour force and in socializing and controlling people'. Discussion of the practice of medicine in the alternative socialist societies which they are striving to impose is condensed into a few lines such as ' ... we cannot specify in advance a utopian blueprint for a socialist health policy'. No, but they conveniently forget that in actual socialist societies such as the USSR medicine may be used as a much more formidable means of social control than in the west. For example, the government puts considerable pressure on doctors with regard to the extent to which they are allowed to issue sickness certificates in ways which may have very adverse effects on the doctor-patient relationship. A book basically sympathetic to Soviet health care[14] admits this:

> The whole issue of the doctor-patient relationship tends to be further complicated (some might say poisoned) by the question raised by official sickness certificates .... These certificates are quite important in Soviet society, for they not only officially absolve the individual from the penalties for unauthorized absenteeism, but they are necessary for him in order to receive sick pay or other benefits. Pressures are often put on physicians by persons who are not, in the strict sense of the word, "sick" but who need, for any number of reasons, the relief provided by the certificates. The state, of course, places counter-pressures upon the physician in order to reduce his latitude in these matters and to minimise the economic costs or losses caused by these excuses. While unexcused absenteeism is not punished as harshly now as it was under Stalin's regime, it is still very much frowned upon officially and exposes the individual to disciplinary and financial sanctions ... The physician must thus be (as a military doctor usually is) constantly on the lookout for malingerers or others who would use the medical excuse for private ends. This situation is, in itself, not conducive to the best relationship between physician and patient. (pp. 135-6)

'Penalties', 'punished', 'disciplinary and financial sanctions' ... are these not words of control and do they not relate to an overwhelming concern with 'maintaining a healthy labour force and in socializing and controlling people'? How can writers such as Doyal and Pennell claim directly that these are characteristics of capitalism and ignore their even more extreme applicability to socialist societies? How can they advocate a socialist alternative to capitalism without addressing themselves to the realities of socialism?

When we turn to the notorious and well documented abuse of psychiatry in the USSR for "treating" dissidents, we are confronted with spine-chilling examples of the use of torture under the guise of "therapy" to try and compel people to conform to the ideology of their Marxist rulers. The recent Report by Amnesty International[15] documents the USSR's use of the psychiatric profession as an agent of social control and of the hideous ill-treatment meted out to "patients" whose "disease" is dissent – aspects of the practice of medicine in socialist societies which our left-wing academics find it convenient to ignore.

This type of thinking applies to the work of many radical social scientists right across the board. Their one-sided criticisms are not reserved for medical care; they are found in studies of all aspects of society, and the pattern is always the same.

They denounce western society and capitalism; they advocate a visionary socialist alternative; and they ignore the harsh realities of socialism as it now exists. Yet, nearly every feature which the Marxists criticize in liberal societies is found in much greater measure in their socialist counterparts. This characteristic of much left-wing social science is so widespread, so influential and so intellectually unacceptable that it needs to be spelt out loud and clear.

First, because liberal democratic societies are "open", committed to publishing material which is critical of their own institutions and practices, it is easy for Marxists and other radicals to document and harp on their defects. Academics such as Professor Stuart Hall[16] of the Open University spend a great deal of time and money documenting the supposed bias and partiality of the western media in the way they provide information and report news – despite the multiplicity of sources of information and the freedom to publish criticism. Contrast this situation with Marxist societies. The major newspaper in the USSR – the official propaganda organ of the Central Committee of the Communist Party – contains nothing written by independent journalists. Its name – *Pravda* – means "truth", but it only publishes the "truth" as defined by the Communist Party. Soviet citizens are permitted to read no alternatives since independent newspapers do not exist, western newspapers are banned, and penalties for circulating *samizdat* literature are exceedingly severe.

Nothing can be published in the Soviet Union without the offical approval of the vast Communist Party censorship organization, *Glavlit*. Even during the famous Khrushchev "thaw" only one or two manuscripts such as Solzhenitsyn's *One Day in the Life of Ivan Denisovich* were allowed through the censorship as very exceptional cases; the whole oppressive apparatus was left intact and still operates its stranglehold today.

True, Khrushchev did release millions who had been imprisoned under Stalin. Yet he retained the vast network of labour camps run by the KGB – the Gulag Archipelago described by Solzhenitsyn – and even extended the apparatus of repression by creating the special psychiatric hospitals where perfectly sane political dissidents and religious believers are subjected to forcible treatment until they accept "Soviet reality". As the Campaign Against Psychiatric Abuse asks: 'How would you like to be: confined to a psychiatric hospital when you are sane? forcibly treated with damaging drugs? locked up with psychotic or violent patients? brutally treated by convict orderlies? ... Your only signs of madness might be that you: wrote a letter to a newspaper criticizing the government; or believe in God ... or write satirical verse; or take part in a peaceful demonstration; or try to start a Trade Union ...'.[17]

The control of information is so complete that people can be made "unpersons" – their faces obliterated from official photographs or their names removed from books and journals; the names of five of the eight Prime Ministers of the USSR since the Revolution do not appear in the Great Soviet Encyclopaedia. Historical events can be completely falsified or hushed up; the worst nuclear accident in the world took place in the Urals in late 1957 or early 1958; tens of thousands of people were affected, hundreds died and hundreds of square miles were contaminated with radioactivity. Yet no mention of this accident has ever been made in any Soviet publication – for the rulers of the USSR it is an event which never happened. We do not deny that there may be some distortion or bias in the presentation of news and information in the west, nor do we claim that this should be immune from criticism. But we do blame Marxist academics like Stuart Hall who lay these faults at the door of capitalism and who exercise massive selectivity themselves in refraining from subjecting socialist societies to comparable criticism.

Other Marxist academics like Professor Ralph Miliband of Leeds University criticize capitalism for the power it gives to the ruling class.[18] They criticize the democracy of liberal societies as a sham and denounce the freedom to choose between political parties as "bourgeois". Yet *all* Marxist societies are ruled centrally by governments drawn from the only permitted political party – the Communist Party. In the Soviet Union, for example, a single list of Communist Party candidates is "elected" at regular intervals by a system in which a "Yes" vote is made openly, while for a "No" vote a citizen has to be seen to go into a separate booth to mark a ballot paper. Members of the ruling class in communist societies have privileges far exceeding those of their counterparts in the west: for example, access to consumer goods in special shops which are closed to the population in whose interests they rule, special housing, and privileged access to education – while those who oppose them are often unable to enter universities.

One final contrast. The crimes for which Richard Nixon was forced to resign – suppression of information and perversion of the course of justice – are common-place, routine, everyday occurrences in the Soviet Union. They are part of the fabric of life, and the system would collapse without them. No wonder the Soviet leaders, who rose to power by massacring millions in Stalin's purges, never believed that Nixon would resign over Watergate. And no wonder they will not permit a free press which could expose them as it exposed the far less serious crimes of Nixon. But perhaps even more culpable is the failure of "social scientists" to evaluate the overall nature of totalitarian societies. They are not liberal democratic societies in which one or two areas of life show reprehensible or deplorable features. Therefore, it is not adequate for social scientists to deal with any aspect of life in a totalitarian state without relating it to the overall nature of totalitarianism. The prime example is the Soviet Union which is the greatest and best organized tyranny the world has ever seen and which has already caused the deaths of more than 40 million people, many of whom were its own citizens. And all other existing Marxist societies show similar oppressive features, including nearly complete control by the Communist Party of information and of all other aspects of life. To treat these societies as anything other than totalitarian tyrannies is to fly in the face of the evidence.[19]

In summary, all of these contrasts between capitalist and socialist societies are so extreme that the neglect of them by "social scientists" must be seen as deliberate, politically motivated and as constituting gross malpractice.

Sociologists who adopt a "reductio ad absurdum" stance

Here we refer to those sociologists who are so committed to explaining everything in social terms that they ignore or deny the importance of other factors in understanding human behaviour or the physical world. Prime examples are found in the sociology of medicine, where sociological zeal sometimes seems to obliterate any consideration of physical pathology, finding all explanations of disease in the evils of society– capitalist society, of course. This is well illustrated in the writings of Karl Figlio who teaches medical sociology at Charing Cross Hospital Medical School. In an article entitled "Sinister Medicine"[20] he supports those who 'reject the physiology in which the body is a system in equilibrium – a neo-classical economic organism'. He quotes two other authors (Berliner and Salmon)[21] who claim 'While scientific medicine views people as unhealthy when they deviate from a statistical equilibrium, we see people as unhealthy when subjected to social assault.' Figlio approves, suggesting:

> ... they are right to try to understand the ways our bodies reflect the internalized conflicts of society. In that sense, disease is a political act, only we don't usually know it ... They are also right to say that our scientific concepts – epidemiological or physiological in these cases – transpose to our bodies a framework which derives from, and then reinforces, our theories of socio-economic structure ...

Really? Why? Where is the evidence for these grand assertions?

In the field of sociology called the Sociology of Knowledge, we find another example of *reductio ad absurdum*, smacking of delusions of grandeur, in the title of a widely acclaimed book – Berger and Luckmann's *The Social Construction of Reality: A Treatise in the Sociology of Knowledge*.[22] This would probably strike the lay reader as arrant nonsense. Surely, he would think, the physical universe preceded any human "construction" by millions of years! Surely, physical and biological reality is what makes humans possible! And, of course, he would be right. Nor is it the provocative title alone which sounds so nonsensical and would deserve that kind of reaction. The opening lines of both the Preface and Chapter I are in the same vein. For example,

> The basic contentions of the arguments of this book are implicit in its title and sub-title, namely, that reality is socially constructed and that the sociology of knowledge must analyse the process in which this occurs (p. 13 – the first sentence of the book).

Now, there *is* a more subtle point to be made, but not in this manner. The world is an object independent of our knowledge, but we can only know and describe it from within our conceptual scheme as it now is. Any coherent conceptual scheme depends on rules, and rules are social. If people do not agree with each other in their judgements of what they perceive, there could be no observation and no science – only private, incommunicable worlds with no standard for separating true perception from illusion. This does not mean that truth is simply what the majority or the dominant class thinks, nor that the ground rules are arbitrary. Nor does the fact that science or mathematics is a social enterprise mean that a correct sociology of science (whatever it did explain) would undermine the truths of science. But these kinds of extreme and absurd claims are just what Berger and Luckmann's statements do suggest. Yet how many sociologists have challenged that title or insisted that we talk, not of the 'social construction of reality', but more modestly and accurately of 'the social construction of our perception of reality'? It is a lack of modesty and a lack of rigour in the use of language that make the claims of Berger and Luckmann appear ridiculous, and deter people in other disciplines from considering any valid arguments they may have – and from taking sociology seriously.

Another variant of *reductio ad absurdum* in sociology – sometimes associated with the sociological concept of "labelling" – is the notion that by perceiving, defining and labelling a person or his behaviour in a particular way, one may materially change his condition and his subsequent behaviour.

Examples of this kind of thinking are found particularly frequently in discussions on mental illness, for example in the work of T. Scheff[23] or E. Goffman.[24] We do not wish to denigrate their work, as it contains ideas and insights that have been influential in sensitizing health care professionals to some genuine problems in the treatment of psychiatric patients in ways which have prompted significant improvements. However, where sociologists have tended to go wrong is by failing to recognize that their insights into the effects of labelling are no new discovery: parents and teachers, for example, have long been aware of the existence of peoples' powerful motivations to live up, or down, to others' expectations of them. Also, they are misguided in their tendency to insist that the effect of labelling is far stronger than it is – or could be; they imply that we are all totally creatures and products of others' expectations. We are not; unless as "radicals" nowadays seem to assume, we are born as identical lumps of infinitely plastic material susceptible to omnipotent social engineering. Therefore, Professor Wing[25] is justified in pointing out:

> Labelling theory is over-generalized. It cannot explain the first rank symptoms of schizophrenia, nor the chronic disabilities which still develop in about one-quarter of patients ... Anyone who deals with schizophrenia (and now I can widen the statement to include other severe and disabling mental illnesses) needs to be skilled enough to use disease theories differentially, to assess the contribution of social factors to the course and present state [of the illness] and to understand the personal reactions of the individual ...

He goes on to claim that some sociologists

> have jumped to the conclusion that no disease theory can ever be held to apply, but this is a clear case of throwing out the baby with the bathwater. What they should be condemning is the misapplication of disease labels. They should be pressing for better diagnosis, not no diagnosis. Otherwise, sociologists are likely to be trapped into an expansionism of their own, just as irrational and damaging to the prospects of reducing disability and suffering as the ones they are criticizing.

This is a sober warning from a psychiatrist who is sympathetic to sociology and keen to develop 'creative partnerships between sociologists and psychiatrists'.

The tendency to debunk and to deride the work of professionals and scientists

Sociologists often appear carping, cynical and negative. Of course, we are not averse to them taking a critical position: this is an academically valid role which, in a free, pluralist society, should be valued. However, they often adopt a stance and tone which appear arrogant and prejudiced. As B. Heraud[26] points out:

> The emphasis by sociologists on negative, sceptical and pessimistic aspects of human endeavour must be seen as part of the history of the subject ... It is both a strength and a weakness ... and the weakness shows itself particularly in the contemporary analysis of the professions, where the sociologist takes a very serious view of his role as everlasting social critic by ignoring or distrusting any of the positive, pragmatic or optimistic forces or expressions of opinion inherent in such institutions or in the wider society. Yet the fact that this position is, in sociological terms, an unreflective and uncritical departure from methodological rigour is, as yet, a point understood and expressed so far by only a perceptive few within the discipline.

Professor M. Jefferys[27] in a paper to the 1980 British Sociological Association Annual Conference referred to certain studies in medical sociology as depicting health care professionals acting not merely in their own interests but actually to the disadvantage of their patients. She claimed that such studies give sociology a reputation for "doctor bashing" and pointed out that the sociological enterprise could be interpreted as motivated by professional self-aggrandizement as much as by concern for the patient. A similar "debunking" attitude, this time towards teaching, is found in a book which is widely recommended on teacher training courses – *Schooling in Capitalist America* by Bowles and Gintis[28] – in which they refer to teaching thus:

> It is easy to imagine teaching as relatively integrated unalienated labour ... given a sufficiently vivid imagination he or she may even entertain illusions of social usefulness.

We suggest that sociological accounts of professions such as medicine or teaching which do not take account of genuine altruistic attitudes and motivations of practitioners are sociologically wrong. They understandably arouse scepticism about the motives of the sociologist and hostility to the implications of his findings. A similar hostility and scepticism is, we suggest, justified concerning some of those who teach social studies of science when they state that there is a 'need to make a separate attack on science so that it can become part of – rather than a falsely conscious model for – socialist theory and struggle' and that one of their main aims is 'to demystify science and bring both science and working scientists into the mainstream of radical theory and action'.[29]

The tendency to ignore the heavy burdens of responsibility carried by professional practitioners

Many criticisms made by sociologists imply a lack of appreciation of what is at stake in the professionals' real world. For example, at a recent sociology workshop, sociologists dismissed nurses' anxieties about their responsibilities as mere "red herrings" to detract attention from "fundamental" issues. This is nonsense. Much of the day-to-day work of nurses and midwives operates at the level of life and death judgements and decisions which do not give much time or margin for error. In debates on health care, sociologists can be as radical and destructive as they choose; but in everyday life, professionals have to decide and to act on their decisions: they stand or fall by them, while sociologists remain safely on the sidelines. It would perhaps help if all sociologists who teach students on professional courses were to bear this in mind – one so often meets depressed and demoralized students whose confidence in themselves and their work has been undermined by sociology tutors to the extent that they either feel like giving up (presumably the desired outcome?) or rejecting everything which goes under the name of sociology (a great pity).

Ideologically partisan teaching

Our final example of undesirable tendencies in the teaching of sociology refers to situations where it is taught in so ideologically partisan a way as to amount to intellectual dishonesty and indoctrination. Apart from the political implications, this gives students academically short shrift. These tendencies occur in a number of other forms of which one is to teach only those sociological approaches that the teacher "believes in" with any degree of enthusiasm or commitment, and to dismiss or ridicule all others. Students have to be exceptionally astute and determined if they are to follow up and study seriously the "pariah" approaches. In some colleges they also run the risk of being awarded low marks if they have the audacity to present work for assessment which is ideologically "unsound". Another way in which this tendency is manifest is in a very partial and selective coverage of topics in a course. For example, many "Science and Society" courses offered to science students, concentrate, as a matter of policy, on case studies of specific controversial issues – such as nuclear power or genetic engineering. These courses are often characterized by a lack of rigorous analysis of the historical growth of science, the nature of scientific knowledge, the social conditions conducive to its development and the distortions of knowledge and truth which can occur when political or ideological influences interfere – as in Nazi Germany or in the Lysenko affair in the Soviet Union. They eschew any comparative analysis of other societies implying, by default, that all problems are associated with (and caused by) the type of society in which we live – i.e. they are part of the "crisis of capitalism". There can be no excuse for academics who adopt a myopic case-study approach and fail to give comparative studies of scientific and technological developments in different kinds of society; ample published material is available and it is the duty of academics to bring it to the attention of their students. Yet a book, *Science, Technology and the Modern Industrial State*,[30] produced by the organization "Science in a Social Context" (Siscon) and funded by the Nuffield Foundation, deals exclusively with problems of science in western societies. It makes great play of President Eisenhower's warning about the growing influence of the military-industrial complex in the USA but nowhere does it discuss the situation in the USSR where the military-industrial complex virtually is the state.

Still in the area of the Sociology of Science, there are many more examples of books which identify capitalism *per se* as the prime cause of many current problems. For example, those by S. and H. Rose[31] which are widely recommended reading, contain statements such as:

One development in the US which has achieved considerable success in directing the movement from its attempts to analyse the role of science has been the mushrooming growth of the pollution movement, suggested by many as having been fanned as a deliberately mystifying attempt to direct campus activities from the Vietnam war ... The politicisation of pollution (as an inevitable product of capitalism) has scarcely checked this tendency.

Characteristically, the writers do not discuss whether pollution only exists in capitalist societies, or whether comparative studies have anything to offer. They are also noticeably vacuous on such issues as how a socialist science will differ in content from a capitalist science – although they seem seriously to imply that there would be substantial differences. Some examples can be found, but it is not certain whether they are sincere attempts at clarification, or exercises in mystification. The reader can judge this for himself in this passage [32] written by Professor A. Sohn-Rehtel (Professor of Social Theory at the University of Bremen, who lives in Birmingham):

my central thesis is that the forms of the social relations of production are the determinants of the forms of thought; in particular, that there is a determinate relationship between the modes of scientific reasoning and the commodity exchange abstraction.

In particular, he claims 'that the Galilean concept of inertial motion is *the* distinguishing feature of modern science' and that 'this concept evolved as a consequence of the nature of the capitalist mode of production.'[33] He also claims that 'Galilean science has produced objectively valid knowledge that can, however, be correctly understood only in a socialist society.' The arguments used to "establish" these extraordinary claims are so vague, and reveal such apparent ignorance of the development of the whole concept of inertial motion, that we find it difficult to believe that anyone could have the audacity to write – or publish – such material. But its publication is perhaps explained by this extract from the preface to the article – 'an account which *appears* not to call for further explanatory factors may *demand* them for Marxist reasons as a condition of replacing a bourgeois academic level of understanding by a political level' (emphasis in original).[34]

It is also interesting that during a December 1979 Conference on the teaching of Science and Society courses various models were advocated. These included the "Use/Abuse of Science" Model; the "Social Construction of Reality" model and various Marxist approaches. The main speaker, R.M. Young, when asked why he recommended a particular brand of Marxism as his preferred model, gave as his criterion of choice that 'it has greater agitational potential' – an answer which aroused no apparent dissent from the majority of teachers present. Similarly, at another Conference in April 1980, one lecturer on a Science and Society course when challenged to make it clear whether his courses were designed to train industrial managers or Marxists replied 'I want to train Marxist managers'.

Similar situations of ideological partisanship occur in the sociological literature on health, welfare and education. There is an abundance of books of the same genre as Bowles and Gintis' *Schooling in Capitalist America* which assert that educational health and welfare institutions in capitalist societies are repressive, that they are tools of the state and that they serve to legitimate the *status quo.* They may do so. But as the late Professor Halmos pointed out when reviewing a book on social welfare[35] written in a similar vein:

... there is a complete silence on the failures of the so-called socialist welfare states in the areas so often featuring in the critique of capitalist welfare states: suicide, drug addiction, alcoholism, crime, mental illness and so on, the catalogue of "social problems" recognized by the fifteen or so contemporary socialist states, are just as frequent in these states as they are in capitalist ones. A book devoted to highlighting the failures of the British Welfare State since 1955 and prescribing a socialist revolutionary answer for this failure has no business to be silent about the record of the socialist precedents in this area of human experience ...

Open University Courses

In this connexion, it is important to consider one of the most influential educational institutions of our time, the Open University (OU). In view of the number of people in this country and abroad who come under its influence directly (in the form of the thousands of students who enrol every year) and indirectly (its recommended texts are widely available and the BBC resources are used for transmission of programmes) it is vital that its academic standards and integrity should be beyond reproach. However, the OU has been running a number of courses which have been so politically biased and intellectually weak as to cause great disquiet. Three public criticisms of such courses – "Schooling and Society" (E 202) by J. Gould (*TES*, 4 April 1977); "Patterns of Inequality" (D 302) by Caroline Cox (*Sesame*, Spring 1977); and "Genetics" (S299) by J.H. Edwards (*THES*, 28 March 1980) – sparked off heated exchanges. The OU defended its position in subsequent correspondence – sometimes in interesting and revealing arguments. What were some of the criticisms?

A recurring theme was the familiar one-sidedness of social and political criticism which concentrates on the defects and problems of capitalist societies while neglecting any comparably critical analysis of socialist alternatives. We are told in the opening pages of "Patterns of Inequality" that 'Poverty and wealth need to be understood in relation to their respective places in the system of capitalism.'

What, we ask with dogged persistence, of "patterns of inequality" in the USSR or Eastern Europe, on which data are now available? The student on this course will not find his attention directed there.

A similarly myopic view is found in the early sections of the "Schooling and Society" course and in the accompanying textbook which a Pro-Vice Chancellor of the OU has agreed is a "Marxist Reader".[36] The contributions to the book revolve around the familiar theme: hostility to capitalism and to the "liberal ideology of education" which is purported to be bound up with it. The tone of the book is set in the Editor's Introduction:

Under a capitalist mode of production there is an unequal distribution of power. It is therefore in the interest of those who hold power to ensure the perpetuation of capitalism.

Although sops to a more eclectic approach may be offered later in the course, students' attitudes are inevitably affected by early work which shapes the "mental set" with which they interpret what follows. We do not suggest the OU staff are so naive as to underestimate the importance of this and can, therefore, only interpret this Marxist blitzkrieg in political terms. It is very difficult for any student who is new to a field of study to be aware of alternative viewpoints and to develop his own self-corrective mechanisms. This is particularly so in the case of OU students who often work under great pressure, as part-time students with other commitments. Naturally, they tend to regard their official OU publications as "Bibles", sources of all relevant information, and rely very heavily on them. One of the standard defences used by the OU staff in answering allegations of bias – that alternative ("conservative") views are put forward on radio and television programmes – is not convincing. Many students cannot possibly devote comparable time to these ancillary parts of the course and, even if they do manage to "tune in", the knowledge gained tends to be more ephemeral than that embodied in the printed course units.

Another equally unconvincing argument put forward by defenders of the OU is that these courses only represent a "tiny" minority of all OU courses. It is not the relative proportion of Marxist to all other courses that is the cause for concern – it would be difficult to conceive of a Marxist mathematics or physics course.* What matters is the gross bias of the courses together with the dishonesty which allows subjects to be portrayed under misnomers. In other words, if the OU staff wish to run a course in Marxist Education Theory or a Marxist Analysis of Patterns of Inequality, let them do so – under the honest title. Then students would know the nature of these courses, and the public would know what it was subsidizing.

Finally, one particularly revealing line of defence which lends credence to our concern about the prevalence of Marxist or other left-wing bias in Sociology and Social Studies teaching was the claim, in some correspondence, that although this sort of biased teaching was very widespread, the OU was uniquely vulnerable to criticism because its work is visible. Most of the other equally ideologically biased teaching is, we are told, going on behind closed doors in other universities and colleges and is, therefore, likely to escape detection!

The Genetics Course has also been attacked by Professor Edwards who, in a detailed critique of its contents, pointed out numerous errors of fact and many significant omissions. He is particularly critical of the course's treatment of the complex subject of human genetics, claiming that most of the sections dealing with the subject suffer from:

> the absence of a sound grounding, and are largely used as a mere handle for vague fact-free sociological generalisations which do little credit to genetics or sociology. A sound basis ... could have been built on what is known in health and disease, which should include the contribution of blood groups to anthropology, the basic problem of transplantation, the commoner indications for amniocentesis, and a basic knowledge of a few common conditions including mongolism, cystic fibrosis, muscular distrophy and thalassaemia. At least one protein, such as haemoglobin, should be discussed in some detail. Further, some help should be given in trying to assess the hazards of mutation and the problems of nuclear power or even war.
>
> On such a basis the student should be better equipped to follow such common tragedies and anxieties as are related to our genetic background, and to improve the deplorable standards of public debate on radiation and of medical journalism. In fact such matters are mostly omitted and the recommended reading gives inadequate help. There are no references to books on blood grouping, on serum typing, on transplantation, on human chromosomes or on human development...

Professor Edwards also pointed out that the course team, in discussing the nature-nurture debate, showed 'their preference of fog for clarity' and concluded:

---

*Although the Soviet Union has tried to apply a Marxist straitjacket to many areas of science including cybernetics, the resonance theory of chemical bonding, Einstein's special theory of relativity and, of course, genetics.

> What went wrong? How did a university, lacking any adequately informed staff, but enjoying the good-will and easy access of advisers in many other universities, manage to go it alone with such assurance and at such expense? ... In a field so open to misrepresentation and with so serious and bloody a past in Germany in the 1930s and in Russia in the 1940s, a democracy can ill afford to have so important a topic misrepresented at public expense with the help of the BBC. The Open University has a responsibility to help to raise the standard of public awareness. In this case it can only do so by rewriting this course.

Amen. We would endorse this recommendation for the other courses, too.

We must emphasize that the traits we have just outlined are not characteristic of all sociology or of all sociology teaching. There is much academically sound work being done by sociologists which is of considerable value to professional practitioners and students in other disciplines. This is why the travesties we have discussed are particularly unfortunate in their results for they tend to:

a) Discredit sociology in the eyes of other academics and of practitioners in the professions and the sciences;

b) Give students intellectual short change, sometimes in the form of indoctrination rather than education;

c) Waste or abuse resources – There was a great explosion of courses in sociology in the 1960s and although student demand has slackened in recent years, many staff remain in post. They obviously have vested interests in doing so, and discussions at Faculty Boards have focused on ways in which, by hook or by crook, staff can retain their posts. In some places, the staff/student ratios are such that, one suspects, many eyebrows would be raised if they were to be made public. In others, initiatives have been taken to expand the domain of teaching into other subject areas primarily in order to increase teaching hours. Some developments in the teaching of sociology on courses such as those we have discussed in this essay have occurred as a result of these initiatives. If the sociologists are willing to teach in ways which are helpful to the students on these other courses, well and good. But if their motivations are purely instrumental and are reflected in the kinds of travesty we have depicted, then their contributions should be treated with caution and, if need be, rejected outright. For in the words of T.S. Eliot, it would be '... the greatest treason: To do the right deed for the wrong reason'.[37]

Conclusions

What criteria should be applied in assessing the quality of sociological teaching on the kind of courses we have been discussing? Obviously, fundamental academic criteria are a *sine qua non* of any teaching in higher education and apply here as in other subjects. These include logical coherence and a commitment to an attempt to take account of all available relevant evidence. Although these are necessary criteria for the evaluation of any scholarly enterprise they may not be sufficient, and the demands of teaching sociology in diverse contexts may require additional attributes. Some of these derive from the nature of sociology itself. It is *not* an exact science – and probably never can be, given the enormous complexity of its subject matter. Men are not molecules: they have feelings, motivations and beliefs which need to be taken into account in any attempts to understand human behaviour; moreover, they are responsive and reactive – possibly altering the situation which is under study and making prediction immeasurably more difficult than in the Natural Sciences. In addition, there may be different versions of "truth" which can exist side by side, competing with each other: for example, American and Russian views of the Vietnam War will diverge in many respects. In other words, whilst historical facts may be well documented, interpretations of events may vary to the point of incompatibility.

Given these characteristics inherent in the subject matter of sociology, there is a great onus on those who teach the subject to do so with a deep commitment to the principle of *pluralism* i.e. to have a regard for different viewpoints and to teach with an appropriate degree of humble eclecticism. We cannot "know it all" or know we know "the" truth. Human reality is too complex. It is thus imperative to avoid dogmatism and to refrain from the attempt to impose any "one truth".

However, we have seen that there are many sociology staff in post who are publicly and politically committed to a stance which rejects pluralism. Many Marxists in particular, believing themselves to be endowed with a compelling vision of "the" truth, tend to reject the canons of the liberal tradition – that precious heritage from Athens: a respect for a plurality of views, open discussion and debate, and a commitment to taking into account all available relevant evidence. They dismiss these as bourgeois delusions or humbug.

It is these "academics" who are currently undermining the foundations of The City of Athens from within its own walls. In their arrogance they act like Comte's High Priests of Society imposing their versions of "Truth" and visions of their Utopia on their students – ignoring the evidence of what their Utopias have become in reality and violating the fundamental academic standards of truth and integrity.

Here we reach an *impasse*. It is clear that our analysis in this chapter reveals a deep dilemma: we have argued that there is potential value in teaching sociology, or social studies, to students on other courses, but we have also demonstrated that much of what has been written and taught in the name of sociology over the last fifteen years is a travesty.

What is to be done?

Ideally, the academic community should put its own house in order by calling to account those who fail to abide by its own standards. This is not a violation of academic freedom but a just requirement that the citizens of Academe should abide by its rules. But this academic community has allowed much of the work we have criticized to pass largely unchallenged.

It is also a fact that many of those sociologists whose work is highly undesirable by our standards are unlikely to mend their ways and, being eager for jobs, often move into the "applied" courses. There is thus an intractable problem. Ideally, sociology would be an asset. In practice, it is often a menace and our educational institutions would often be better off without it. There is no easy solution but the following steps might alleviate the situation:

i.   *Drastically reduce* the number of sociology and social studies departments throughout the country. One measure which might achieve this in the maintained sector, especially polytechnics, would be to raise the number of students required as a minimum intake before a course can run. At present, in polytechnics the minimum is 24; if this were raised to 40 it might make it much harder to keep courses running and departments open.

ii.   Recommend that sociology should be *taught as a post-experience or post-graduate subject*. Students can gain infinitely more from the subject if they have previously had a thorough grounding in another academic discipline, or in the discipline of "real life". As a subject it requires considerable maturity and the requirement of some other professional or academic experience would enhance the benefit to be derived from it. It would also make it harder for staff to teach in ways which are so divorced from the constraints of reality.

iii.   Try, where possible, to *appoint* to posts involving teaching sociology to students on other courses, staff who have *direct experience of work* in those, or related fields. E.g., scientists with qualifications in History/Philosophy/Sociology of Science or nurses with Social Science Degrees may be in a better position to present the insights and challenges of sociology to scientists or other professionals, than those who hold purely academic qualifications. This would facilitate our fourth proposal.

iv.   Those responsible for organizing the teaching of sociology to students on their courses should ensure that the type of sociology taught is of maximum help and relevance to their students. For example, Professor M. Jefferys,[38] writing about teaching sociology to medical students, argued that sociologists should *identify* with some of the explicit and implicit goals of medicine and its various practitioners. The same principle would apply to teaching sociology to students in education and science. This is a very different approach from the one-sided "doctor-bashing" and "science-knocking" attitudes which characterize some courses. It does not imply uncritical acceptance of the *status quo* but a balanced appraisal of problems and achievements.

v.   The fifth and related suggestion is that one of the criteria we should use is the extent to which at least one of the goals of teaching should be the *enhancement of the outcomes of the professional practice* to be undertaken by these students. This does not mean that we emasculate sociology's critical functions, but that we have sufficient respect for the students on these courses and for the enterprises in which they are engaged, to attune our sociology to the optimization of their endeavours. This is an approach that has already been practised by many sociologists and is nothing new. See, for example, some of the work of Digby Anderson in his collaboration with health care professionals,[39] or the partnerships between G. Brown and J. Wing[40] in the study of social factors in mental illness.

   If this is done, the inhabitants of Athens and Jerusalem may find that they have much to offer each other. The current hostilities and suspicions which exist in some quarters may be replaced by mutual respect and fruitful dialogue. For we agree with Professor Wing[41] that we need 'creative partnerships . . . based on a realistic appraisal of each other's talents and limitations. This is the way forward now.'

Notes

1. Armstrong, P.F. *Servicing the Professions: Spurious Legitimacy in the Development of Vocational Training.* Paper presented to the Annual Conference of the British Sociological Association, Lancaster, 1980.
2. Frankenberg, R. *Functionalism and After? Theory and Developments in Social Science Applied to the Health Field.* International Journal of Health Services (1974) 4,3, pp. 411-427.
3. Gouldner, A. *The Dialectic of Ideology and Technology* (Macmillan, London, 1976), p. 186.
4. *Report of the Royal Commission on Medical Education* (HMSO, London, 1968).
5. Tuckett, D. (ed) *An Introduction to Medical Sociology* (Tavistock Publications, 1976).
6. Wing, J.K. *Sociology and Psychiatry.* Paper presented to the Annual Conference of the British Sociological Association, Lancaster, 1980.
7. Briggs Report. *Report of the Committee on Nursing* (HMSO, London, 1972).
8. Clark, J. *Bevan's Masterpiece or Bevan's Folly? The NHS – Should we start again?* Address to the Royal College of Nursing Professional Conference, 1978.
9. Cox, C.A. *Who Cares? Nursing and Sociology: The Development of a Symbiotic Relationship.* Paper presented to the British Association for the Advancement of Science, Bath, 1978; published in the *Journal of Advanced Nursing* 1979, 4, pp. 237-252. This article discusses and gives examples of ways in which sociology may make a valuable contribution to nursing and also warns against some of the undesirable developments in contemporary sociology.
10. Owen, G. (ed) *Health Visiting* (Bailliere Tindall, London, 1977).
11. See, for example, some of the studies discussed by F. Naylor in this book such as *Pygmalion in the Classroom* (Rosenthal and Jacobson, 1968), or *Social Relations in a Secondary School* (Hargreaves, 1967).
12. Council for National Academic Awards *Regulations and Conditions for the Award of the Council's First Degree* (1974) Regulation 4.1.3.
13. Doyal, L. with Pennell, I. *The Political Economy of Health* (Pluto Press, 1979).
14. Field, M.G. *Soviet Socialized Medicine: An Introduction* (The Free Press, New York, 1967).
15. Amnesty International *Prisoners of Conscience in the USSR: Their Treatment and Conditions*, 1980.
16. See the Working Papers of the Centre for Contemporary Cultural Studies, Birmingham University, directed by Stuart Hall until his appointment in October 1979 as Professor of Sociology at the Open University.
17. Campaign Against Psychiatric Abuse for Political Purposes *Your Disease is Dissent* (CAPA 1980).
18. Miliband, R. *The State in Capitalist Society* (Quartet Books, 1973).
19. The literature on conditions in the Soviet Union and other Marxist states is now so extensive that the following list is not comprehensive. What it does indicate is the range of material neglected or ignored by many "social scientists".

(i) **Censorship and the Press**
Conquest, R. *The Politics of Ideas in the USSR* (Bodley Head, 1967).
Medvedev, Z. *Ten Years after Ivan Denisovich* (Macmillan, 1973).
Nogee, J. (ed) *Man, State and Society in the Soviet Union* (Praeger, 1972).
Reddaway, P. (ed) *Uncensored Russia* (Jonathan Cape, 1972).
Labedz, L. (ed) *Solzhenitsyn: a Documentary Record* (Penguin, 1970).

(ii) **The Gulag Archipelago and the KGB**
Solzhenitsyn, A. *The Gulag Archipelago*, 3 vols. (Collins/Harvill, 1974-76).
Conquest, R. *The Great Terror* (Macmillan, 1968).
Conquest, R. *Justice and the Legal System in the USSR* (Bodley Head, 1968).
Conquest, R. *The Soviet Police System* (Bodley Head, 1968).
Barron, J. *KGB* (Hodder & Stoughton, 1974).
Myagkov, A. *Inside the KGB* (Foreign Affairs Publishing Co., 1976).
Conquest, R. *Kolyma; the Arctic Death Camps* (Macmillan 1978).

(iii) **The Treatment of Dissenters and Minority Groups**
Tokes, R. *Dissent in the USSR* (Johns Hopkins University Press, 1975).
Bloch, S. and Reddaway, P. *Russia's Political Hospitals: the Abuse of Psychiatry in the USSR* (Gollancz, 1977).
Medvedev, Z. and Medvedev, R. *A Question of Madness* (Macmillan, 1971).
Grigorenko, P.G. *The Grigorenko Papers* (C. Hurst, 1976).
Bukovsky, V. *To Build a Castle: My Life as a Dissident* (Deutsch, 1978).
Conquest, R. *Religion in the USSR* (Bodley Head, 1968).
Beeson, T. *Discretion and Valour* (Collins/Fontana, 1975).
Amnesty International *Prisoners of Conscience in the USSR* (1980).
Conquest, R. *The Nation Killers* (Macmillan, 1970).
Institute of Jewish Affairs *Soviet Antisemitic Propaganda – Evidence from books, press and radio* (1978).
Medvedev, Z. *The Medvedev Papers* (Macmillan, 1971).

(iv) **Science and Nuclear Energy**
Sutton, A. *Western Technology and Soviet Economic Development* (3 vols.) (Stanford University Press, 1968, 1971, 1973).
Medvedev, Z. *The Rise and Fall of T.D. Lysenko* (Columbia University Press, 1969).
Joravsky, D. *The Lysenko Affair* (Harvard University Press, 1970).
Medvedev, Z. *Soviet Science* (Oxford University Press, 1979).
Medvedev, Z. *Nuclear Disaster in the Urals* (Angus & Robertson, 1979).
Medvedev, Z. *Two Decades of Dissidence* (4 November 1976); *Facts behind the Soviet Nuclear Disaster* (30 June 1977); *Winged Messengers of Disaster* (10 November 1977); all in *New Scientist*.
"Soviet Science and Technology" in *Survey,* Vol. 23 No. 1 and No. 2, Winter 1977-8 and Spring 1978.

(v) **Totalitarian Nature of Marxist Societies: Domination by Communist Party**
Shapiro, L. *The Government and Politics of the Soviet Union* (Hutchinson 1965).
Fainsod, M. *How Russia is Ruled* (Harvard University Press, 1963).

Shapiro, L. *The Communist Party of the Soviet Union* (Eyre & Spottiswoode, 1970).
Fainsod, M. *Smolensk under Soviet Rule* (Harvard University Press, 1958).
Conquest, R. *Agricultural Workers in the USSR* (Bodley Head, 1968).
(vi) **Privileges of Communist Party Members**
Djilas, M. *The New Class* (Allen and Unwin, 1966).
Sakharov, A.. *My Country and the World* (Collins/Harvill, 1975).

These books can be supplemented by many authoritative articles and documents from journals such as *Survey* (Oxford University Press, edited by Leo Labedz); *Religion in Communist Lands* (Keston College, Kent, edited by Xenia Howard-Johnston); *The Chronicle of Current Events* (a samizdat journal distributed by Amnesty International); the publications of the *Campaign Against Psychiatric Abuse*, and many others.
A similar list of sources could be compiled for the People's Republic of China and for all other existing Marxist/Communist societies.

20. Figlio, K. *Sinister Medicine? A Critique of Left Approaches to Medicine,* Radical Science Journal 9 (1979) pp. 14-68.
21. Berliner, H. and Salmon, J. *The Holistic Health Movement and Scientific Medicine: the Naked and the Dead* Socialist Review (1979) 43, pp. 31-52.
22. Berger, P. and Luckmann, T. *The Social Construction of Reality: A Treatise in the Sociology of Knowledge* (Allen Lane, 1967).
23. Scheff, T. *Being mentally ill* (Aldine, 1966).
24. Goffman, E. *Asylums* (Penguin, 1961).
25. Wing, J.K. op. cit.
26. Heraud, B., *Sociology in the Professions* (Open Books, 1979).
27. Jefferys, M. *Doctor's Orders. The Past, Present and Future of Medical Sociology.* Paper presented to the Annual Conference of the British Sociological Association (Lancaster, 1980).
28. Bowles, S. and Gintis, H. *Schooling in Capitalist America* (Routledge and Kegan Paul, 1976).
29. From the editorial in Radical Science Journal (1975) 2/3, pp. 3, 6.
Lest it be thought that this is a "fringe" journal with no significant influence, it is probably worth stating that it is edited by a collective whose members teach courses involving social aspects of science at some major institutions of higher education. For example, the editorial collective has included B. Easlea, Lecturer in Social Studies of Science, Sussex University; D. Griffiths and B. Werskey, both Lecturers in Industrial Sociology, Imperial College, London; D. Dickson, former science correspondent of the *Times Higher Educational Supplement* and Washington correspondent of *Nature*; R.M. Young, formerly of the Wellcome Unit for the History of Medicine, Cambridge University, and Fellow of King's College; and M.F.D. Young, Senior Lecturer in the Sociology of Education, London University Institute of Education, and a member of the Sociological Studies Board of the Council for National Academic Awards (CNAA).
30. Pavitt, K. and Worboys, M. *Science, Technology and the Modern Industrial*

State (published for Science in a Social Context (Siscon) by Butterworth, 1977).

31. Rose, H. and Rose, S. *The Radicalisation of Science*, and *The Political Economy of Science*, both sub-titled *Ideology of/in the Natural Sciences* (Macmillan, 1976).

32. Sohn-Rehtel, A. *Science as Alienated Consciousness*, Radical Science Journal (1975), 2/3, p. 73.

33. From the editorial introduction by the Radical Science Journal Collective to the article cited above, p. 69.

34. Op. cit. p. 70.

35. Halmos, P. Book review of *Ideology and Social Welfare* by V. George and P. Wilding (Routledge & Kegan Paul, 1976) published in *The Times Higher Educational Supplement*, 18 June 1976.

36. Dale, I.R., Esland, G.M., and MacDonald, M. (eds), *Schooling and Capitalism: a Sociological Reader* (Routledge & Kegan Paul, 1976).

37. Eliot, T.S. *Murder in the Cathedral* (Faber and Faber, 1935).

38. Jefferys, M. op. cit.

39. Anderson, D.C. *Health Education in Practice* (Croom Helm, London, 1979).

40. Wing, J.K. and Brown, G.W. *Institutionalism and Schizophrenia: A Comparative Study of Three Mental Hospitals 1960-1968* (Cambridge University Press, 1970).

41. Wing, J.K. *Sociology and Psychiatry*, op. cit.

VI

Quality or Equality: Educational Standards and the Examination System

Alan Grant

Educated at grammar school and the universities of Leeds (B.A.), Warwick (M.A.), and Leicester (Post Graduate Certificate in Education). Senior Lecturer in Politics and Public Admini- stration at Oxford Polytechnic (since January 1980) he was Lecturer in Government and Politics at Buckinghamshire College of Higher Education (1971-9) and has lectured at Moorpark College in California, the University of Maryland and for the Open University. He was elected to Buckinghamshire County Council in May 1981 and is a member of its Education Committee. He is a Governor of four schools and a college, and the author of The American Political Process.

This chapter looks at the various ways in which politicians and educationalists espousing egalitarianism have attempted to change the system of public examinations in this country. The role and influence of the National Union of Teachers and the Schools Council in this process is considered. The motives of these bodies are questioned: in advocating reforms that merge existing examinations and in introducing new ones at various levels; in replacing external assessment by indepen- dent boards with papers set and marked by teachers; in altering established grading systems and reducing specializa- tion. The chapter also analyses in some detail two recent reports – of the Waddell and Keohane Committees – which advocate changes in the examination system and highlights the weaknesses and inconsistencies in the cases submitted for reform.

In celebrating its fifteenth birthday in 1979 the Schools Council was moved to remark: 'Like other teenagers we've come in for some knocking and even our relatives don't always understand us as they should. Some think the Council an indulgent extravagance.'[1] The Council's annual budget for 1979 was just under £3m. supporting over a hundred active projects but it has come to the public's attention, particularly as it has reached its adolescent years, as the source of numerous sweeping proposals to reform the public examinations system. The late 1970s witnessed schemes for a common examination at 16-plus, N and F level examinations to replace GCE Advanced Level, the proposal for a Certificate of Extended Education (CEE) at 17-plus for the "new sixth formers" and, in March 1980, the Schools Council initiated a move to introduce a new Intermediate (I Level) examination. There have also been many plans for alterations to and modifications in the grading systems of existing examinations.

This hectic spate of activity on the examination front either coincided with or followed shortly after the "Great Debate" on education. Parents and users of educational qualifications might, therefore, be forgiven for thinking that all these fresh approaches were specifically designed to safeguard or improve academic standards in our schools. Unfortunately, nothing could be further from the truth. Long before Mr Callaghan's sudden conversion to traditional Conservative concern for standards in education, the Schools Council had been pressing for change. Indeed these proposals germinated in the trendy 1960s and early 1970s when progressive opinion still held almost unrivalled sway in educational circles; many of them have only recently borne fruit at a time when both the intellectual climate and the government have changed.

At first sight it may be surprising that left-wing politicians and progressive educationalists should be searching for more ways of testing and evaluating children. Surely they are the people who tell us that our educational system is already too hidebound by examinations, that the curriculum is dominated by such concerns and that it inhibits innovation and limits teaching methods? And do not these same experts find that dividing children by examination performance is doctrinally unacceptable as well as being extremely difficult as a logistical exercise? The Waddell Committee, for example, complained that the separation of GCE O Level and CSE tends to "mark off" pupils from one another.[2] Christopher Price, a Member of Parliament who is now Chairman of the new Select Committee on Education, Science and the Arts, told the Labour Party Conference in 1970:

If the 11-plus exam was wrong so was the 14-plus, the 16-plus, the 18-plus and the filtering and selection mechanism for university and higher eduation.[3]

On the basis of these objections some educationalists advocate the complete abolition of examinations. In January 1979 the Advisory Centre for Education proposed their replacement by reports describing all aspects of pupils' performance and character written by their teachers.

The history of public examinations since 1945 helps us to clarify this apparent paradox. Many progressives and socialists are intellectually and emotionally opposed to all examinations that show people are not equal. Examinations encourage rivalry and competition, promoting individual effort and unequal attainment. In order to create a classless and egalitarian society they will have to go. However, tactically they have recognized that the abolition of examinations could not be sold immediately to parents, employers and most sensible teachers. They could not convince ministers at the Department of Education and Science, even Labour ones concerned at the electoral consequences. The approach would therefore have to be a more subtle and long term one; a subversion from within rather than a frontal assault. The attack on established academic examinations – GCE O and A Levels – would be a parallel campaign with the drive to abolish selective secondary education. However, the attempts to reduce public respect for academic examinations and to alter the curriculum and what actually goes on in the classroom are even more insidious and a greater threat to educational standards than universal comprehensivization of the state sector. In a school structure as decentralized as Britain's the examination system run by independent boards associated with the universities is the principal means by which national standards are safeguarded. What is more, changes in that examination system affect both the maintained and independent sectors of secondary education.

A number of different approaches have been tried by the progressive lobby; some have been spotted and repelled, others have crept through with the aquiescence of politicians and a public mostly lacking in vigilance or under-standing of the repercussions.

A Common Examination at 16-plus

One line of attack is to recommend a new examination designed for pupils who are unable to meet the academic requirements of an established one. The next move is then to campaign for a merger of the two – hence the proposals for a common system at 16-plus. On the face of it the case for merger is logical enough. It is said to be confusing as well as creating administrative and time-tabling problems to have groups taking different papers by separate boards. We are told how difficult it is to decide which children should take the more or less academically demanding papers and, of course, the new examination suffers from having a "low status". The National Union of Teachers, the majority of whose members are not involved in public examinations teaching, argues:

> In maintaining two quite separate examinations designed for pupils of different ability ranges, the present system is as divisive, and hence educationally indefensible, as the co-existence of grammar and secondary modern schools.[4]

What is more, progressives support a common examination at 16-plus because it would open the floodgate to the development of mixed ability teaching throughout the comprehensive school, another of the egalitarians' priorities for eradicating inequality. They oppose streaming and setting by ability despite an HMI Report showing that mixed ability teaching works well only in exceptional circumstances and evidence that it is highly unpopular with parents.[5]

The Schools Council as an educational quango heavily influenced by the National Union of Teachers and pervaded by progressive opinion, has been occupied with proposals for a common examination at 16-plus since 1970, and formally presented the package to the Secretary of State in 1976. The Conservative Party was extremely sceptical; in 1977 its spokesman, Norman St John Stevas, wrote:

The Schools Council has bought forward its proposals for a common exam at 16-plus. They are not convincing. They have failed to overcome the problem of testing the able child as well as the least able....

The imposition of this exam would encourage a common curriculum for all abilities, which in itself is undesirable. It is argued that a common curriculum would make the task of the teacher easier. The implication is that it would no longer be necessary to treat children differently. In my view the egalitarian philosophy that so opposes success, which underlies the concept of the exam, would cause lasting harm. This proposal, in which employers also have no confidence, should not go forward.[6]

Mrs Shirley Williams established the Waddell Committee to review the proposals and consider how they could be implemented. It reported in July 1978 in favour of a common system and the Labour Government hastily accepted the recommendations in its White Paper, *Secondary School Examinations: A Single System at 16 plus* (October 1978). With the election in May 1979 of a Conservative Government, Mr Mark Carlisle pronounced himself unsatisfied that the proposals would safeguard standards, particularly those associated with O Level. Six months later he announced that on reflection he had decided that O Level and CSE should be merged into a single system, but that his new system would ensure the continuance of the GCE Boards being responsible for setting and marking papers for those aiming at the top three grades in the new seven-grade integrated scheme.

Teacher Assessment and Control

Another familiar approach is to recommend that externally assessed papers be replaced by those set and marked by teachers. This system is used in the CSE Mode III and has been one of the major stumbling blocks in obtaining acceptance and status for CSE as it has been regarded by many as an easy option. In 1977, 25 per cent of CSE entries nationally were by Mode III and as the recent HMI Report on Secondary Education makes clear such courses are frequently planned for those who have difficulty with a more academic approach. The report notes it is common to provide '... O-Level for the top band... CSE for the middle band and CSE Mode III.... for the lowest band'.[7] This is despite the fact that CSE Mode I and III are supposed to be equal in difficulty and status. The Schools Council has consistently advocated that there be a major extension of such practices in a new 16-plus examination and more tentatively recommended internal assessment as having a part to play at A-Level. Many supporters of teacher-assessment see Mode III style examinations as a major step down the road to teachers' reports replacing examinations altogether. They ignore the distortions of the teacher-pupil relationship, the dangers of bias, the problems of comparability of standards and the fact that a bright child from a poor school may well be blighted by the reputation of the institution he attended. Moreover, the teachers' unions have tended to support this approach because it removes one of the very few ways in Britain in which their members are held accountable by independent bodies for what they actually achieve in the classroom. The unions would prefer that there were no external checks at all on their members' competence and teaching effectiveness. While these independent indices do exist the unions also consistently oppose the publication of examination results by local education authorities. The NUT, in particular, opposes parents and taxpayers having the right of access to information about the schools for which they are paying. Only teachers, according to the union, can understand the results; other people would make invidious comparisons between schools or different authorities without understanding the grades or the significance of "social factors."

The same pressure groups campaign to have examinations administered by boards on which serving teachers (i.e. union representatives) are a majority. The CSE Boards are run in this way and the Keohane Committee recommended that for the proposed Certificate of Extended Education 'committee(s) of examining boards controlling the CEE examination should have a majority of serving teachers.'[8] The Schools Council should, according to both the Waddell and Keohane committees, be responsible for national coordination of the new 16-plus and CEE examinations.

Examination Grades

At the same time the progressives have been very busy playing down the significance attached to grades showing different levels of performance in existing examinations. In 1975 failing was abolished in GCE O-Levels. Grades were to be awarded on an A - E scale despite the fact that only A - C were representative of passes under the previous system which had six pass grades and three fail grades. CSE candidates who cannot even achieve a minimal performance do not fail, they are "ungraded". Bernard Levin remarked in an article in *The Times*:

> I see that a Yorkshire headmaster has finally blown the whistle on the General Certificate of Education by refusing to hand out, at his school's speech day, O-Level certificates recording pupils' attainment of grades D and E, on the not entirely unreasonable ground that these grades establish that the pupil who achieves them has in fact *failed* in the examination, and the good dominie, at the risk of sounding so unfashionable as to be thought positively deranged, says that pupils ought not to be applauded by the school's entire complement of scholars (no doubt with attendant parents) for failing.
>
> Well, schoolmasters always were a rum lot, and a Yorkshire schoolmaster may be presumed to be rummer than most. This one, at any rate, shows that he simply has not grasped the vital principle that lies at the heart of our new educational system, and which was promptly encapsulated to perfection in the words of our old and valued friend, A. Spokesman. Asked to comment on the maverick headmaster's decision, he said first that the D and E grades did indeed represent marks lower than the failure line. But he added in his characteristically ineffable way: 'The concept of pass and fail was abolished two years ago to try to be fairer to those of moderate ability'.[9]

When Mrs Thatcher was at the DES she vetoed a Schools Council proposal to replace the existing A-Level examination grades with a new 20 point scale with an indicated unreliability of three grades. The idea had been condemned by teachers involved with A-Level as hopelessly vague and complex and it was scorned by those in higher education who saw it as utterly meaningless for their selection purposes.

Under the present system of A-Level grades established in 1963, guidelines have been established so that a certain percentage of candidates are awarded each grade. The distribution of grades over all the boards has conformed closely to the guidelines with only marginal fluctuations from one year to the next. Therefore, approximately 10 per cent of entrants pass at grade A, 15 per cent B, 10 per cent C, 15 per cent D, and 20 per cent E, while 30 per cent obtain either an O-level pass or Fail. This system, therefore, does not provide an indication of how standards are fluctuating over time and whether, for example, a student who in 1979 received an A grade in English Literature would have done so in 1969. The same percentage of a much larger absolute number of candidates taking A-levels over the last twenty years achieve pass and fail grades. We cannot tell whether the standards required to obtain a pass have improved or declined and yet Labour politicians – and Mrs Shirley Williams – have no difficulty in claiming that standards are improving because more children are staying on and passing A-levels. Despite national concern over educational standards the Schools Council in its March 1980 report proposes to expand the percentage of entrants who obtain the narrow middle-range C grade at A-level rather than deal with the fundamental issue of monitoring and comparing performances over time.[10]

Reducing Specialization

Yet another strategy used in the campaign to erode the value of academic examinations is to attack their specialization and propose changes which would "broaden the curriculum" and delay choice. Students would be required to take more subjects but to what would inevitably be a lower standard than A-level. The Schools Council proposed that sixth formers should take five subjects, three to normal (N) level and two to Further (F) level.[11] Each N-level course would have half the study time and an F-level course three-quarters of the study time of an A-level. There was also a recommendation that total study time between examined and non-examined work should be in the proportion of 70 per cent to 30 per cent. While it is true that not all advocates of broadening the curriculum were so motivated, it is clear that many progressive reformers saw this as a further opportunity to hold back the bright student and reduce the inequalities of achievement.

Opposition to the N and F proposals was so widespread that Mrs Williams, who originally supported the reforms, was obliged, in 1979, to announce that the Labour Government would not, after all, abolish A-levels. Universities and polytechnics argued that it would be impossible to maintain the standard of honours degrees if they were expected to build on N- and F-levels in the sixth form without increasing the length of degree courses from three to four years, and the cost of adding the extra year to degree courses was estimated at £300m. in 1978. It does not appear that the Schools Council consider the economic repercussions of their proposals as having any great significance.

However, the Schools Council is nothing if not persistent and, undaunted by the rejection of N and F levels and accepting that – for the time being at least – A-levels will continue, it served up a re-hashed N-level as a new Intermediate (I) level examination. The I-level was intended to be about half the scope of an A-level and about halfway between A-level and O-level in the examination hierarchy. The Schools Council suggested that it could be taken by those in the sixth form for whom A-level was inappropriate but who were academically more able than those "new sixth formers" for whom the Council had already designed the CEE at 17-plus. In addition, A-level students might take some I-levels in their non-specialist areas to broaden the sixth form curriculum.

The Conservative Government issued a consultative paper "Examinations 16-18" in October 1980 in which it argued that, in practice, any new examination could not realistically serve the interest and needs of both these groups.[12] The Government says that an Intermediate level examination might have a valuable but modest role to play in improving educational opportunities in sixth forms for those taking two or three A-levels already by allowing, for example, an arts subject specialist to develop skills in mathematics or science. However, it believes that further work would only be justified if there were a firm indication that universities, colleges and employers would value and use such a qualification as a factor in selection for their courses or for employment. It also warns that resources for I-level courses would need to be found by "re-deploying existing levels of provision". The Government concludes that Intermediate courses would not be suitable for those sixth formers who find A-level too academically demanding, as had been suggested by the Schools Council.

The Waddell and Keohane Committees

On the occasions when the Schools Council proposed a common 16-plus examination and a new Certificate of Extended Education for 17-year-olds, the Government established a steering committee or study group to consider the plans and advise whether they should be given official recognition. Both bodies were headed by an appropriate academic and both supported the principles of the Schools Council's proposals while expressing some reservations or qualifications on how they should be implemented. For anyone interested in this legitimization process the composition and working of these bodies is of considerable concern. The Keohane Study Group, for example, was looking at proposals for a new examination intended for those who would stay into the sixth form but who would not be aiming for higher education, people who would mostly be seeking employment after the CEE. It was also to consider the relationship between CEE and other qualifications available, mainly in further education, for the same age and ability group. Despite these terms of reference the Committee had only two representatives from industry and two from trade unions out of a total of twenty-four members. The Keohane Report says:

> Nor did it seem practicable to conduct a survey of employer opinion with regard to courses and examinations for the young people concerned.... we benefited from the advice of our employment members.[13]

The Central Policy Review Staff's very useful document *Education, Training and Industrial Performance* noted that the Keohane Committee had been established because there was concern that the experimental CEE had too little relevance to employment and that the Committee had recommended approval of CEE subject to the incorporation of a larger vocational element and compulsory tests in mathematics and English. The CPRS discovered no indication that employers found CEE of value and stated that there were strong arguments against sanctioning the CEE when many further education courses existed for pupils of broadly the same ability and aspirations. The "Think Thank" concluded:

> We recommend that in coming to a conclusion the Government should attach particular importance to the extent to which any innovation in examinations is likely to prepare young people better for

employment and help employers recruit appropriate individuals. The CPRS would therefore attach much more weight to increasing the participation of young people in "foundation" level vocational courses than in the continuation of an examination along the lines of CEE.[14]*

The Waddell Committee was considering the reform of GCE O-Level and CSE which at present provide the basic qualifications for many areas of business and commerce. However, the Waddell Committee included only one representative from industry (the Chairman of the Education and Training Committee of Birmingham Chamber of Industry and Commerce) and also admitted 'we did not undertake any survey of employer opinion....'[15]

Both Committees were also aware that they were under considerable pressure to prepare reports quickly so that decisions could be taken as matters of urgency. This encouraged cutting corners and taking on trust a lot of the Schools Council's research and arguments. The Keohane Report notes that in setting up the committee Mrs Williams had indicated that she expected it would take about a year to produce a report. Therefore the Committee did not think it practical to undertake detailed studies of individual CEE syllabuses and examinations or extensive research of a kind more appropriate to the Schools Council. Instead the committee's role would be to provide "a broad assessment."[16] When the group found evidence of a drop in the number of candidates for the CEE pilot examinations – a matter one would have thought to be of vital importance in making any assessment of the practicability of CEE – the report states:

> In the time available to us we were not able to seek the views of the schools and colleges on the reason for this decline.[17]

The Waddell Committee was also not so concerned with whether the cat should be skinned but merely what difficulties would have to be overcome in the skinning:

> In considering the issues before us, we did not consider it our business to embark on a fundamental reassessment of the strengths of the arguments for a common system. The Secretary of State had already acknowledged these and did not ask to have them reconsidered.[18]

Throughout the reports there are inconsistencies and contradictions, claims that are not supported and conclusions that do not follow easily from the evidence provided in the reports. The Waddell Committee argues in paragraph 8 that the present system of separate O-Levels and CSE is confusing to the general public and to the "users" of the certificates, but in paragraph 48 it admits that the system has the confidence of the users as tests of performance and, in paragraph 27, that a common system is by its nature complex. The Keohane Committee concedes that the Schools Council's previous predictions of the number of children staying on into the sixth form were not fulfilled and that a dramatic fall in such numbers is now projected for the period to 1994. It also recognizes that in 1978 candidates in CEE pilot examinations took on average only 1.4 subjects and a mere|one per cent took the five subjects which the Schools Council had envisaged as a full CEE course, while the number of potential candidates in 1991 would fall

---

* In October 1980, the Government issued a consultative paper "Examinations 16-18" in which it effectively followed the advice of the CPRS by rejecting the Keohane Committee's case for the CEE. Instead it argued that this target group of students would be best served by provision of a vocationally orientated examination broadly along the lines recommended in "A Basis for Choice", a report published in June 1979 by the Further Education Curriculum Review and Development Unit (FEU).

within the lower part of the projected range of 52-76,000.[19] Despite the evidence of considerably less demand for CEE than that foreseen when it was originally proposed and the fact that a great variety of more vocational courses were already available, the committee concluded that it was an appropriate time to establish a totally new examination.

The Waddell Report is particularly suspect as a piece of sound and honest intellectual advocacy. Admittedly the committee was faced with an almost insuperable problem: how to make credible a proposal suggesting that examinations could be devised that could cope adequately with fully 60 per cent of the ability range (at present O-Level is designed for the top 20 per cent and CSE for the next 40 per cent). The committee did not undertake any new research itself but set up a ten member Educational Study Group which then investigated and summarized the work that had been done on the feasibility of a single system. The evidence came mostly from the studies and joint examinations organized by consortia of GCE and CSE Boards and feasibility studies sponsored by the Schools Council. Many of the joint examinations adopted the "common examination" approach – the ideal for the advocates of a common 16-plus because there is no need for prior choice between papers and all candidates study the same syllabus and take the same examination. Misgivings about the value of the evidence shine through the bland officialese of the Group's report which is hidden away as Part II of the Waddell Committee findings in a separate pamphlet. The evidence 'varied in force and weight' and the joint examinations had been 'mounted quickly and were developed before an overall research strategy could be devised.'[20] (Surely even the most trusting observer might be tempted to ask why there should be this sort of hurry in a matter of such long-term significance?) The results of the research however show that a genuine common examination was *not* feasible in nearly every major school subject.

The ESG Report gives the game away time and again with comments such as that for History:

> ... examining techniques... did not prove wholly adequate to meet the demands of assessing the range of ability concerned. Many of the difficulties arose because the schemes adopted a common examination.[21]

However the drafters tried hard to end each section on individual subjects with the conclusion that a common examination was feasible and the Group was satisfied that techniques existed to overcome the difficulties. The Waddell Committee – unable to realistically support a common examination – instead recommended 'a common system' of examinations where 'all grades... must be awarded on a single scale and all certificates must bear a common title'.[22] In practice this would mean alternative papers and questions in almost every subject. Very little research had been done on how such examinations could be devised or operated and the report skates over the problem of deciding which children should take which papers (one of the major criticisms made of the existing GCE/CSE dualism). Despite all that had been revealed it was no great surprise that the Labour Government, while paying lipservice to the need to complete 'a good deal of development work'[23] reached the conclusion that the Waddell Report had provided evidence that a common examination system could be established satisfactorily from both educational and administrative standpoints.

One effect of establishing a number of different committees and advisory bodies to make and consider individual proposals for reform is that none of them takes an overall view or tries to assess the inter-relationship of the schemes. The result is a very disjointed approach to what should be one system of examinations. The Keohane Committee, for example, had to consider the CEE and other further education courses without any rigid assumptions about the future of 16-plus examinations, and just before it completed its report it was informed by Mark Carlisle that A-levels would definitely continue. Keohane's attempts to estimate the likely demand for CEE was also hindered by such uncertainties as to whether at some future date an Intermediate-level examination alongside A-Level might be introduced. Therefore the Secretary of State is left to try to make some sense out of a plethora of unrelated and overlapping proposals and forge a coherent policy on examinations. The rapid turnover of Ministers at the DES has not contributed to such a development.

Conclusion

In typical British style the public examination system has grown up on a piecemeal basis in response to the changing needs and demands of higher education, employers and parents. There is clearly room for improvement and modifications may be made without threatening the edifice that has been established. Alternative methods of assessment – projects, oral examinations, multiple choice tests, for example – can all be extended and developed to meet new demands and test skills in more appropriate ways than traditional written examinations but within the framework of an independent external examination system.

Organic development is both natural and healthy. Unfortunately, many educationalists and politicians on the Left in Britain are not interested in these sorts of reforms. We have seen that the overriding concern of many of them is to create uncertainty, instability and lack of confidence throughout both the examination and the wider educational system. For the extremists the primary objective is to abolish all examinations as a major step down the road to the socialist utopia; for the moderates and social engineers the aim is to give everybody a prize just for taking part, and nobody's sensibilities are to be offended by failing until such time as the need for examinations no longer exists; for the educational bureaucrats who may share these longer term ideals, the short and medium term goal is to keep the research projects and feasibility studies, the steering committees and the advisory groups, the quangos and the departmental enquiries in business and the taxpayers' money flowing in.

No one connected with education believes that examinations are the only things that count when judging the success or failure of our schools. We are all concerned that children develop an ability to express themselves, a sense of cooperation and a desire to discover things for themselves. The examination system should not become a straitjacket that deters experimentation and prevents curriculum development. However, it is essential to recognize the important roles of the examination system particularly in relation to selection, the development of ability in specialized areas and in the maintenance of standards in our schools. The emphasis for too many educationalists and politicians has not been on developing high standards, disciplined learning and pride in work and achievement – the characteristics that young people and the nation require in order to prosper and succeed. Their concern has been to promote equality rather than quality and to use the schools as instruments of social engineering where "middle class" values and standards are decried and condemned. As Maurice Kogan has shown, educational policy making is to a large degree initiated internally within the system itself, and the climate of opinion within the social science intelligentsia, the educational press correspondents and the leaders of the professional bodies has been of great importance in influencing official decisions by successive governments.[24] Most of the proposals for changes in the examination system have come as a result of these internal forces rather than from any discernible public pressure. It has been the purpose of this paper to point out that the motivations of the advocates of reform have not always been consistent with the priorities and concerns of the country as a whole and to argue that educational policies which have wide and important repercussions should not be left to these unrepresentative and often politically extreme elites.

Notes

1. Schools Council Newsletter No. 30 (Summer 1979), p. 1. An inquiry headed by Mrs Nancy Trenaman of St Anne's College, Oxford, reported in Autumn 1981 that the Schools Council should divest itself of power politics and be reduced in numbers, particularly of its teacher-union members. The inquiry was set up in March 1981 by the then Secretary of State, Mark Carlisle, in response to criticisms of the Schools Council's activities.
2. Waddell Committee Report, Part 1 (Cmnd 7281-1, July 1978), p. 3, para. 8.
3. Quoted in Rhodes Boyson, *Battle Lines for Education* (Conservative Political Centre, July 1973), p. 13.
4. *Examining at 16 Plus* (National Union of Teachers, November 1978), p. 2.
5. *Mixed Ability Work in Comprehensive Schools, Matters for Discussion No. 6* (HMI series, July 1978); *Sunday Times* Survey, 22 October 1978.
6. Norman St John Stevas, *Better Schools for All* (Conservative Political Centre, 1977), pp. 30-31.
7. *Aspects of Secondary Education in England; a survey by HM Inspectors of Schools* (DES 1979), p. 119.
8. *Proposals for a Certificate of Extended Education*, the Keohane Study Group Report (Cmnd 7755, December 1979), p. 16, para. 44.
9. *The Times*, 29 July 1977.
10. *Secondary Examinations Post 16: A Programme of Improvement* (Schools Council, March 1980), Appendix A, p. 15.
11. *Examinations at 18 plus: the N and F Studies*, Schools Council Working Paper 60 (Evans-Methuen Educational, 1978).
12. *Examinations 16-18*, A Consultative Paper (DES and Welsh Office, October 1980), p. 5, para. 25.
13. Keohane Study Group Report, p. 2, para. 7.
14. *Education, Training and Industrial Performance* (Central Policy Review Staff, 1980), pp. 28-9, paras. 46-48.
15. Waddell Committee Report, p. 17, para. 53.
16. Keohane Study Group Report, p. 2, para. 7.

17. Ibid., p. 20, para. 56.
18. Waddell Committee Report, p. 4, para. 11.
19. Keohane Study Group Report, p. 14, para. 38; p.30, para. 93; p. 47, para. 139.
20. Waddell Committee Report, Part II, p.10, para. 14.
21. Ibid., p. 38, para. 118.
22. Ibid., Part I, p. 6, para. 21.
23. *Secondary School Examinations: A Single System at 16 plus* (Government White Paper, Cmnd 7368, October 1978), p.7, para. 16.
24. Maurice Kogan, *The Politics of Educational Change* (Fontana 1978), Chapter 10.

Change and Obstacles to Change

VII
Education Vouchers

Marjorie Seldon

Founder and Hon. Chairman of Friends of the Education
Voucher Experiment in Representative Regions *(now in its
seventh year), Marjorie Seldon has written widely in national
and local publications on the voucher system and has appeared in a number of radio and television debates. She is also
Vice-Chairman of the special education committee of the
National Council of Women of Great Britain. Married to free
market economist and author, Arthur Seldon, she has three
sons: the youngest, Anthony, is author of* Churchill's Indian
Summer.

*Why is there continuing crisis in education? What does real
parental involvement mean? Can the high costs and huge
bureaucracy in state schooling be cut? Can we create a market
in education and allow parents to choose the school they want
and give a verdict on others? A hundred years of growing state
education has created so much failure – of schools, of little
reward for each taxpayer's pound, of children's chances in
employment – that the time has come for radical change. Spain
now has vouchers equal to state-school cost for use in private
schools; British Columbia pays one-third of the cost. In Britain
many parents would change to private schools with the help of
vouchers. This would protect the independent sector from
threatened political interference. When about a quarter of all
children have transferred from state schools under a voucher
system, there could be a progressive reduction in taxpayers'
funding of education.*

Education is always in the news; and mostly it is bad news: teacher strikes, caretaker strikes, demonstrations, Councils "mugging" education, pupils mugged in playgrounds, shortage of textbooks, of maths teachers, closure of schools for handicapped children, of village schools....

There is no end to the dismal headlines. Little wonder that the idea of radical reform in the financing of education is gathering support in Britain and all over the world: Australia, Canada, Spain, Germany, the U.S.A., New Zealand. For most countries endure school crises that parallel or exceed ours. In the eyes of a consumer of state supplied services the reason is obvious. Education is run in the interests of the producer. Parents are the only people with no vested interest in education except their children. And the poorer and less articulate they are, the less their influence. No one now living in Britain has experienced a market in education in which schools, public and private, offer their "goods" to parents, of all social classes, who in turn would choose and pay for their preferred school out of their own pocket and with a return of taxes.

The growing populist movement for education vouchers, which gives the parent his child's share of state education finance, alarms the leaders of the teachers', civil service and public employees' unions. Good teachers have no reason to be anxious. But the others see the cosy world in which they have called the tune for local authorities and government coming to an end. They have mounted a strident campaign to fend off this "threat" to their jobs. Their unsupported allegations are that parents are incompetent to choose schools: only the experts "know"; vouchers would be impossible to run because the queues for, say, Highbury Grove School would stretch from Islington to Charing Cross....; supplying information would call for a "bureaucratic bonanza and a paper mountain"[1] at vast expense to the taxpayer. There is no evidence, rather the reverse, for any of these objections.

Administration would be no more complicated than the issue of family allowance books. Every child of school age would be issued with an annual book containing three vouchers, one for each term. The value of the vouchers would be the division of total expenditure by the number of children of school age including the 4.8 per cent of children at present in independent schools.

The 1981-82 Revenue Estimates published by the Inner London Education Authority show the cost per pupil as £1011 for primary, £1375 for day secondary, and £4175 for boarding secondary schools. State school costs per pupil (voucher value) should include a proportion of capital cost and upkeep of buildings, repairs and replacements of fabric and equipment due to vandalism as well as wear and tear, and salaries of teachers, administrators, caretakers and cleaners. It is doubtful whether the full expenditure on these items is incorporated in local authority calculations. Nevertheless, the costs given by ILEA approximate closely to January 1981 fees in the independent sector which average £1012 and £1322 respectively for day primary and secondary schools, and £2185 and £3053 respectively for primary and secondary boarding schools.

When parents had chosen a school and "paid" for it with the voucher, plus any topping-up from their own pockets, the school would obtain its income from central or local government by applying for the cash represented by the value of its vouchers. Its income would be spent on teachers, text books and so on, as it thought fit. Money raised by parents could be spent on staff or equipment rather than peripheral frills. Schools would be induced to issue prospectuses which would be more informative than the reluctant offerings of local authorities. The difference in approach is that schools obliged to attract pupils would *for the first time* have an interest in disseminating detailed information to would-be customers.

On almost every public issue, whether cheap air fares to Hong Kong or allowing parents to choose schools, Labour is invariably on the side of bureaucracy. Opposition from Conservatives and Liberals is harder to understand.

In the many public debates at party conferences and elsewhere, the ambiguity of a near-total authoritarian state education system in a country with a democratic political ethos and a capitalist economy has never been explored. The state runs teacher training colleges, it has financial control over schools attended by 95 per cent of all children, it owns the school buildings, it employs the teachers. It appoints most school governors.

Schooling is compulsory from five to sixteen. Yet parents are seldom able to choose a school; and because they are not the paymaster, they cannot influence it. The state cuts the vital link between the provider and the user. Parents are unable to vote with their feet, so no one knows whether they approve of a school or not.

The experience of Germany under Hitler and of China and Russia today should warn us of the danger that state education will be manipulated by the political party in power. Yet it is not only behind the iron curtain that state-controlled education indoctrinates children. Now that the voting age is eighteen, the influence of politically motivated teachers is more important than when it was twenty-one. Enfranchised young people have had barely two years' experience of the outside world and employment, or none at all if they have been sixth-form students. Their vote is likely to reflect the opinions and values of their teachers. Conservative teachers are less inclined to exert political influence than their articulate left-wing colleagues. Parents may complain if they think their adolescent children are suborned, but these are not grounds on which the educational authority would allow a change of school.

Auriol Stevens, education correspondent of *The Observer*, described a play performed by the pupils of a primary school: '.... centre stage, a pink-coated huntsman speculated as to whether one could train one's dogs to chase coal miners instead of foxes'. She thought the play showed '... a balanced understanding of the issues'. In a voucher system, schools with left-wing 'understanding of the issues' could exist only if sufficient *parents* were prepared to support it with their vouchers. Indeed it is an integral part of voucher financing that no school would be prohibited if it were within the law. This is in contrast to the ideology of socialists who would outlaw any school that was not a state comprehensive. The theory that state education is the cornerstone of democracy has little basis in reality.

If private schools are included in voucher experiments, the exaggerated problem of the too-popular school would vanish. Some of the 100,000 women teachers supposed not to be teaching[2] might be induced to start schools. Parish councils, religious organizations, groups of parents, and teachers could set up schools as they are already beginning to do as a consequence of worsening state education. Frustrated West Indian mothers in London have recently taken their children out of the state system and started their own Seventh Day Adventist School. Its fees are £ 600 a year but it already has 300 pupils and a waiting list. And there is no reason why private entrepreneurs able and willing to run efficient schools should be excluded. In the long run there is little doubt that we should see an expansion of private schools to meet demand. In the short term, the Kent County Council Feasibility Study found that the children whose parents wished to move them could be accommodated by the state and private schools named as their preferences.

The Suppression of Choice in Education

Of course, people will want to be reassured that there are more benefits of all kinds on parents'-choice schooling than in the status quo. There is a wide-spread belief that the State had to intervene in schooling in the nineteenth century to spread literacy. Professor E.G. West[3] claims 'it was as if it jumped into the saddle of a horse that was already galloping'. The first state subsidy was made in 1833 but since the beginning of the century poor people throughout Britain were paying a few pence a week so that their children could learn to read and write. These memorial verses to a Scottish schoolmistress tell a story common to many towns and villages at this time:

> Imagine a woman o' three score and ten
> She fends off the worst o' poverty's shock
> By skuiling [schooling] the bairns o' hardworking folk
> For weekly, as Monday comes round,
> There's tuppence sent with them for auld Eppie Brown.

In 1835, Henry Brougham, Whig statesman and former Lord Chancellor, said 'We have such a number of schools... furnished by the parents themselves from their own earnings and by the contributions of well-disposed individuals in aid of those whose earnings were insufficient, it behoves us to take the greatest care how we interfere with a system which prospers so well'.

But the subsidies to schools continued relentlessly – so did the taxation on food and tobacco so that the Government could pay them. In 1870 Forster's Education Act created board schools allegedly to fill up the gaps left by private schooling, but in effect they subsidized schools to compete with unsubsidized schools. Board schools supplied books, slates, etc. free of charge. Their fees, typically at 3d a week in 1870, were lower than the 6d charged by many private schools. Forster, the "Father of English Education", perpetuated and enlarged the state's role in education. The implementation of his Bill resulted in the mulcting of working class parents through taxation so that they could no longer afford to pay for the private schools which many preferred.[4] 110 years later, this is still happening. Taxpayers and ratepayers are now paying for one education bureaucrat to every teacher in Manchester, a City Council which, not surprisingly, has a financial crisis of Doomsday proportions. The country's educational expenditure is now nearing a staggering £ 12,000 m.

If state education was unnecessary to spread literacy,[5] are there other reasons which defend it against the proposed breach of its monolithic structure? Its supporters say that equal opportunity, social cohesion, common culture and protection of children ought to make state education inviolable.

Concepts of equal opportunity vary but purists might insist that it means that there should be equal amounts and quality of schooling for everyone, that every pupil achieves a minimum standard by the end of his schooldays, and that each child reaches his potential. The inability of state education to achieve any of these goals, with some fortunate, and quite fortuitous, exceptions, is obvious. Zoning prevents poor people buying houses in an area near a good school, the best teachers are generally not in poor schools, and talent and ambition are stifled in the many inefficient state schools.

The claim that state schooling creates social cohesion or a melting pot of all cultures and all social backgrounds does not withstand the reality of inner city schools with their over-high proportion of immigrant children nor with the community strains caused by unemployable school leavers. Common culture should mean toleration of differences, not extinguishing them by schools so uniform and so large that the individual struggles to keep his identity, and the good teachers become discouraged.[6]

Finally, it is an insult to 98 per cent of parents to insist that they haven't the wit or the responsibility to choose schools. The words of Sir Robert Lowe, Gladstone's Chancellor of the Exchequer, are as pertinent today as they were in 1868: 'Parents have one great superiority over the bureaucrat, their faults are corrigible faults of ignorance, not of apathy and indifference.' It may be that, for a time, public guardians as envisaged by William Humboldt in 1844 to protect children from malevolent parents, might be appointed by an attenuated education authority to advise on schools for children until parents learned the art of choice suppressed by state education. There would not be many. However limited her intelligence or disorganized her home, the desire of any mother[7] to be as good as her neighbour in exercising this new power to choose or reject a school would ensure that parents who now seem indifferent to their children's prospects would not remain so. Adam Smith thought that '... after twelve or thirteen years, provided the master does his duty, force or restraint can scarce ever be necessary to carry on any part of education'. If this premise can be accepted then older children can be expected to share the decision-making process which the voucher makes possible. Younger children, even from the age of five, perceive (as do their parents) that they have a personal interest in literacy and numeracy.

The last resort of the statist is to claim that parents' choice would disrupt the smooth running of the bureaucratic empire. Schools are now filled with children, teachers and caretakers are employed, block grants are sent out. The question is whether the money required for the salaries of many of these officials, sometimes duplicating themselves in Whitehall and town hall, could be spent more efficiently by bursars employed by the schools. A school in the market is certain to perform better and cost less than one without the spur of competition. Moreover schools operating in a competitive market and without the shackles of bureaucratic salary-fixing (closely monitored by the unions) could pay higher salaries for mathematics or language graduates.[8]

The Kent Initiative

Fortunately, thanks to the perspicacity and courage of Kent County Council, we have a blue-print, a voucher field study conducted with the advice of Dr William Taylor, Director of the University of London Institute of Education and Professor Mark Blaug of its Economic Research Unit. The school district of Ashford was chosen with 15,000 school children, 44 primary schools and eight secondary. 23 independent schools within a radius of 20 miles were also included. 1500 parents were interviewed and questionnaires were sent to 2000 more in a cross section of social groups. All 750 teachers in the district were asked to complete questionnaires and heads were also consulted. The results revealed information which could be used by other Local Education Authorities for voucher trials.

90 per cent of the parents interviewed felt they ought to be able to choose their children's schools. 68 per cent said they had insufficient say or influence. They were told the voucher might be worth around £ 300 per annum for primary and £ 500[9] for secondary schools and were asked if they would use it in a private day school with fees varying from £ 500 to £ 1,400 per annum. 16 per cent chose a private day school and most of these said they would be prepared to top up the voucher. This was confirmed by the Harris/Seldon 1979 study *Over-ruled on Welfare* (Institute of Economic Affairs) which demonstrates that preferences for private education have been suppressed.

Their new evidence is that if parents had vouchers even of only two-thirds of average school costs, the demand for private schooling would have risen from an estimated 30 per cent in 1965 to 51 per cent in 1978. And as a country we would be spending millions more on the education of our children because the private purse would add to the public purse.

In the Kent Study 72 per cent of parents said they should be allowed to use the voucher for private schools. The predominant reasons parents gave for transferring children were falling standards and slack discipline. They disliked large schools, had little objection to mobile classrooms (which some schools would need to accomodate voucher pupils) and almost one-third would transfer if the school changed from GCE to CSE examinations. The survey found that there would be little difficulty in meeting primary school preferences because of the falling birth rate. Two of the secondary schools would have surplus capacity and one would require extra classrooms to meet the hypothetical demand for places.[10] The independent schools were very flexible in their willingness to accept pupils who had said they wanted places.

Teachers in the survey had received a letter from the National Union of Teachers and the National Association of Schoolmasters and Union of Women Teachers suggesting they should make unhelpful and obstructive replies to the questionnaire. It showed little faith in the form-filling ability of their supposedly intelligent members by supplying a table indicating "recommended" answers. Sixteen questions were asked and the following are typical of the unions' proposed replies:

1. Would you be in favour of a voucher system which would operate in the maintained sector only? ANSWER: No.
2. Would you be prepared to teach in a school where pupils were admitted by voucher? ANSWER: No.
3. Do you think that parents should be able to use a voucher towards private school fees? ANSWER: No – it will weaken promotion prospects.

Despite this, 39 per cent said they would continue to teach in voucher schools. In the four years since the Kent Study, teachers have had more unemployment, so it is a fair prophecy that all but a few would prefer to keep their jobs rather than refuse to teach in voucher schools. As in the Californian experiment described later, many teachers would find they liked the happier atmosphere of a school which parents had chosen for their children and the closer co-operation of parents in dealing with any problems of individual pupils. The fears which teachers expressed in the Kent Survey were of redeployment, dislike of mobile classrooms, objections to letting parents know their qualifications and experience, and of giving information to parents about their children's progress.[11] All these are familiar trade union responses which have no direct connection with the quality of education.

Teachers who find themselves in schools with drastically falling numbers (rejected by parents) could be offered employment in other schools[12] or, say, two years severance pay. No clauses guaranteeing employment "for ever" should be included in the contracts of teachers employed after the start of voucher financing. No one questions that among many conscientious teachers we have some whose skills are indifferent and who are lazy. It would not be unwelcomed by some of their own profession if parents were able to guide their children's feet from the classrooms of these incompetents.

No one was more dismayed than Mrs Shirley Williams at the findings of the Kent Study that many parents, including manual workers, were dissatisfied with state education. She grew up in an affluent intellectual family and developed a passionate belief that the poverty and limited horizons of working people could be ended by an all-powerful state dispensing largesse in education (and elsewhere). The possibility that these beneficiaries have come to resent the exorbitant demands in taxation by the state to pay for the "largesse" has been borne upon her since the 1979 General Election in which she lost her seat. Since then, her thinking on education has produced an improbable idea that pupils in independent schools might be induced (for a time) to change places with state school pupils and, since her translation to the SDP, an attempt to convert her new colleagues to the Labour shibboleth of abolishing private schools.

Voice must be reinforced by Exit

Many Conservatives and some Liberals have sympathized with the growing desire of parents to be able to choose their children's schools. The anxiety to meet these wishes is reflected in the new Education Act, but its sponsors have failed to understand the nature of the problem. Rights have been given to parents subject to the convenience of the local authority. Creating appeals tribunals for parents refused their choice of school is an extension of the parent's role as supplicant. Parents are not satisfied merely with more "voice" especially as many dislike confrontations or are inarticulate. They want the right to escape from an unsatisfactory school. And they don't want to have to explain their reasons for disliking it to a paid official of the local authority. The controversy stirred up by the Assisted Places Scheme is disproportionate to the 2 per cent or so of children who will benefit. It is no substitute for a voucher system for children of *all* abilities and *all* incomes.

We hear a little less these days about parent governors and parent/teacher associations. A year or two ago many of all political parties thought that an extension of these palliatives (or substitutes for individual choice) would involve parents of all kinds, create social cohesion, deal with problems of misbehaviour and unsatisfactory schools, and so on. There was no end to the euphoria. But there was no end either to the unwillingness of most parents to "join up".

The advocacy of the voucher system by Dr Rhodes Boyson will be written in history as the courageous campaign of one man to show his political colleagues that the consumerism of the 1970s could not be confined to the supermarket and the travel agent. Parents were restless; they wanted something better than the offering of the local authority. Comprehensivization, which many had supported initially, was increasingly resented. The grammar schools were fighting a losing battle. In the accents of working-class Lancashire Dr Boyson told the people of Britain they could and should have the right to choose schools. In 1976 he persuaded his colleagues in the House to propose a new clause for Labour's Education Bill:

> On request from a local education authority, the Secretary of State shall authorise the establishment of a schools voucher scheme devised and run by the local education authority in question, on an experimental basis, for a period of time agreed to by the Secretary of State and the authority. During this period of time the secretary of State shall monitor the results of such an experimental voucher scheme.

The essence of the voucher was distilled in the debate by Mr Reginald Eyre who said 'the use of the voucher would produce early evidence of the need for correction and improvement in a school as a result of the choice of parents', and Mr Michael Brotherton 'I pay, as we all do, vast sums in taxes. Is it not right that we should be given vouchers so that we can decide where the money we have paid towards the education of our children should be spent?'

Many Conservative members made eloquent speeches on behalf of the Motion. Labour Members expressed shocked disbelief in the ability of parents to choose schools and the rigidity of their views has a parallel in the unwillingness of any educational bureaucrat to change his mind once he has given a decision. On a three-line Whip Conservative Members voted for the Motion.[13] This made it Conservative Policy and it appeared in the Party's pre-election document *The Right Approach*. It is, therefore, difficult to understand Mr Edward Heath's riposte to Sir Keith Joseph – see "Some Questions and Answers" at the end of this essay – that a Voucher Bill 'hadn't a chance in hell of getting through Parliament.' Mr Heath, himself, voted in the "Ayes" lobby in 1976.

The Enemy at the Gate

Some years ago, Dr Boyson wrote in *The Spectator* that independent schools should not be complacent at the demise of the grammar schools '... for' he said, 'the barbarians are coming up the hill and will soon be at your gate'.

Mr Neil Kinnock and the Labour Party's Education Committee are now at the gate with proposals to take away charitable status, entitlement to rate relief, to outlaw covenants and other arrangements which enable parents to meet the fees. More extreme proposals include charging the schools for their teachers' training in state colleges and the reduction of higher education grants to their pupils. Could it happen? It has in Malta, where the Socialist Prime Minister, Mr Mintoff, as determined as Mr Kinnock to end private schooling, has refused to allow private schools to raise fees to keep pace with inflation and has removed all state subsidies. Religious orders may have to pay income tax on the notional salaries of nuns and priests teaching in their schools.

'It appears to me that the day you sanction compulsory rating for the purpose of education, you sign the death warrant of voluntary exertions...'. These were Gladstone's words in 1852, and we who live today may see them come true. There is only one defence of the independent schools, and that is to expand. When private schooling ceases to be a privilege[14] confined to the better-off, the Labour Party will fear to lose votes by tampering with it.

If the SDP's *Discussion Paper on Education* forms the basis of its policy, then private education has another Enemy at the Gate. 'Private schools help to divide Society ... the competitiveness they promote is destructive ... there should be no element of public support existing ... charitable status ... support should be withdrawn ...'. If the SDP thus emerges as "willing to wound", how long will it be "afraid to strike"?

The Voucher Experiment in California

So far there has only been one experiment with vouchers in the world. This was at Alum Rock, California, a small school district near San Francisco with a white, black and Mexican population. A five-year voucher trial was mounted in the early 1970s with a grant from federal funds of 15 per cent of the school budget. Some of this funding was used to provide extra cash for children thought to be disadvantaged, some for the extra transport costs, and some for the paid counsellors thought to be necessary. In the event parents rapidly learned what to look for in the schools, and counsellors became redundant.[15] One lesson to be learned from this very limited trial with vouchers is that parents were not in a hurry to make changes. There was not chaos with crowds clamouring outside a particular school's gates for admittance as *The Times Educational Supplement* groundlessly fears. This responsible attitude of parents is borne out by the Kent Study.

Secondly, teachers in Alum Rock who had stridently opposed the start of the scheme changed their attitude and after a year or two asked that voucher financing of schools be written into their contracts.

Some observers of the Alum Rock experiment complained that parents failed to use their power to dominate schools and that the experiment was more or less taken over by the bureaucrats. They overlook what happens in the competitive sector of British education – the private schools. Fee-paying parents do not spend their time urging Heads to alter the curricula or the discipline. They show dissatisfaction if they feel it by removing their children. Alum Rock gave parents the option of withdrawal from an unsatisfactory school. It gave them exit instead of argument – which is all they had had before. We can accept the verdict of the District School Superintendent, Dr William Jefferds: 'Alum Rock will never be the same again'.

Now that the experiment has reached its pre-destined end, the district has an "open enrolment" system. This means the parents can make a free choice between the schools, subject only to the absolute right of children to enrol at their nearest school. The system of financing which is the crucial voucher feature, pegging school cost to the individual child, continues. So the income of the school will still rise and fall according to the number of pupils it attracts.

Voucherism in America is at its height. Public esteem of state schools is low[16] with a consequent rise in the number seeking private education. Not surprisingly, there is a surge of interest among black parents who want vouchers to help them to private schools. A group of black parents in Harlem, led by Mrs Babette Edwards, appealed to the Democratic Party to put vouchers on its agenda. They complained of the ill effects of state schooling on black children: high crime rates, illiteracy, failure to achieve higher education and jobs, and so on. They wanted vouchers for use in private schools, community schools and for private tuition. Now, the Congress of Racial Equality has made the support of vouchers one of its major campaigning points.

Every education convention, it is said, in America last year had a debate on vouchers, and Professor Stephen Sugarman, whose Californian voucher initiative with his law colleague at Berkeley, Professor John Coons, failed in 1979 to get enough votes to make a referendum mandatory, is confident that they will eventually succeed and that either California or one of the other three or four states with much popular support will "lift off". Open enrolment trials (but without the finance pegged to the child as in Alum Rock) have taken place in Richmond, Northern California, and in school districts in Milwaukee. They have shown that voluntary transfers do not lead to racial segregation. Indeed, some schools now have significant numbers of the ethnic minorities where there were few before.

A German observer of the American scene, Dr Ulrich van Lith, an economist from Cologne University, says that by now there would have been voucher financing in some states if there had been unanimity between the proponents. In California, the electorate were confused between three voucher proposals and there was unwillingness by advocates to make common ground. The most highly favoured, the Coons-Sugarman proposal, wanted to restrict the power of the schools to choose pupils and the right of parents to top-up fees. They are likely to make some concessions in their next round to enlist more support. President Reagan is known to be favourably inclined to vouchers and/or tax credits and has appointed a "Task Force" on education chaired by Professor W. Glenn Campbell, Director of the Hoover Institute of Stanford University and a friend of Milton Friedman. An impetus will be given to vouchers and tax credit installations in the USA by Professor Coleman's March 1981 Report to the National Center for Education Statistics. Professor Coleman's conclusions are favourable to private schools. He finds that they achieve more than state schools and the latter fail to provide the more egalitarian outcomes that are one of the goals of public schooling. Can there be much doubt that a Coleman Report for Britain would have similar findings!

Politicians in Australia and New Zealand are interested. In Australia, it looked as if New South Wales would undertake an experiment. They got as far as a feasibility study. The Federal Minister of Education continues to ponder its political attractions, but as with the New Zealand politicians everyone seems to be waiting for everyone else. Meanwhile dissatisfaction with state schooling continues,[17] and the influence of voucher groups in both these countries is spreading.

In Germany the voucher movement has at last started, fuelled by fears that the domination of education by the state will lead to indoctrination of the young and, as many parents fear, an anti-religious bias.

The start of voucher movements is connected with popular unease at state education. Thus in Sweden an organization called "Knowledge in School" heralds the end of the "conformistic" public debate. Dr Carl-Johan Westholm of the Swedish Employers' Federation writes that the organization which seeks a change from monolithic state schooling has a membership representing grass roots in all Parties and a dominance of "disappointed Welfare Socialists".

Spain gives the World a Lead

The dramatic move by Spain surprised the world when in 1980 a Bill was passed to give vouchers to parents using private schools equal to the cost of a state school place. This follows an international conference of private school parents at Tarragona in March 1977 when a memorandum was passed urging all Western European Governments to give vouchers for private schools. The value of the voucher was at first in dispute because the Spanish independent schools argued that the state cost per pupil was set too low by the bureaucracy.[18] A Spanish correspondent tells me that the Bill is implemented in the current school year but it is too early to assess how much movement from state schools has taken place.

And in British Columbia

In 1978 British Columbia passed Bill 33 to give parents using private schools a "voucher" equal to one-third state school costs. This has been described as a foot in the door for a market in education. It has severe limitations, restricting (or constricting) a free market. The most important one is that schools accepting voucher pupils must have existed for five years. The supply of schools (involving the creation of new schools) cannot therefore be helped by vouchers to meet the demand. Because of this many independent schools are already over-subscribed and have no reason to be enthusiastic about accepting voucher pupils. But Dr Daniel J. Brown of the University of British Columbia writes[19] that there has nevertheless been a distinct movement towards the private schools with one "very entrepreneurial" school achieving an expansion of 20 per cent of pupils. Dr Brown gives figures of state and private school costs showing that the latter are the lower. He attributes this to greater parental involvement with parents giving 'time and materials' (from classroom help to plumbing and electrical work) and to 'lower teacher salaries'. Dr Brown estimates that a 30 per cent transfer of pupils from state to private schools would have to take place before the taxpayer recouped the cost of the voucher funding. This is because, apart from those who are already in private schools, transfers from state schools would not immediately reduce the number of teachers, nor the upkeep of buildings nor, importantly the state employees, bureaucrats and others "needed" to run the system. In short, the savings would be marginal to set against the cost of the private school vouchers. However, as privatization got under way, as it would in an unrestricted voucher scheme, fewer officials would be necessary and the taxpayer would not fund teachers to teach in empty classrooms. Some might find it expedient to teach in private schools even at lower salaries. In Britain village schools would not have had to close if teachers could have accepted salaries within an economic budget.

And in Holland

Private schools in Holland do not arouse the emotion they do in Britain and there are many more of them. This is because the state funds private schools equally with state schools. Grants are given to independent (including denominational) schools matching the running costs of state schools. This has the effect of making almost all schools wholly free-place but economists argue that direct funding to schools makes competition imperfect because it reduces incentives to keep costs low. A voucher system, especially if vouchers for use in private schools are at a percentage of state costs, makes independent schools competitive in reducing the topping-up element to their fees.

Vouchers now for Parents in Britain

The appointment of Sir Keith Joseph as Secretary of State for Education brings new hope that we may, at long last, have voucher financing experiments in Britain. At the Conservative Conference he said, to loud applause, that he had thought of the possibility of the Government introducing a voucher system as a 'way of increasing parental choice even further.' He added: 'it is now up to the advocates of such a possibility to study the difficulties, and they are real, and see whether they can develop proposals which can cope with them.' Thus, Kent, which had delayed its proposed experiment because of teacher obstructionism and lack of support from central government, now has what amounts to an invitation to present proposals to Sir Keith and Dr Rhodes Boyson (Minister for Schools).

An increasingly attractive alternative to local authority initiative, which would circumvent Union militancy, teacher strikes, caretaker strikes etc. would be to allow parents to vote with their feet and depart from state schools by giving them a voucher, as in Spain, for use in private schools. The Institute of Economic Affairs' Survey (p. 108) indicate that transfers from state schools, even with a voucher of two-thirds value, would soon reach 50 per cent of all pupils and this is borne out by a survey discussed in the *Daily Express*, 22 November 1980, which finds that 57 per cent of parents in ILEA comprehensive schools 'wished they could afford to send their children to private schools'. The number of children leaving state schools would, as in British Columbia (p. 113), probably have to be 25-30 per cent to achieve a down-turn in public expenditure on schooling. Fifty-fifty state and private education would mean very large savings indeed to the public purse.

If, however, we move in the direction of local authority experiments then the education voucher would be "educational".

The distribution to every parent of a piece of paper marked with the value to be obtained by the child in notional "fees" in a state school and the current fees in a private school would instruct parents of all social classes in the use of choice by *personal* payment. Transport vouchers would have to be given to children entitled to free school meals, but everyone else should pay. The strident objections which parents recently made to increased charges would be very much less, or non-existent, if combined with their own choice of school. Parents would soon make reciprocal arrangements on cars (three-quarters of all parents of schoolchildren own cars), strike good bargains with private hirers-out of buses and taxis, etc.

Text books, too, should be paid for by pupils with a secondhand pool such as many private schools run, so that there could be buying and selling at the start of each school year. A Science teacher wrote in *The Guardian* that in the 1950s his school only had to discard 2 per cent of worn-out books each year: now it is 20 per cent. Free text books are not cherished by their owners, and many vanish each year with school-leavers, not intentionally, but there is no penalty for such carelessness.

Lower Taxation would allow Charging

Lower taxation would in time make possible increased payment from parents' pockets. The value of the voucher could be progressively reduced over several years so that the state subsidy lessened and we reached a market in which parents bore the financial responsibility for their children's education. There would still be state schools but they would charge fees, as elementary schools did until 1891 and grammar schools until 1944. There would be many more private schools of all kinds. And if it was thought desirable to "protect"[20] unsophisticated parents, it could be obligatory for schools to join an Association of Private Schools whose main function would be to run an inspectorate.

The End of State Domination

State domination of education means that education is in the political arena. It is vulnerable to the manipulation of trade unions, subject to fashionable doctrines of educationists and the whims of politicians. It is inefficient in maximizing the potential of individual children and so of all children. And it is expensive. The money acquired from rate and taxpayers to pay for each school pupil is now very close to the average fees of private schools. As the dissatisfaction of parents mounts, it becomes certain that if parents were given the money now spent on their behalf they would use it more carefully and to better effect for their children.

State education has had its day, and politicians must grasp the nettle of radical change. If they do not they will lose the votes of millions of parents who feel let down by the Government's refusal to return some of their taxes so that they can choose and influence school education.

Some Questions and Answers

1. Is there a danger of raising false expectations on the amount of choice a voucher scheme is likely to make practicable?

   Answer There would be some disappointed parents unable to have their first choice. Even so, they would have more satisfaction than now because the second or third choice would be *theirs* and could be made from schools in a wide area and including private schools. Zoning and bureaucratic choice would disappear. Disappointments would diminish as all schools responded to parental choice and parental wishes.

2. Would the taxpayers' investment in bricks and mortar be lost if unpopular schools closed down?

   Answer There is little satisfaction for the taxpayer in paying the costs of a school that parents don't want – probably for very good reasons. The unpopularity of the school would soon end if a trickle of parents decided to use their vouchers elsewhere. This would alert school governors who would remove its defects. If they failed, the buildings and plant could re-open under new management. Any Education Officer can give examples of unpopular schools with first-rate buildings and equipment. The voucher trial at Alum Rock showed that good teachers, not good buildings, drew voucher pupils.

3. Would unpopular schools worsen, be filled with difficult and disadvantaged children and become sink schools?

   Answer We have these kinds of school now, often in inner cities. If we gave the parents the opportunity to remove their children to other kinds of schools, in other areas, there would be some exodus, particularly of immigrant children within a strong family structure. Others would stay, but more parental involvement could be expected and more co-operation with teachers. Teachers and pupils would feel the challenge to improve. No one can say whether the operation of a voucher system would succeed in changing such schools, but the lot of these children would not be worse and might well be better (see p. 112).

4. Cannot poor schools be improved by spending more tax money on them?

   Answer The argument that schools can be improved by injecting more state money has been disproved both in ILEA schools and in the USA. Nothing changes, except for the worse.

5. Would not the introduction of vouchers increase state expenditure at a time of cut-backs?

   Answer This is alarmist propaganda of the statists, Left and Right. The costings in the Kent Feasibility Study were for mobile classrooms, employment of bursars, additional transport costs and the cost of including private school pupils. Falling rolls have made some mobile classrooms redundant (Strathclyde, n. 10), bursars would make some staff redundant at County Hall (see p. 107), transport to chosen schools need only be paid for poor children. If vouchers were made available for state and private schools, then voucher value could be calculated by dividing state schooling expenditure by the total number of school children. The inclusion of the 4.8 per cent of children in private schools would result in a voucher a little lower than current state cost per pupil which would oblige state schools to trim their budgets. But it would not cost the taxpayer more and savings would result as civil servants became fewer. If vouchers were only available for private schools, as in Spain, then there would be dramatic savings, especially on a two-third value voucher, as parents transferred children to private schools and topped up their vouchers. Equal access for poor children could be achieved by giving them full-value vouchers.

Notes

1. These are the words in which the Times Educational Supplement describes the excuses given by local education authorities for postponing compliance with the new Education Act that they should supply information to parents about each of their schools.
2. E.G. West, *Education: A Framework for Choice* (Institute of Economic Affairs, 1967).
3. E.G. West, *Education and the State* (Institute of Economic Affairs, 1971).
4. '... many parents were prepared to pay a fairly high fee to avoid sending their children to Board schools' and '... the abolition of fees in Board schools in 1891 was the death blow to the private schools', E.G. West, *Education and the Industrial Revolution* (Batsford, 1975).
5. The Registrar General's returns in 1871 showed that 80.6 per cent of the population (male) were literate and that literacy had risen by some 5 per cent in ten years. His returns in 1881 showed a similar 5 per cent rise in literacy. The conclusion is that state education achieved no more than wholly private provision. It is legitimate to speculate that our present illiteracy rate of around 7 per cent would be less if we had more private schools. Slow learners and persistent truants – the core of illiterates – would be a challenge to the private provider as they are not to those whose classrooms are filled whether teacher performance is good or not.
6. Private schools have been able to be more innovatory than state schools because of their autonomy, the only restriction being the approval of their clients. The latest example is the American International School in London, a "school without walls". Under a voucher system state schools would be able to try new ideas if parents were not opposed. Many state school teachers would welcome this.
7. Mothers are more closely involved with their children and seem more willing to make sacrifices for them. But this is a general observation which fathers may dispute!
8. I have been told by the head of a mathematics department in a large boys' secondary school in the Home Counties than an advertised vacancy for a mathematics teacher was answered by a girl with a CSE grade 1 pass in mathematics.
9. Average costs are now higher (see p. 104). Gordon Richards, a former chairman of Brent Education Committee, believes that the figure would be higher still if some bureaucratic and other costs had been included in the average figure.
10. Strathclyde Education Authority paid £ 239,000 for the disposal of 85 surplus mobile classrooms. They were subsequently sold by the contractor for a handsome profit. The redistribution of mobile classrooms in a voucher system would probably make new ones unnecessary.
11. 40 per cent of teachers thought that details of their qualifications and experience should be withheld from parents and 13 per cent thought that parents should not be told their children's standardized tests results – 47 per cent *only* if parents asked.
12. But if parent support had failed because of incompetent teaching these

teachers could not be inflicted on children in other schools and should be offered severance pay as the sole option.

13. Mr Nigel Forman (Carshalton) abstained.

14. Labour's working party on Education condemns private education as 'undermining the confidence and morale of state schools, promoting the snobbish idea that a bought education was better than one which is free, setting the elitist values of success in public examinations and university entrance as the standard by which all schools should be judged' (*The Times*, 30 June 1980).

15. The ability of parents to make judgements on schools was noted as long ago as 1861. The Newcastle Commission reported the evidence of one of their Commissioners: 'It is a subject of wonder how people so destitute of education as labouring parents commonly are, can be such just judges as they also commonly are of the effective qualities of a teacher.'

16. 'If morale has ever been lower in public education, few people alive today know or remember when.' School Superintendent Hayes at the 1980 convention of the American Association of School Administrators.

17. In March 1980 a letter from an indignant parent was published in the *New Zealand Herald*. After complaining at the quality of state schooling and high taxation, the writer said that if everyone could afford private schools there would be a mass exodus from state schooling.

18. See p. 104 (costs in British state schools).

19. Daniel J. Brown, *The British Columbian Experience*.

20. There is no "protection" from inefficient suppliers equal to the market. Competition would eliminate inadequate private schools. In the 1950s an exhaustive inspection of the many private schools then existing was undertaken by the government; only nine teachers were found to be inefficient. Such criteria for efficiency would not readily be undertaken now in the state sector.

VIII
The National Union of Teachers –
Professional Association or Trade Union or ...?

Fred Naylor and John Marks

Fred Naylor was educated at grammar school and Pembroke College, Cambridge (Open Exhibitioner in Natural Sciences). He researched at Cambridge for four years and has published papers in the Journal of the Chemical Society *on Synthetic Antimalarials and Peroxidase action. Has taught in the private sector before transferring to the state sector. Was Head of the Science Department of Leeds Modern School and Head-master of the City of Bath Technical School. Sixth-form Curriculum and Examinations Officer, Schools Council, 1968-73. At present on secondment to Bath College of Higher Education, lecturing in Education.*

The National Union of Teachers (NUT) is the most influential educational pressure group in the country. This chapter analyses many of its policies and statements and concludes: that the NUT is not representative; that despite having most of its members from primary schools, it has been a major influence in determining what goes on in our secondary schools; and that it regularly assumes that educational advance is just a matter of spending more money on schools. Many of the NUT's policies are virtually identical with those of the Labour and Communist Parties and are anti-educational in that they have not led to more boys and girls learning more and better. In short the influence of the NUT must be reduced if there is to be any really radical improvement in educational standards in Britain.

Introduction

For good or ill, trade unions are a major influence in Britain today. This is as true of education as it is of many other spheres of our national life. So how that influence is used is a legitimate matter of public interest – particularly when it concerns such a vital matter as the education of the next generation, not to mention the annual expenditure of about £ 8000m. of public money.

It is against this background that we consider the National Union of Teachers (NUT). For, although the NUT is the most overtly political of the teacher organizations, the way it works is not widely known or understood – even, we suspect, by many of its own members.

So we offer this analysis of the NUT as an aid to understanding what it is and how it works. We will not be concerned with the personal services the NUT offers its members[1] but with its influence in the wider educational and political debate. Our analysis will inevitably be influenced by *our* political values just – as we shall contend – as the NUT's operations are influenced by the political values of those who control its activities. The question is not *whether* political values influence educational decisions but *which* values are so involved and what these values mean in practice.

We contend that on many of the issues on which it speaks so frequently and so influentially, the NUT is not representative of the great majority even of its own members; that the NUT's influence on *secondary* education has been out of all proportion to the number of members it has in this sector; that the effects of many of the NUT's most characteristic and cherished policies are strictly anti-educational in the sense that they have not led to more boys and girls learning more and better; that the NUT regularly takes it for granted that educational advance is just a matter of pouring more and more resources into schools without any comparable commitment to discovering how far any purely educational objective is, in fact, being attained; and that, for all these reasons and others, the influence of the NUT needs to be drastically reduced.

The National Union of Teachers

The National Union of Teachers (NUT) is the largest organized group of teachers in the country. It claims a membership of more than a quarter of a million serving teachers, has an annual subscription income or more than £ 3m. and total assets of more than £ 7m.[2] The NUT was originally an organization of teachers in elementary schools and this is still reflected in the membership figures. Primary school-teachers make up nearly 60 per cent of the membership and for many years only about a third of all graduate teachers were members (at present data are not available on members' qualifications). About one-third of the membership is male and two-thirds female. The membership is maintained by a vigorous recruitment policy, especially in the colleges of education, and it is possible that the membership figures contain significant numbers of student teachers.

Influence on Education Policy

The NUT is the most important pressure group in school education; its influence has been particularly marked in educational policies affecting *secondary* schools despite its predominantly *primary* school membership. For example, it has strongly supported the moves towards a state secondary system consisting entirely of comprehensive schools, and it has long been an advocate of merging the GCE O-level and CSE examinations into a single examination.

It might be thought that the policies supported by the NUT would reflect the views of its members. However, there is evidence that the power exercised by the NUT is *power for teachers' representatives* rather than *teacher power*; that is, the policies adopted are those supported by the Union leaders rather than the majority of members. For example, an NOP opinion poll for the *Times Educational Supplement* (TES) in 1974 showed that 72 per cent of all teachers *opposed* the elimination of grammar schools and only 26 per cent of secondary and 18 per cent of primary teachers favoured Labour's and the NUT's fundamental policy of complete comprehensivization. As John Gretton's commentary in the TES observed: 'It really is a massive vote, by all sectors of the profession, against the principal trends of educational policy over the last ten years'. He added that it should worry a union like the NUT that its members' and its executive's attitudes evidently 'point in different directions'.

Three years later another NOP poll for TES showed exactly the same proportion (72 per cent) opposed to the elimination of grammar schools. The poll and its findings were fiercely attacked by Fred Jarvis, general secretary of NUT. The TES replied in an editorial (9 September 1977):

> In a BBC news programme Mr Jarvis attacked the sample used by NOP and virtually accused NOP and TES of loading the sample and the questions to obtain pre-determined results.
>
> There is no justification for Mr Jarvis' complaint. The sample was properly constructed. The constituent groups within the sample were properly identified. Interviewees were selected at random within these groups... the results are honestly obtained and honestly presented.
>
> Mr Jarvis' trigger-happy attack on the integrity of this newspaper and National Opinion Polls should not be allowed to conceal his failure to come to grips with the underlying issue: the strange dissonance between the attitudes of the teachers in primary and secondary schools and the attitudes struck by the leaders of the National Union of Teachers.

The NUT influences policy both directly, by its explicit policy statements, and indirectly, by commenting on policy proposals and DES regulations while they are still in a formative stage. The union is also a dominating influence on many key educational committees and organizations. Major examples are the Schools Council and the Teachers' Panel of the Burnham Primary and Secondary Committee which negotiates teachers' salaries.[3]

Recently the policies of the NUT have been affected by the growth of the Rank and File movement, a Marxist teachers' organization of Trotskyite leanings which is at odds with many of the union's hierarchy, including even the significant number of Communist party members and sympathizers who are prominent in the union's activities. At the 1980 NUT annual conference, the Rank and File delegates shouted down Mark Carlisle, the Secretary of State for Education and Science. They were angrily denounced by the union's President, who issued a statement claiming that the Rank and File group made up not much more than 10 per cent of delegates at the conference. This is deeply disturbing. If the NUT conference is representative of its members, it means that there are more than 25,000 extremist Marxist revolutionaries teaching in our schools. If the conference is not representative, it means that such revolutionaries have a significant and disproportionate influence on the policies and activities of the most influential educational pressure group in the country.

The power and influence wielded by the NUT are thus considerable. Let us now see, in more detail, some examples of how they are used.

The policies of the NUT

The NUT has policies on a multitude of issues. Much union policy and activity is necessarily directed towards bread and butter activities like salaries, conditions of service, pensions and the like which are a routine part of the work of any union. What we are considering are NUT policies on some important wider issues of educational debate. By looking at what it advocates and what it opposes, by reading its leaflets and other publications, it is possible to build up a picture of the nature of the NUT. Such a picture will inevitably be incomplete, but hopefully it will reflect some of the essence of the NUT's purposes – or, at least, of the purposes of those who control its wider educational activities.

We contend that such a study shows that:

(a) although the NUT is not affiliated to the Labour Party,[4] many of its policies are virtually identical with Labour's educational policies and even with those of the Communist Party;[5]

(b) the NUT champions an extreme form of egalitarianism in a way that undermines academic standards and even threatens to subvert society;

(c) the NUT is afraid of rational debate. It deals with most educational issues in an emotive way and has a largely pragmatic notion of the "truth";

(d) the NUT is committed to teacher control in education. It does not trust parents and wishes to wrest control of children's education away from their parents.

Now let us look at the evidence for these statements.

(i) Comprehensive schooling

The NUT first gave its support to the idea of comprehensive schools as long ago as 1943.[6] But in the early days this support was cautious. In 1959 the union called for 'a long period of experimentation' and argued that 'the issue should not be decided until there was sufficient evidence available to permit a confident answer in strictly educational terms'. However, these admirable sentiments were abandoned in 1964 when, in its evidence to the Plowden Committee, 'the union came out in favour of the abolition of selection and the adoption of the fully comprehensive school as the model for the future'. After that time, the NUT supported comprehensive reorganization wholeheartedly and unequivocally. In 1966 the Annual Conference supported 'the reorganization of secondary education under a system of comprehensive schools'. In 1969 the NUT urged the government 'to make the necessary legislative changes to bring about comprehensive education by *abolishing selection** for secondary education' and called for the abolition of the grammar schools and 'a unified system for *all** children'. In 1972 the NUT reaffirmed 'its belief in the comprehensive system as providing the only satisfac-

---

*Our italics throughout section (i).

tory basis for equality of opportunity' and urged the government 'to *compel** authorities to submit plans for secondary reorganization along genuine comprehensive lines'. In 1974 the NUT joined with the Campaign for Comprehensive Education[7] (CCE) in organizing a national symposium on the theme "Comprehensive not Coexistence". A joint NUT/CCE survey *Comprehensive or Coexistence – We must choose which we want* written by Caroline Benn and published in 1974, concluded that: 'toleration of a divided system and all forms of 11-plus selection must be ended, and renewed attempts made to secure a policy whereby *all* schools still catering for only a limited attainment range be widened to cater for the full range. It is not more comprehensive schools which are required, but a comprehensive system.... for the comprehensive reform to actually work and to benefit the country, all schools had to be involved.'

In 1975 the NUT went even further in calling for 'the achievement of a fully comprehensive system of education without selection at 11-plus or *any other stage**' and for 'the incorporation of *all** direct grant and independent schools into the system'. The union also decided to 'give support to members who refuse cooperation in selective procedures'. And in 1977 the NUT condemned 'the action of all who obstruct the development of comprehensive education and denigrate the achievements of these schools'. So, in a few short years, the cautious 'experimentation' of 1959 – (awaiting an answer 'in strictly educational terms') – has become the totalitarian insistence on equality (no selection at any age), uniformity (*all* children and *all* schools must be involved), compulsion (to *compel* authorities) and hostility to criticism (condemns the actions.... of all who denigrate...).

(ii) A common public examination at 16+ to replace GCE and CSE[8]

In parallel with its campaign for comprehensive secondary education, the NUT has also campaigned long and hard for a common examination at 16 in which '... there would be no artificial divison between "pass" and "fail" '. And it has recently claimed that 'in maintaining two quite separate examinations, designed for pupils of different ability ranges, the present system is as divisive, and hence educationally indefensible, as the coexistence of grammar and secondary modern schools'.[9]

The NUT campaign started in the mid-1960s. Although it had welcomed the introduction of the CSE in 1965, the NUT began, almost immediately, to press for the merging of O-level and CSE. In May 1966, the Schools Council stated that 'Within the foreseeable future, there is.... no question of abolishing the ordinary level GCE examination, nor of changing the distinctive character of either the GCE or the CSE examinations; all that is at issue is the possibility of devising a method of describing results which would be common to both types of examination...'

But the NUT had other ideas. It now claimed to find inherent educational contradictions in the existence of two kinds of examination and 'refused to accept that it was impossible to create a single examination which could discriminate throughout the ability range...'[10]

During the late 1960s the NUT continued to develop its ideas for a common syllabus and examination, requiring no differentiation between pupils and no selection. The new examination would be primarily teacher-controlled and would strongly encourage Mode 3 (teacher-assessed) examinations in which teachers mark their own pupils' work. These ideas were set out in an NUT policy statement in

March 1970, which called for only two grades above the O-level pass grade (instead of the existing six) and which advocated the abolition of the pass/fail concept. Furthermore, 'there should be no interim stage between the present system of GCE O-level and CSE examinations and the proposed examination, that is, there should be no stage of common certification of two separate examinations.'

This latter possibility was still all the Schools Council would contemplate – until July 1970 when its Governing Council met to consider proposals for new sixth-form Q and F examinations. According to the NUT[11]: 'In July 1970 the Governing Council of the Schools Council supported the union's view in adopting the resolution "that there should be a single examination system at the age of 16+".' In fact the Schools Council reached this decision at a five-hour meeting during which the 16-plus examination was never debated and was never even on the Agenda. The humiliating rejection of the Q and F proposals, and the desire of the Governing Council to salvage something from the wreckage, gave the NUT the opportunity it needed. Managing to blur the distinction between a common examination and common certification, the NUT pushed its resolution through. Since the NUT is the largest and best organized group on the Schools Council – holding special caucus meetings before important Council meetings – it has established itself as a dominating influence in a body that has shown a strong preference for decision by consensus.[12]

Anxious to be seen to be doing something, the publicly financed Schools Council proceeded to devote much of its resources (currently running at more than £ 3 m. per annum) to pursuing 'the single examination system'. The Council set up a working party to consider the proposals in detail. It met six times and had before it papers from specialists in different areas of the curriculum which considered the feasibility of a single examination system. *These papers were never discussed.* Thus, the working party ignored, for example, the warning by the consultant in French that a common examination was nonsensical and that a non-common syllabus masquerading as a common one was little more than a piece of chicanery.

The subsequent role of the Schools Council has been well summarized by Adam Hopkins.[13]

.... from 1970 onwards the Council was very much occupied with its proposals for a new exam. at sixteen-plus to replace O-level and CSE; and these seemed to imply the most radical extension yet of teacher-power, with a heavy reliance on the Mode III principle. Considerable research was conducted by the Schools Council into possibilities for an exam. of this kind and by 1976 the proposals were ready. It was, however, clear to all who scrutinized them that there still remained a good deal of confusion over the administration of the exams. (mainly because of differences of opinion between the school-centred CSE boards and the more university-centred approach of the GCE boards). Much of the research had been into the possibilities of an exam. that could be common to all. This had been abandoned in favour of proposals for a common system. But the common system itself remained under-researched, and open to the criticism that while the most able might not be fully stretched, the least able would be somewhat confused. When the main decision-making body of the Schools Council debated the proposals, the universities, the GCE boards and the independent schools were heavily opposed. But the teacher unions were, of course, in favour. And so, because of the composition of the Schools Council, the sixteen-plus proposals were accepted and forwarded to the Secretary of State for Education. This was a major defeat for the universities and all who identified themselves with university values, and it appeared to many observers to be a naked bid for power by the teachers.

The Inspectorate at the DES attacked the new examination in a Yellow Paper, leaked to the press in September 1976. Again, in Adam Hopkins' words:

... the Yellow Paper pointed out all the obvious difficulties in the sixteen-plus proposals and simultaneously launched a fierce attack on the Schools Council. Despite some 'good quality staff work', its performance on examinations and the curriculum had been generally mediocre. Moreover, it said, 'the influence of the teacher unions has led to an increasingly political flavour – in the worst sense of the word – in its deliberations'... Partly because of the Schools Council's injudicious exam. proposals, teacher power was one of the main targets the Yellow Paper shot at.

But, according to the NUT, two months earlier:

In July 1976 the Governing Council of the Schools Council fulfilled the hope expressed by the union, in deciding 'that the Secretary of State be asked to establish a Common System of Examining at an early date'. The features of the proposed new system were virtually identical to those recommended earlier by the union.

The Schools Council also recommended that the central co-ordinating role in the new system should be played by – the Schools Council! And not surprisingly

... the Schools Council's proposals were warmly welcomed by the union, which hoped for a favourable decision on the part of the Secretary of State and no further delay in their implementation.[14]

However, the Secretary of State, Shirley Williams, did delay. She set up the Waddell Committee to reconsider the Schools Council proposals.[15] This committee conducted no further research, but it did summarize the costly research which the Schools Council had sponsored. This research showed that, in nearly every major subject, a common examination was *not* feasible. Despite this the Waddell Committee decided in favour of a common system, albeit with alternative papers or parts of papers *in nearly every major subject*, and recommended that 'a central body (probably the Schools Council) should be responsible' for co-ordinating the new system; however, it did reject the idea that teachers should be in a majority on such a body.

Again not surprisingly, the NUT warmly welcomed the Waddell Report (June 1978) and Shirley Williams' White Paper (October 1978) which accepted most of the Waddell recommendations.

However, in July 1979, the incoming Conservative government had second thoughts about some of the proposals in the Labour government's White Paper. In response to this the NUT has returned to the attack. In particular the union

(i) 'regrets the Government's decision not to establish a central authority within the Schools Council';
(ii) strongly opposes the GCE boards being left in control of O-level standards;
(iii) strongly advocates complete teacher control – 'teachers should have the majority voice on all committees primarily concerned with... examination policy... and on subject panels';
(iv) recommends the widest possible use of common examination papers for all candidates;
(v) 'urges most strongly that the use of Mode 3 [teacher controlled] syllabuses... should be encouraged.'[16]

As the union says, '... a truly comprehensive system of education demands a comprehensive system of examining....'.

So for nearly two decades, the NUT has singlemindedly pursued its aims for secondary education. The union has stressed uniformity rather than diversity. Equality and a common system came well before academic attainment in its scale of priorities. One type of school for all, no selection either within or between schools, a common public examination which everybody passes, the abolition of anything which is seen as socially divisive – these are the themes which underly NUT policies for secondary schooling.

All these policies are much nearer realization now than they were twenty years ago, and the history of this period testifies to the political effectiveness of the NUT in imposing its ideology and its determination to wear down all opposition. The NUT – a union with most of its members in *primary* schools – has been a major influence in determining what now goes on in all our *secondary* schools. We will not get secondary schooling on the right lines in this country until the influence of the NUT on secondary education is considerably reduced and the views of parents and the public given much greater weight.

(iii) Parental choice and the NUT

The NUT has a record of opposition to any significant degree of parental choice and has even advocated the reduction of the existing limited choice available to parents.

For example, in 1970 the NUT Annual Conference approved proposals which claimed that it would be entirely proper to limit parental choice.

> By comprehensive education.... we mean the absence of selection procedures which either directly or indirectly prevent each school from having a representative cross-section of the full ability range.... if legislation is to have more force than a pious hope, it is necessary to limit parents' choice of school. It was for this reason among others that we suggested... that parental choice should not be exercised contrary to public policy. We believe that comprehensive schools have the educational advantage of enabling children to mix with a cross-section of their contemporaries, and that these two advantages far outweigh the restriction of what in theory is a universal liberty but what in fact is a liberty that has never existed for the large majority of persons.

This is still the official policy of the NUT who thus put a higher premium on the asserted social and educational benefits of the comprehensive policy than on increasing the freedom of parents to choose the education best suited to their children.[17]

And this opposition to any significant extension of parental choice is clearly shown in the attitude of the NUT to education vouchers.[18] In October 1978, the NUT published a pamphlet in its Fightback Series with the title *The Case Against Education Vouchers* in which it categorically states that 'the union has made clear from the start its total opposition on educational grounds to any voucher scheme' and calls the Kent experimental voucher scheme 'a totally unjustifiable gimmick'. Yet many of the arguments in the pamphlet are either irrelevant or unsound. The NUT start by claiming that the major point of a voucher scheme is 'to allow parents the *unrestricted right* to choose the school they wish their children to attend' (our italics). This is false: no-one has ever claimed that a voucher system could do more than *increase* the degree of parental choice above its present low level.

The NUT then go on to claim that, if schools had to admit all who wanted to go there, this could lead to overcrowding, fluctuating intakes from year to year, and so on.

What they do not consider as a serious possibility or advantage is a considerable *increase* in the degree of parental choice above its present low level. They also object to the need for popular schools to select from those who want to go there. To the NUT this is 'a potentially very dangerous privilege, not unlike that enjoyed by independent schools.'

The NUT pamphlet dismisses "the right to choose" as 'an emotive phrase, calculated to appeal to indignant parents who feel that their choice is at present too restricted[19] and goes on to refer to opposition from teachers which the NUT itself helped to organize.

The NUT then argues against vouchers by claiming that a voucher scheme would lead to extra costs and seems incapable of considering the possibility that vouchers could *replace* much of the present administrative structure in education, based on local authorities, rather than be considered as an *addition* to the present system.

Finally, the NUT claims that it is not alone in condemning vouchers – Mrs Shirley Williams and the Labour Party, when in government, had pledged 'total opposition' to such schemes. Instead of vouchers, the NUT calls for small class sizes and the employment of more teachers as the main answer to problems in our schools.

(iv) Falling rolls and the NUT

The hostility of the NUT to parental choice is also shown in their attitude to falling rolls in schools. As the total school population falls due to the falling birth-rate, a naive observer would think that this would make relatively more places available, even in popular schools, and thus that there would be scope for greatly increased parental choice. But that is not the view of the NUT which, instead, pushes for a policy euphemistically called 'planned admission levels' which in practice is likely to mean that, as the school population falls, all schools, popular and unpopular alike, should contract together. This, of course, protects the unpopular schools from the cold winds of change.

One example of this policy is shown by a discussion document issued in July 1979, by the General Secretary of the Greenwich Branch of the NUT. This document strongly opposed parents having more choice of school when over-subscription became less of a problem. Instead it suggested that all schools should be reduced in size and that parental choice should be limited in the same way as before. 'We suggest', said the document, 'that few parents will take on the Authority and any new legislation strengthening the rights of parents will have to be tested before it can be allowed to defeat highly desirable educational developments'. So much for the NUT's interest in listening to what parents have to say.

According to the NUT, Shirley Williams 'was about to legislate to allow local education authorities to limit the intake in each school year' so that resources '... are not squandered in an unseemly rush following the unwise exercise of "parental choice". What arrogance! By what right does the NUT dare to say that all of us who, as taxpayers, employ their members are, as parents, unwise in our decisions?

(v) Educational Standards and the NUT

The NUT repeatedly states that it is concerned with improving "standards of education". However, what the public means by "improving standards" can be very different from what the NUT means by this phrase.

If we read NUT publications we find repeated references to the need to increase expenditure on education, to employ more teachers, to reduce class sizes and to lower pupil/teacher ratios. What we do *not* find are repeated calls to improve standards of educational attainment or standards of morality and behaviour. And the NUT never seems to ask questions about value for money – it appears to believe that more resources automatically mean better education.

As an example of this let us look at the series of leaflets and pamphlets produced by the NUT during 1979 and 1980 in its "Campaign against the Cuts". 'Oliver Twist asked for more.... government policy means.... *less education for your child.*' 'Scrooge lived to regret *his* meanness.' 'Protest about the threat to education standards.' These were some of the phrases used by the NUT. We are also told that 'there is no leeway in the service' and that 'after the years of cutback in education, there is no room for "economies".'

It is claimed that staffing levels will be reduced and that therefore class sizes and pupil/teacher ratios will increase. Little mention is made of the fact that the school population is falling rapidly and that expenditure per pupil will therefore actually be *increasing* in the near future. And absolutely no mention is made of the fact that, over the last thirty years, expenditure on education has increased by a factor of four *in real terms* and that pupil/teacher ratios have fallen from 30.4 to 22.3 in primary schools and from 21.1 to about 16.3 in secondary schools. So, by the criteria emphasized by the NUT, educational "standards" have risen dramatically. But there is no evidence that standards of attainment or behaviour have risen as dramatically over this period and a disturbing amount of evidence that there have been some actual declines. And one question the NUT pamphlets never ask is whether extra resources for education are best spent on more teachers or in other ways. For example, how many people realize that expenditure on school books and equipment could be approximately *doubled* if pupil/teacher ratios were to return to those existing only four or five years ago? You would certainly never learn this by reading NUT pamphlets about the "cuts".[20]

And while the NUT have pressed, successfully, for more money for education and more teachers, they have not been in favour of more information being gathered or published about standards of attainment in schools. The NUT has a record of opposition to the publication of school examination results and to the testing of levels of attainment of pupils in individual schools. And it has not welcomed proposals to publish information about the qualifications of teaching staff. Finally, on standards of discipline and behaviour, it is the NAS/UWT rather than the NUT which has done most to alert the public to growing problems here.

(vi) Educational research and the NUT

The NUT is quick to publicize research which seems to support its policies. For example, the NUT believes that 'the educational justification for comprehensive schooling is... conclusive' and that comprehensive education '... is the best way to meet the educational needs of all children, whatever their abilities and home backgrounds. Whilst any vestige of selection remains, many children will be deprived'.[21]

So it is not surprising that the NUT should have extensively publicized the research report, *Progress in Secondary Schools*, published by the National Children's Bureau in July 1980, with three separate articles in the NUT weekly newspaper *The Teacher*. The headlines were 'Comprehensives are just as good', 'Comprehensives Vindicated' and 'Bright children do just as well in comprehensives as grammar schools'. The editorial is unstinting in its uncritical praise of comprehensive schools: '... their achievements must be one of the great educational triumphs of the century'; and it concludes by hoping '... that the research will do something to balance the totally lopsided picture which has misguided public opinion for so long'. But when the NCB report was severely criticized[22] and these headlines shown to be false, *The Teacher* failed to inform its readers of the nature of these criticisms.[23]

It is worth noting in this context some of the criticisms of London's comprehensive schools made in a recent report by the HM Inspectorate on the Inner London Education Authority (ILEA).[24] There is no lack of resources – indeed the provision in ILEA comprehensive schools is so generous that the situation must come close to the NUT's ideal as set out in the pamphlets mentioned earlier. The ILEA does spend much more each year per child than the national average* and its pupil/teacher ratio is amongst the lowest in the country. It spends twice the national average per child on books and equipment and three times as much on support staff. So by the criteria espoused by the NUT, educational standards are very high in Inner London. Yet the academic attainments of many children are poor by any standard and are well below their capabilities. In the Inspectorate's own words:

> The retention of mixed ability grouping up to the end of year 2 or 3 for all or the great majority of subjects is not uncommon in ILEA schools and is most often accompanied by a continuation of undifferentiated teaching; this frequently occurs at a level barely suitable for the middle of the ability range in the group, leaving the least able unheeded and the most able unchallenged.
>
> ... in many schools the pace of work is too slow and the level of teacher expectation too low ... the consequence of this is that many enter year 4 unprepared to face O-level or CSE with any justifiable confidence at the end of a further two years in school.
>
> In years 4 and 5 the pace does not accelerate beyond that noted in years 1-3... roughly two-thirds of the classes observed do not show any urgency of approach and the work does not appear to fit in to a logical scheme of work continuing progression towards a clear goal.... It is evident that many teachers underrate the capacities of pupils whatever their level of ability.

And ILEA public examination results are well below the national average and '.... make it clear that many pupils in ILEA secondary schools are under-achieving'. There could hardly be a more striking contrast between the very high "educational standards" in Inner London, in the NUT's sense of that term, and the very poor results which many of London's children take with them as they leave school.

(vii) The NUT pamphlet *Race, Education, Intelligence*

In September, 1978, the NUT published a pamphlet *Race, Education, Intelligence: A teacher's guide to the facts and the issues* with the aim of answering '... some of the questions in the minds of many people – adults as well as children – concerning the concept of "race" and its relevance to teaching and learning'.

This whole subject is one of considerable complexity and controversy in its

---

* £1260 per head in 1981/82 compared with £821 nationally.

scientific and in its social aspects. So any contribution to debate on these issues needs to be written with considerable care, balance and sensitivity if it is not to be misleading or harmful.

These problems have long been recognized. For example, in 1950, UNESCO issued a statement on Race produced by a group of scientists who had examined the scientific evidence for the existence of innate differences between races. This 1950 statement aroused some hostility and was replaced by another statement in 1951. There were so many reservations even about this revised statement that in 1952 UNESCO published a book *The Race Concept: Results of an Inquiry* setting out the background to the statement and detailing the considerable reservations that had been expressed.

Since 1952 the debate on these topics has continued both in scientific and political circles. However, our understanding of many important questions is still very far from complete, and the only verdict which can be given on many issues is "not proven". So any publication intended as "... a teacher's guide to the facts and the issues" ought to aim to give teachers some understanding of the different aspects of this many-sided debate. But this was not what the NUT chose to do. Instead Professor Steven Rose[25] of the Open University and some of his colleagues were invited to write the pamphlet. This was an extraordinary choice since Professor Rose has been one of the principal protagonists of one viewpoint – the Marxist or "radical" science position – and has been one of the most committed polemicists writing in the whole debate. It was rather like inviting Lenin to give a balanced account of the Russian revolution.

If the NUT were really interested in giving a balanced account of the issues, it should surely have invited some other participants in the debate in addition to Professor Rose, preferably including an expert in genetics, which Professor Rose is not. This would seem to be the only prudent and academically honest course for a union consisting largely of primary school teachers whose knowledge of modern genetics must, of necessity, be somewhat limited. Instead Fred Jarvis preferred to appeal to the sheer and unevidenced authority of his Executive: 'it is the belief of the Executive that the views put forward by Professor Steven Rose, Dr Ken Richardson and their colleagues are essentially correct'. Thus we now have a new criterion of truth in complex social and scientific matters – the belief of the NUT Executive. We suggest that this criterion has some affinities with that reigning in Soviet agriculture under Stalin and his protégé, Lysenko – 'henceforth ... conformity with the rural policy of the Communist Party would be the criterion of truth'.[26]

We do not have space to discuss the pamphlet in detail, but when it appeared it was criticized by Professor Eysenck, Professor of Psychiatry at London University, as being 'extremely biased and factually incorrect'. Six months later *New Scientist* persuaded Professors Eysenck and Rose to publish, side by side, their answers to four questions on race, intelligence and education. In our view these *two* contributions[27] would have given teachers a more balanced picture of the debate than the NUT pamphlet did. But this is not the view of Professor Rose, who sees the disagreement between himself and Eysenck as a Zoroastrian conflict between pure light and total darkness: 'the issues at stake are the distinction between sense and nonsense, biological knowledge and magical prescientific thinking'.

The pamphlet itself is a mixture of scientific facts, confusing statements and references to the Nazis and other racist groups. It tells us that one recent writer,

Leon Kamin, has concluded that 'there was no evidence from which to deduce that there was any heritable component to I.Q. differences at all', but it does not mention the contrary conclusions reached by most other recent writers on this subject.[28] And it also tells us that 'the determinants of "civilization" and the development of different human societies should be sought in social, economic and historical factors, not in biology'. In view of this categoric statement it is extraordinary that the authors should use the genetic defect, phenylketonuria (PKU) to illustrate one of their arguments. For this is an example where irreversible mental retardation has a known genetic cause. Moreover, it is a case where biochemical knowledge of specific metabolic pathways has enabled us to prevent this otherwise inevitable mental retardation. So biological and genetic knowledge here has a clear and beneficial social effect: it leads to higher intelligence for many individuals, just because of our growing understanding of a complex interaction between heredity and environment, and our consequent ability to intervene effectively.

Ostensibly the reason for publishing the pamphlet was to promote social harmony in a multi-racial society. The UNESCO report *The Race Concept*, mentioned above, warned that confusion between the concepts of race and culture provided fertile soil for the development of racism; the report concluded that it was essential to define race biologically in order to avoid this confusion. Yet Professor Rose and the NUT deny that this is possible. They claim that 'in biological terms the concept of "race" is meaningless for human populations' and seem intent on dissolving race into a social category. Could it be that the NUT and its pamphleteers might actually be engaged in confusing the issue?

The Marxist prophet Herbert Marcuse despaired of the working classes of Western Europe and the United States. They were too prosperous ever to bring about the social revolution in the way that Marx had anticipated. So Marcuse looked to other groups to spearhead the revolt against capitalism. If, for example, black people could be identified with the lower classes, then racial struggles could be used to breathe life into the faltering class struggle. How convenient it would be if, at the intellectual level too, the debate on race could be subsumed into the debate on class. And isn't this what the NUT pamphlet claims to have done?

The Real NUT – What is it?

Ostensibly the NUT is both a trade union, negotiating its members' salaries and conditions of service, and a professional association, consulted continually by Ministers and the DES on all major questions of educational policy.

It is the single most influential organized group in education, and its claim to this influence depends on its large membership.

We believe that the NUT's influence on education in this country should be drastically reduced. Why? Because its official policies do not represent its members' views. Because its predominantly *primary* school membership does not justify the major role it has played in policy for *secondary* schools. And because the NUT is a combination of a left-wing political pressure group and a trade union acting largely in its own interests; it is not primarily a professional association either in the policies it supports or the values it encourages.

It is not a professional association because it is not primarily concerned with the quality of education. As we have seen, by "improving standards" the NUT means more resources devoted to education, more teachers employed and lower pupil/teacher ratios – all of which have been "achieved" over the years; it is much less concerned with standards of educational attainment or behaviour and has strongly resisted attempts to remove incompetent teachers from the profession.

It is a trade union in the basic services it provides for its members and it acts like many other trade unions in the way it has attempted to obtain teacher control over all aspects of education in schools – policy, curriculum, salaries and resources, organization and public examinations. It is extremely hostile to effective parental influence in schools; one of its main objectives is to see as many teachers in employment as possible, preferably all as NUT members.

That it is a left-wing political pressure group has been shown by our examination of the policies it has consistently advocated – complete comprehensivization, the abolition of selection, a homogenization of the system of public examinations, social engineering as a major aim of education; by the growing influence of far left Marxist groups in its activities – whether they are the provocatively militant disruptions of the Rank and File group or the rather less flamboyant orthodox Communists with their greater staying power; and by some of the people it calls upon for advice – such as the Trade Union Research Unit at Ruskin College, Oxford, or Caroline Wedgwood Benn of the Campaign for Comprehensive Education, or the Marxist Professor Steven Rose of the Open University.

Conclusion

1. Politicians and the public should recognize the NUT for what it is – a combination of a well organized and vociferous but unrepresentative left-wing political pressure group and a conventional trade union acting in its members' interests.
2. We therefore recommend that the influence of the NUT on educational policy must be reduced – by Ministers ceasing to defer to it on so many issues; by reducing its influence on bodies like the Schools Council which are dominated by the NUT; and by making every effort to emphasize the differences between the attitudes of many of its members and the political ambitions of those who control it.
3. The reduction of the influence of the NUT is a necessary but not sufficient condition for any really radical improvement in the standard of education in this country. This will never be achieved unless both politicians and the public understand *why* it is necessary. It was in the hope of contributing to such understanding that this chapter was written.

Notes

1. In these matters, there is relatively little to choose between the various teacher organizations.
2. The total membership of other teachers' organizations is roughly equal to that of the NUT, but individually these organizations are appreciably smaller; the National Association of Schoolmasters/Union of Women Teachers (NAS/UWT) has about 120,000 members; the Assistant Masters' and Mistresses' Association (AMMA) has about 90,000; the Professional Association of Teachers (PAT) has about 20,000.

3. The NUT has sixteen members on the Teachers' Panel of the Burnham Committee compared with six for the NAS/UWT, four for the AMMA and five for various head teacher organizations. On the major Schools Council committees, the NUT are not so predominant numerically but they are by far the largest single group and, hence, can exert a major influence on decisions. For example, under the 1978 Schools Council constitution, the NUT has eleven members on both Convocation and the Professional Committee, while the next largest group, NAS/UWT, has four, while on the pre-1978 constitution the NUT preponderance was even greater.

4. If it were so affiliated it would lose much of its support. At present it can identify with the left-wing of the Labour Party, whilst appearing to be politically neutral.

5. Consider some of the educational policies of the Communist Party (*A Survey of Left-Wing Plans for Transformating Education*, Common Cause Publications, 1980).

    Local authorities should be given full legislative powers to bring voluntarily aided schools into the local comprehensive systems.

    The final objective is to bring independent schools for the wealthy into the system as their continued existence is a threat to democracy.

    The practice of parental choice should be discontinued because it reintroduces selection into the comprehensive system.

    Neighbourhood schools should be encouraged.

    Smaller classes and the provision of adequate resources are needed to enable the transition to one-stream or mixed ability teaching.

    GCE and CSE examinations should be replaced by a single examination at 16+.

    Now compare these policies with those of the NUT as set out in this article. This book also contains much other useful information about left-wing influences in education, including a section on the NUT.

6. *The NUT View on Comprehensive Education* (NUT, July 1970) is the source for most of the pre-1970 quotations in this section. The rest come from resolutions passed at NUT Annual Conferences.

7. The CCE is a pressure group which has Caroline Benn, wife of Tony Benn, as one of its main organizers.

8. See also "Quality or Equality?" by A. Grant, p. 89, this volume.

9. *Examining at 16+ – the case for a common system* (NUT, November 1978).

10. The NUT have continued to reject the collective wisdom of examination experts right up to the present.

11. *Examining at 16+ – an NUT policy statement on proposals for a single system* (NUT, May 1980).

12. The NUT attaches considerable importance to maintaining this influence (see the sections dealing with the Schools Council in the annual NUT reports).

13. Adam Hopkins, *The School Debate* (Penguin 1978), p. 104.

14. See Note 11. This leaflet neatly summarizes the stately public duet between the NUT and the Schools Council on this subject over the last decade. Throughout the appearance is given that these two bodies are independent of one another.

15. See Alan Grant, "Quality or Equality?" p. 89 this volume, and John Marks, *GCE/CSE Merger: the Threat to Academic Standards* (National Council for

Educational Standards Bulletin, Spring 1980) for a fuller discussion of the Waddell Committee report.

16. The recent HMI report on secondary education admitted that it is quite common to provide '... O-level for the top band, CSE for the middle band and CSE Mode III for the lowest band....'. So much for the comparability between Mode I examinations which are externally set and marked, and Mode III assessments, which are largely controlled by the pupils' own teachers with only minimal external checks.

17. In doing this, the NUT set themselves against both the United Nations Declaration of Human Rights which asserts: 'the prior right of parents to determine the kind of education that shall be given to their children', and the European Convention which speaks of 'the right of parents to ensure the education of their children in conformity with their own religious or philosophical convictions'.

18. See Marjorie Seldon, "Education Vouchers", p. 103, this volume.

19. 68 per cent of parents interviewed in the Kent feasibility study said they should have more choice.

20. See *Education Statistics* (Chartered Institute of Public Finance and Accountancy) for up-to-date and detailed information on educational expenditure.

21. *Comprehensive Schools: Does Mrs Thatcher know what she is doing?*, (NUT, September 1979).

22. See "Cause for Concern", p. 185, this volume.

23. See Fred Naylor, "Educational Myths and Research", p. 167, this volume, for another example of inadequate reporting in *The Teacher* relating to the effectiveness of mixed ability teaching.

24. *Educational Provision by the Inner London Education Authority*, a report by HM Inspectors (DES, November 1980).

25. See Caroline Cox and John Marks, "What has Athens to do with Jerusalem?", p. 67, this volume, for some discussion of Professor Rose's writings and some published criticisms of the Open University course "Genetics", which was the responsibility of a course team chaired by Professor Rose.

26. S.G. Solomon, *Controversy in Social Science: Soviet Rural Studies in the 1920s* (Minerva, Winter 1975), p. 544.

27. "Race, intelligence and education", *New Scientist*, 12 March 1977, pp. 849-852.

28. See, for example, the article by Professor P.E. Vernon referred to by Fred Naylor in "Educational Myths and Research", p. 167, this volume.

IX
Knowledge, Debate and Choice in Education

Digby Anderson

M.Phil. and Ph.D., he has taught in both sectors of higher education and was, until May 1980, Research Fellow at the University of Nottingham. His books include Health Education in Practice, The Ignorance of Social Intervention *(with E.R. Perkins),* Self-Assessment in the NHS, *and* Evaluating Curricula Proposals – a Critical Guide. *He is at present Director of the Social Affairs Unit whose projects include "Cases for Contraction?" (welfare state), and "The Culture in Decline?" (ideology).*

Both Conservative and Labour administrations have suggested that 'debate' has a crucial role to play in justifying educational change. This chapter argues that contributions to this debate have failed to clarify criteria, lack proportion, are superficial, permeated by wishful thinking, complacent and weighed down with ideology, vested interest and rhetoric. The 'debate' is not up to the task expected of it and is no substitute for informed parental choice about schools.

Over dinner[1] I suggested to a couple of educationist friends that their four-year B.Ed. teacher training courses could be cut down to five days. They were not angry. They thought it was a great joke. I pointed out that my suggestion, unlike the four-year courses, was considered and serious. Then they said I must be mad. I said I had not been, at least up to the skate. Then they asked me for my reasons and I made my first mistake. I assumed they wanted to hear my reasons and, dismissing the obvious inclination that it was they, the voracious consumers of others' time and money, who ought to be giving reasons, I fell to.[2]

I pointed out the pitiful state of the "discipline" called education with its inconclusive research and its total lack of practical wisdom. I argued that no one knew enough about teaching, at least enough that was agreed, useful and interesting to occupy one year, let alone four; that previous generations of teachers had learned what is obviously a craft and art by imitation, apprenticeship and socialization, and that they had not done too much harm; that the peculiar new needs of our peculiar new schools could be dealt with by later in-service training, and that their tedious recurrent novelty and extreme peculiarity were arguments against long periods of central, general training. Of course, I was happy to accept that all teachers should have degrees in these days when the dole queues exude them, but they should be degrees in the subject taught.

I realized that it was important to have good teachers and thought that this might mean more careful selection procedures and two-year contracts for the first twelve years. Warming to my own ideas I explained how "having" good teachers, unlike "acquiring" good teachers, meant continual monitoring and accountability. Surely if "teaching" was enough a science to take four years, it was enough a science to be able to evaluate itself and kick out the incompetent, unproductive and tired teacher. Was there no point short of rape at which contracts should not be renewed? What about teachers who did not own a book apart from a Cortina Manual, and so on. Then I started on what is an open secret in "higher education" – the awfulness of so many of the departments which are responsible for the elastic teacher courses: the extraordinary attempts to cling on to students, to courses, to jobs in the face of falling demand by merging, redesignation and the discovery of new, urgent and awesome needs; the bright new prospectuses for dull old practices; the frantic pursuit of novelty and trendiness only exceeded by the stolid perpetuation of staff who are anything but novel.

I spoke with personal experience of the contributing specialists, the psychologists "of education", the sociologists "of education", and the philosophers "of education" who most reluctantly have to be "relevant" to the training needs of future teachers, but who confuse simplification with application, and, to their own immense relief, produce little of the former and none of the latter. Especially the sociologists wend their own jargon-ridden relativistic way occasionally illustrating it by educational example and suggesting no practical interactional application short of the Trotskyist millennium.

We talked of lesser known breeds, such as those aspiring technicians who would make a discipline out of an overhead projector, and the notorious ubiquitous schemers who, disdaining detail and argument, find that all problems, be they in teaching or management, fall at the approach of a box, an arrow, and a flow chart. Their boxes, charts and diagrams are metaphors, not models, and unhappy metaphors at that. Certainly if they have any contents they are not the stuff of actual teaching. And to complement these pseudo-scientists, who would mistake the ornaments of science for its rigorous procedures, come the "humanists". These are trendies who want to "facilitate personal growth and liberation", who "enhance life styles" and insist on "sharing" a discussion; these are the bores who go on and on and on and on about something called "the community", but know nothing about actual catchment areas. These are the child-centred sentimentalists whose disdain for subject structures and any notions of failure, deficit or sin, point to a wholly anarchic relativism. And all these jolly people, while bitching about each other in private, live off the cumulative effect of each other's inadequacies to create a sense of a wide and complicated subject, a subject in which the laxity of the entrance requirements is only exceeded by the laxity of the terminal assessment.

As the teal, the salad, the cheese and fruit came and went so did my educationist friends' replies and they were as intemperate as my assertions. A good evening then – but of no consequence for the education system. That system is the product of rigorous research and *reasoned* debate by professionals, elected representatives and public servants. Or is it? Is this "public" debate very different from the dinner conversation?

Characteristics of Educational Debate

There is obviously one difference – the public debate is not much fun. Its participants have managed to take up a topic which is of crucial interest to parents, children, industry and government, an interesting even exciting topic, and turn it into the most tedious, flabby, cliché-ridden exchange of the last decade. Another difference is that this debate has been bigger than the dinner discussion and, by sheer virtue of its size, is likely to have included *some* nice argument. But in several ways the two discussions have been similar or as the platitude runs "have encountered similar problems".

Lack of Conclusion

The public debate has been *inconclusive* – which has not prevented politicians drawing lots of conclusions from it. (*I* think it has one conclusion, but more of that later.) When I say it has been inconclusive I mean that there is a yawning gap between the actual evidence and the arguments matched only by that between the arguments and detailed working out of policies in the schools and universities.

Criteria and Rules not set in Advance

This lack of conclusion may be partly because of a second quality. The criteria for winning the arguments are made up *after* the arguments. Take again the case of opposing lengthy teacher training. If such criticism is ever to bite, the reluctant, bashful trainers must state publicly what they would take as reasonable proof that their courses were a criminal, pretentious waste of time and, occasionally, talent. At least to start with, we do not require measures of success, but measures of failure: we do not need to be able to distinguish between the chimera of a good course and that of a better one merely to identify an appalling one. For what has happened in social criticism is that the institutions which are criticized have been allowed to place themselves beyond the reach of telling criticism. Some accept no minimal standards for themselves; others ensure that the standards are impractical, that they can never be applied in practice. One way or the other they emasculate criticism, and our society with it.

An instance: the Universities' Council for the Education of Teachers has just published a discussion document on the one-year postgraduate certificate in education course.[3] Non-graduate teachers attend three year or four year courses in which they learn what and how to teach. Graduates attend a one year course which is all on teaching. This involves theory and practice (in schools) and is called the P.G.C.E. The writers of the U.C.E.T. report want to see changes in the P.G.C.E. They also want wide *discussion* of their ideas. Now the taught part of the P.G.C.E. course has always enjoyed the reputation among its students of providing a tranquil extension of student life in which some reading and courting and dozing can be done. It is not the course which produces the highest pre-examination suicide rate (though in fairness students *do* worry about teaching practice). It is then a pleasant interlude for graduates before joining a school or dole queue. Apart from the cost to the taxpayer, it has never been shown to do much harm to anyone. Of course it is far too long; most of the essential academic work could be done in a few weeks. No one, except those who derive income from it or who share a trade union collusive brotherhood with them, has ever thought it has much to do with the practical problems of teaching. Now the U.C.E.T. committee has sensibly argued that its academic content (the sociology, psychology, etc.) should be related more intimately to teaching practice and that the central focus should be the work a teacher does in the classroom. Theory is to be 'developed so as to illuminate and inform practical judgements'.

Then the report goes mad. Members of the committee were, of course, well experienced in the P.G.C.E. course, and as is often the case when people write about their own experience and passions, probably with the best of intentions, they became indulgently and wildly enthusiastic. One year is not enough. One year is far from enough. There are so many wonderful and important things which need to be done (all related to the classroom) that, though the report does not recommend extending it, it makes it very clear that a much longer course is what it would prefer. Several things are of interest here. First there seems to be no *principle* for relating course length and content. True, the committee writes a minimal list of topics, but we all know that such lists can be summarized in three items, or sub-divided to thirty – lists are elastic. Nowhere do they *argue* for the increase in time, they assert it. Secondly, like many in social intervention, they move directly from what needs to be done to what is proposed. Such a direct move is arrogant. It supposes that they *know* how to do what needs to be done. Obviously the length of a course should be tied to what can actually and demonstrably be done in it, and not to what might be nice or to what "is needed" (such people do not dream of *considering demand*, they *absorb need*). The whole report seethes with a woolly idealistic liberalism which confuses the desirable and the practical, and persistently over-estimates the capabilities of teacher trainers and the development of their discipline. There are, of course, many books on teaching and there is no doubt that reading and writing about it could be extended for ten years or more. It is even possible that students could *think* about education for some time. But it is certain that while some of the books are simple, next to none are deeply practical; while some sociologists and psychologists can make their subjects accessible to non-specialists, none have much expertise in a psychology or sociology of practical teacher action. While there are a few studies allegedly of classrooms, most of these are of themes or topics abstracted from classrooms; while there are lots of guides on how to start and plan theoretical lessons, there are few on how to continue and maintain actual lessons. In short, while trainers can offer help on practical teaching, such help is very much of the order of tips, hunches and discussion.[4]

For the fabled discipline of *practical* teaching just does not yet exist. Few researchers are interested in it, preferring the experimental or the ideal to the actual. What little work has been done shows it to be a vastly complicated subject (at least to be explicit about) and one can only presume that the committee have not seen such research or they would not display the contempt for the practical, which they do in their assumption that a course on it can be put together in the near future, let alone a longer course. Now this criticism is very casual. It should convince no one. But the intriguing question is what *would* the critic have to do to convince the partisans of lengthy teacher training to abandon their case, their courses and inevitably their jobs? What sort of evidence would they accept? Why have they not specified such evidence – the criteria in advance? What on earth is the use of a polite invitation to discussion if the rules are going to be made up by the other side after the guest has had his "go"? If anyone could show the U.C.E.T. committee the sheer inadequacy of current general knowledge about practical classroom teaching by some agreed criteria, would they then back down? Would they stop their imperialistic advance, allow their students back into their courtships and slumber, and await the production of a little more knowledge before anticipating its creation, and inflating and institutionalizing its dissemination?

Argument from Need – Lack of Proportion

In this discussion of the P.G.C.E. case we have seen two other qualities of the education debate: the advocacy of a policy on the grounds of need, rather than on the grounds of having the ability to deliver a "solution". Indeed policies are often advocated in the face of little or no idea of the technology of their implementation. Discussants find that arguments are settled by a fantastic system of "need bargaining" which makes liberal use of the subjunctive.

Secondly we should note the lack of any principles of proportion between evidence, arguments and action. From the critics' point of view the educational establishment is like a damp sponge. Despite the massive rhetorical use made of "evidence" by politicians in educational debate, the critic should be aware that the sponge reserves the right to ignore evidence it does not like and, more important, to keep the critic guessing as to what might be considered "evidence" in this or that case. If the sponge maintains its superior composure by refusing to spell out the rules of *adequacy*, it enhances that composure by refusing to spell out the rules of proportion. Thus it is not clear how much, and what sort of, evidence one would need to justify the introduction of an evaluative sacking and payment of teachers or to reinstate Latin. Nor is it clear, were one's evidence seen to be satisfactory, how *much* Latin would be introduced or how *many* teachers sacked. A

Schools Council research project has recently argued for more health education in schools.[5] I think its argument is strong; but it wants health education for eleven years, and *I* think eight weeks would be enough. Certainly, one of the most worrying aspects of change in schools is not that it occurs, but that it does so in inflated quantities and prematurely. Nor is such change confined to schools. In the polytechnics, too, courses have been started on subjects whose state of development[6] in no way justifies their being taught except in a minimal or experimental way. Throughout the education system this lack of proportion has resulted in the systematic confusion of experimentation, trial and standard practice.

Superficiality

Teachers are fond of saying to politicians, parents, curriculum innovators and others that outsiders do not understand the realities of the classroom. Outsiders' suggestions are accused of superficiality – 'they sound imposing but...'. Now, this gambit is, we know, the stock in trade of the practitioner protecting his patch, but that should not blind us to the fact that much of the education debate *is* superficial. For example the title of a recent HMI paper promises grand things: *A View of the Curriculum*.[7] But inside we find that it is a very distant view indeed. The Inspectors rule out discussion of teaching methods, and thus the actual activities of teachers. Instead they limit their role to finding new names and combinations for unknown and autonomous practices. Their debate is about surface phenomena. They move around empty tea chests called Humanities, Science and the like, building little piles and shapes. What they contain no one knows. But one expects the results of the exercise will be as nominal as the analysis. Nowhere in this publication does one get the feeling that the authors know what happens in classrooms or that they could specify what their recommendations would look like, in practice rather than on the timetable (except perhaps in one appendix). Similarly DES advice tends to cut off at a critical point deferring to the autonomy of local teachers. Such deference looks, at first sight, like a gesture of humility, of mutual professional recognition but often it is simply a way of avoiding specification, or of giving guidance on the principles and methods of specification. The examples I enjoy best are those in which teachers are exhorted to 'adjust' curricula to 'the needs of the local community'.[8]

Personal and Vested Interest

In the dinner discussion it was inevitable that the parties should start to explain away each other's arguments by the personal interests of the speakers. People do get their interests mixed up in their opinions. That is a fact of life. But it cannot be shouted too loudly that parties to a public debate also have vested interests which are most harmful when they are least obvious. We do not expect teachers to oppose their own security of employment even if they were capable of thinking that two-year contracts might be an incentive. We do not expect senior tax paid bureaucrats in local education authorities to cut back on themselves in times of stringency. Nor should we expect education reseachers, curriculum developers, and inhabitants of university education departments to be critical detached scholars.

Not only are these departments full of ex-teachers, they have also shown scant interest in developing education as a wider discipline than school teaching or lecturing in colleges of further education. Education is, of course, an aspect of many institutions and itself part of wider fields such as knowledge organization, storage and retrieval and "communication". As a discipline, it could be developed to be of enormous use to industry, to individuals and to society. But apart from occasional attempts, for example, in adult education, educationists in universities and polytechnics have preferred to cater for one known and restricted market – school teachers. This may be something for which we should be grateful. However, in restricting education to school servicing they have submerged an intellectual discipline in an organized interest. They now depend on the continuation of extensive and long formal teacher training for their living and it would be naive and unfair to expect them to approach the issue of the length of teacher training in a detached way.[9]

Such vested interests partly explain the sustained push towards more and longer courses. Throughout the 1960s and 1970s, new disciplines of pastoral counselling, curriculum development, educational technology and school management have been sired by vested occupational interest out of elastic social sciences. One intriguing thing about these novelties, and another characteristic of established education argument, is the way that points are *hoarded*. Educationists do not so much debate points as collect them. The typical modern educationist is not simplistically progressive. True, he is "interested in" community teaching, pastoral care systems, curricula grids, project work, de-sexing texts, decision making, relative standards, child centredness, adjustment to sub-cultures, classes in road safety, opening things up, facilitation and gypsies. But, at the same time, he is reluctant to drop existing practices to make way for these exciting developments. There are well known exceptions: certain subjects and certain modes of assessment have been dropped. Manifestly, too, certain standards have disappeared. But the reactionary critic should not see the modern educationist as a vandal replacing literacy, numeracy and exams with relativism, road safety and subjective assessment. Rather he is a squirrel whose wish to add new and silly things is matched by a reluctance to be critical *finally* of existing provision. The result is sometimes moderate compromise – sometimes bedlam. Even progressive curricula developers have noticed this, complaining about the piecemeal and unmethodic adoption of their wares. If there is one thing that progressive and reactionary critics might agree about, it is the need for an education stock-take and clear-out. Of course the refusal to stock-take, to jettison failed curricula, tired practices and exhausted teachers, to cut out irrelevancies and the rest, is a useful argumentative resource for the educationist. He can reject points he does not like on the grounds that the school curriculum is full up, that teachers are stretched to their limits and so forth, and he can adjust those points he does like so that he likes them even more. The critic is totally frustrated; even if he wins a point, it may never be implemented and if it is, he will not recognize it. Somehow, the educationist's myth that his world is busy and crowded, and that none of its practices or inhabitants is dispensable, must be replaced by a realistic assessment that eleven years of compulsory education is a very long time. Taxpayers, parents and pupils have a right to expect a great deal from it.

No Agreement on Terms of Debate

The failure to stock-take is an aspect of the suffocating complacency which the NUT and DES exude with respect to teachers and standards. Individual teachers do speak of tragedies and alarms, of pupils and teachers who are total wastes of time, and of wholly inane practices. But the largest teacher organization – protected as it is by a system which compels customers in, denies effective parental choice, limits searching accountability, hides the relative merits and failures of different teachers and schools, and covers all with bureaucratic cotton wool – is so established that one can expect no more from it than ritual tinkering. It is difficult to establish whether the education machine simply needs a routine service or a major overhaul. But, what is unnerving to the critic is that the modern educationist sees, in what any outsider would take as a simple service, a major, radical and threatening repair. For example, schools' staff selection methods are as fallible as anyone else's. It is obvious that almost total job security and classroom autonomy will have resulted in some corrupt teachers and some lazy functionaries. To review staff's performance every few years, reward the good and eject the bad, is simple servicing. Yet, I have a feeling that de-standardizing pay rates and sacking the worst fifth of teachers and functionaries to allow in some of the highly qualified – or, at least, lengthily trained – and enthusiastic products of our teacher training academies, would not please civil services or teaching unions. When you have been cocooned in cotton wool, a whisper sounds like Concord. All this makes for a very odd debate since the various parties cannot even agree on terms such as a *"radical* change" or *"minor* adjustment"!

The squirrel-like, complacent and cotton wool qualities may explain the odd reaction of educationists to financial stringency, a reaction which has totally failed to include an evaluative assessment of expensive novelties introduced into the system over the last twenty years. For example, once upon a time there was little expenditure on educational broadcasting, and even less on audio-visual aids. In the fuss about cuts in each of these, it seems that they were not assessed. What economies did they produce? What practices did they enable teachers to discontinue? The modern educationist does not think like this. He sees new techniques as supplementary, another or extra way of doing something. This may be all very well in Utopia, but it is of little help to a government trying to economize. More seriously, in the context of this chapter, it is infuriating for both the "negative" and the "constructive" critic who would join the education debate.

Argumentative Protectionism

In discussing these issues we have seen two other qualities of the debate. The first might be called "argumentative protectionism". Points are evaluated according not only to their worth but to who makes them.[10] Teachers "know" about the classroom; the NUT "knows" how teachers feel about comprehensives; the Inspectorate "knows" that with a little tinkering all will be well; the LEA Directors of Education "know" what happens in their Authority; education researchers "know" that streaming is unsatisfactory. These claims to knowledge are often advanced contrastively in that they deny the knowledge of others and their right to speak, or suggest that others "know" inadequately or partially. Without implying that all "know" equally, it is fairly obvious that most parents do know a lot about changes in their children as they go through school. They may not do statistics, but they and the teachers are exposed to the results of what teacher trainers infelicitously call the "chalk face". It is also true that many of the "authoritative" agencies have less adequate knowledge than they pretend, and even less right to talk on behalf of others. The debate has not even started to address rival claims to knowledge about education.

Open Secrets Closed

The fact that teachers and LEAs as bodies are often thought to know best may obscure the other fact that they also "know" as individuals. This private knowledge in my experience (and how else does one gain access to it?) often conflicts, in particular, with the public knowledge of teachers, generating the phenomenon "open secrets". Things are admitted, even proclaimed, in every staff room, every day, which are contradicted at the NUT annual jamboree. Many of the unpleasant things I have alleged about the education system are as nothing compared to the vitriol that an intelligent, hard working, teacher will release against some of his fellows after a couple of gins. Teachers know that there are unsatisfactory teachers – they have to take their classes when they pretend to be ill; they have to repair the damage done to pupils when they arrive in their own classes. Teachers have seen their incompetent colleagues promoted as schools expanded under comprehensivization. Teachers laughed about the jugglings that went on following the local government reorganization. In higher education the bodging that has gone on following the "reduction" of teacher training is a standing and sick joke. The same teachers whose union proclaims that all schools are wonderful (or would be if given more money) will advise any friend enquiring about the educational future of his children on the widely varying merits of the local schools. In short, many teachers do not recognize their schools and colleagues in the cardboard concepts touted by education debaters although they will not publicly admit it. The reseacher who finds the key to releasing these "open secrets" into public debate would be doing an invaluable service to that debate.

Formal Knowledge deeply Rhetorical

Not only is the everyday knowledge of parents and teachers more worthwhile than is often admitted, but the formal wisdom of reseachers and bureaucrats is less scientific than is often claimed. Recent research into School Council curriculum projects,[11] for example, has shown that the claim that these schemes for schools are "based on research", let alone are "the results of the research", should be treated at best as metaphorical, at worst misleading. Like most research behind social policy there is a gap between findings and recommendations. The research does not point exclusively to any single recommendation nor does it detail the technical means for achieving recommended ends in any sort of practical detail. This gap between finding and policy is filled by rhetoric – by appeals to sentiment, by contrived contrast by organized argument, selective citation, arbitrary development and "creative" presentation of "data".[12]

Conclusion

The public debate on education that I have heard is not so different to the immoderate discussion at dinner. It has not spelt out its rules and criteria; it is full of wishful thinking – confusing intention and ability; prone to "need bargaining"; lacking principles of proportion; superficial and distant from classroom realities; evasive; subverted by personal and vested interest; obsessed with hoarding its points, practices and personnel and unable to stock-take or discriminate alternatives; suffocatingly complacent to the extent of seeing simple evaluation procedures as a major threat; restrictive about who can contribute what to the debate; scornful of "outsiders" (those without a vested interest); interested in formal corporate pronouncements and disdainful of "open secrets"; exaggeratedly reliant on less than scientific research and bulging with rhetorical ornament.

This does not mean that it is a bad debate. That depends on what it is used for. There are some people who would make such debate the key factor in determining what happens in our schools. They would have committees of professionals, delegates, and bureaucrats debate in the way I have described, then force our schools into a pattern which conforms with the "results" of their debates. I have tried to show that the debate cannot reasonably be expected to play such a role. What happens in our schools should be the result of parents' thinking and choosing their children's education. For that we need different sorts of schools. We need genuine choice between them. We need reliable information about them and we need public debate to help parents choose. This educational debate *has* an important role to play as *one* factor in helping educationists provide variety and parents choose schools and curricula for their children. But it cannot replace choice not only because it is wrong for committees of vested interests to decide what education children should be forced to have but because their debate is nowhere near *good* enough to justify rigid and unilateral education policies. It is a dream to think that good schooling can come out of committees discussing education research. It is a nightmare to think that, by multiplying the research and committees, one can find the perfect school. To think like that is grossly to exaggerate the rigour and policy implications of research and the level and quality of the argument about research. The myth that the experts know best and can decide for us is a crucial factor in the ideology of collectivism and totalitarianism. It is immoral and unrealistic.

Notes

1. It will be readily apparent that this is not a conventional research paper. Indeed, its main object is to challenge the adequacy of conventional research and debate in education. It is based on the author's research (see notes 2, 4, 8, 12), and on casual and verbal reports encountered in and outside research. Its assertions should then be treated with caution. If the reader wonders why more conventional methods were not used, I can only reply that I would have had to change the topic to fit the methods and I consider the topic worth treating.

2. It is assumed, I think in general rightly, that those who criticize should provide evidence. The exception may be, as in this case, where the individual critic is criticizing an organization which is supposed to be accountable and which has vast and elaborate means of producing defensive evidence. There the function of the critic is surely to insist on that accountability and to provoke the organization into producing the evidence for its defence (if it can find it). This issue is addressed in Anderson D.C., "Imperialist Manoeuvres in 'Public' Education and Welfare", *Institute of Economic Affairs Readings in Political Economy No. 25* on Local Government, 1980.

3. Hirst P.H., for the Universities' Council for the Education of Teachers Working Party on the P.G.C.E. Course, "The P.G.C.E. Course and the Training of Specialist Teachers for Secondary Schools", *British Journal of Teacher Education*, Vol. 6, No. 1 (January 1980) pp. 3-20.

4. The order of help for teachers is discussed in "The Rhetoric of Practicality', chapter 6 of Anderson D.C., *Evaluating Curriculum Proposals – A Critical Guide* (Croom Helm, London 1980). Further discussion of problems with the practical are in Anderson D.C., "The Formal Basis for a Contextually Sensitive Classroom Agenda", *Instructional Science*, Vol. 8, No. 2, 1979; Sharrock W.W., "On the Possibility of Social Change", in Anderson D.C. (ed.), *The Ignorance of Social Intervention* (Croom Helm, London 1980); but the impetus for all these discussions of practicality is the work of Garfinkel H., especially *Studies in Ethnomethodology* (Prentice Hall, Englewood Cliffs, 1967) and "Some Sociological Concepts and Methods for Psychiatrists" *Psychiatric Research Reports*, 1956, pp. 191-2. Two papers at the 1981 American Educational Research Association Conference also look at this issue from other perspectives: Olson J.K., "Innovative Doctrine into Practice" and Harris I.B., "Effective Communication for Guiding Practitioners".

5. Schools Council, *Health Education Project 5-13*, and forthcoming 13-18, (Nelson, London 1977).

6. For example the spread of courses on Cultural Studies or Media Studies; Leisure Studies; Health Studies; and Women's Studies.

7. *A View of the Curriculum*, HMI Series: Matters for Discussion (HMSO, London 1980).

8. Discussed more fully in Anderson D.C., "Curriculum Innovation and Local Need". *Journal of Curriculum Studies* 11, 2, 1979.

9. This remark is not abusive. I am suggesting that it is difficult to *see* something in a detached way if one's own fate is caught up in it, not that it is seen one way and explained another. A little sociological evidence on this may be found in Becker H.S., et al., *The Boys in White* (Chicago University Press, 1961).

10. Becker has something to say about this too. In Becker H.S., "Whose side are We On?" in *Sociological Work: Method and Substance* (Allen Lane, London 1971) he discusses the problem of accounts from the top down and the bottom up.

11. Anderson D.C., *Evaluating Curriculum Proposals*, op. cit. The Projects analysed in this research were Schools Council, *Moral Education in the Secondary School* (Longman, London 1972); *Health Education Project 5-13*, op. cit.; *Religious Education in Primary Schools* (Macmillan, London 1977); and *Mass Media and the Secondary School* (Macmillan, London 1973); and

Schools Council/Nuffield, *Humanities Project* (Heinemann, London 1970).
12. Anderson D.C., "Writing and Winning Sociological Arguments", *Proceedings of the British Sociological Association Annual Conference*, University of Lancaster, 1980 (British Sociological Association, 1981).

X

Distortions of Education by the Vested Interests of the Bureaucracy and some Possible Remedies

Stanislav Andreski

A professor at Reading University (Head of the Department of Sociology) he was born in Poland which he left in 1940 and served in the Polish units with the British army until 1947. He obtained his bachelor's, master's and doctor's degrees as an external student at the University of London. Has worked as a researcher or teacher at Rhodes University, South Africa, Manchester University, Acton Technical College, Brunel College of Technology, School of Social Sciences, Santiago, Chile, the Nigerian Institute of Social and Economic Research, City College, New York, and Simon Fraser University, Vancouver.
His publications include Military Organization and Society, Elements of Comparative Sociology, Parasitism and Subversion: the Case of Latin America, The African Predicament: a Study in Pathology of Modernization, Social Science as Sorcery *and* The Prospect of a Revolution in the USA.

Many features of the present situation in education appear incomprehensible, as they stand in flat contradiction to the publicly proclaimed goals of education. This chapter shows that these features can be explained by the vested interests of the bureaucratic-educational complex, short-sightedly pursued under the smokescreen of ultra egalitarian phraseology, and with an almost total disregard for the long-term interests of those whom state education is supposed to serve.

The Rise of the Bureaucratic-Educational Complex

The literature of education and sociology is full of condemnations of the ways in which education is made to serve the perpetuation of hereditary privilege. There is some truth in these allegations even today and they were fully justified a hundred years ago. In a situation of straightforward inheritance of social positions, privileged access to education is irrelevant: a lord was a lord whether he was educated or not. With the introduction of examinations as the condition of entry into public administration and the liberal professions, easier access to education entailed a greater chance of entering a remunerative occupation. Throughout the nineteenth century in Britain, until the last decade in Spain, in many poor countries even today, access to education depended, or depends, on the parent's ability to pay for it and dispense with the offspring's earnings. In the affluent welfare states of today no one who is both able and determined is debarred from access to education at any level by poverty. The relative poverty and low level of education of the parents affect less their children's educational opportunites than their desire to go on with schooling, whereas in the backward and more steeply stratified societies education is usually greatly desired as a route for escaping from hard life, but poverty presents an insuperable obstacle. It would be an exaggeration to say that family background and connections no longer affect educational opportunities in the affluent societies, but they seem to matter less in access to education than in access to jobs of the lucrative or prestigious kind.

The elimination of the financial bars on access to education was intimately connected with the extension of the electoral franchise which obliged the politicians to do (or at least to appear to be doing) something for the masses. Opening education to the children of the poor cost the old privileged classes less than would a re-distribution of wealth, and yet it had great electoral appeal. It can hardly be coincidental that the longest steps on this road were made during the two world wars, when inducements were needed to elicit the participation of the masses in the war effort. These concessions also appeared attractive as genera-lized public investments in the economy which demanded ever larger numbers of highly skilled personnel, as it seemed wasteful to allow the supply of such people to be limited by the inability or unwillingness of many parents to pay for the education of their children.

The utilitarian and "machiavellian" motives were reinforced by the changes in the prevalent attitudes to the inheritance of status. The latter seems natural and just when the extended family or the clan is a cohesive and multi-functional entity, enduring through generations and collectively responsible for its members' welfare, misdeeds and debts, but which also accumulates the credit for their past and present merits and achievements. The disintegration of such entities based on kinship, the passing of most functions of the traditional family to commercial and bureaucratic organizations, the increasing fragility of the bond of marriage, participation of each individual in many intersecting but not identical social circles, and frequent movements of people from one group to another (i.e. social mobility) have destroyed the justification for attributing rights and duties to anything larger than an individual. With this outlook – which we might call individualism – permeating legislation as well as moral notions held by the public, an advantage derived from inheritance appears arbitrary and impossible to justify.

Inequality resulting from individual achievement is compatible with the ubiquitous individualism but inequality of opportunity is not.

Under the impact of these circumstances all the states which could afford it have set up provision of more or less free education at all levels, entailing the creation of a large sector of public employees. As in nearly all other fields, the ratio between those on "the firing line" (in this case those who teach) and those engaged in directing or administrating them has been steadily changing in favour of the latter; partly because of the increasing "roundaboutness of production" (to use Alfred Marshall's expression) and partly in consequence of the Parkinsonian tendency of all bureaucratic bodies towards hypertrophy. In recent decades most of these employees have organized themselves into unions whose functionaries have become another element whose special vested interests are distinct from those whom they are supposed to represent. Not the least important among the forces which have shaped the situation in recent years was the propensity of many politicians to use educational policy as a "pie in the sky".

As I pointed out some years ago,* education offers a particularly rewarding field for buying votes with post-dated cheques. There is an analogy here with monetary inflation: faced with claims which exceed disposable wealth, governments buy temporary peace with each powerful sector in succession by giving them more money. The drawback is, of course, that within a year or so an addition to the supply of money will affect the prices and provide grounds for new claims. The advantage of educational promissory notes is that honouring them can be delayed well beyond the date of the next election. The starting point is that many electors feel that they would have been able to get better jobs had they had more education, and are therefore pleased when they hear that their children will stay at school longer and obtain better "qualifications". What parents seldom realize is that by the time their children get the diploma they did not get, its value as a passport to a better job will be severely reduced if the number of diploma holders increase faster than the number of good jobs. The length of post-dating of educational promissory notes encourages not only a quantitative inflation of the certifying papers but also a disregard of the job market, which has prompted a proliferation of non-vocational courses, since these, as a general rule, cost less than more technical courses, and therefore, permit the issue of promissory notes most cheaply.

This process stimulates, and is stimulated by, another slippery slope of politics: namely, the temptation to buy votes by offering places in the administrative machinery, the clamour for which grows with every increase in the diploma-holding class. A common result of the two processes is to push the size of the administrative machine far beyond what is needed for the performance of its useful functions, often to the point where the productive economy is crushed under the burden. A vicious circle thus generated was the main cause of the collapse of constitutional government in Uruguay, Chile and Argentina.

Once the administrative and educational machines attain a certain size, their personnel acquires a weight in the electoral process additional to its pull as a bureaucratic pressure group, and thus becomes more able to influence policies to suit its vested interests. These interests, however, are often pursued in a short-sighted or even self-destructive manner, as a numerical proliferation of personnel

* *The Prospect of a Revolution in the USA.*

(particularly when accompanied by a crushing of the productive sector) must cause a lowering of their average income and status. Moreover, the overproduction and the consequent unemployment of graduates seldom fails to produce ferment and disorder which can make life very unpleasant even for the highest dignitaries, as can be seen on the example of Italy, where lawlessness is largely due to the great aggravation since 1968 of the over-production of graduates in law which has been endemic in Italy for decades.

The Vested Interests of the Complex

To understand the impact of the bureaucratic-educational complex on educational policy we must bear in mind the divergence between the interests of teachers and administrators. In almost every occupation there is a tension between the purely economic motive – the desire to get most money for least work – and the satisfactions of craftsmanship – the pride and enjoyment in work well done. The relative strength of these motives depends on individual inclinations, the general mental climate and the nature of the work. There are jobs which are so tedious and unpleasant as to give no room for satisfaction in craftsmanship, but this is not the case with teaching, where contact with developing children elicits in many people the heights of dedication, provided the conditions of work are not thoroughly off-putting. However, in the higher ranks of administration there is no direct contact with the pupils and no opportunity to derive satisfaction from helping young minds to develop, and therefore the motive of craftsmanship is directed towards the functioning of the administrative machine: its smooth running and growth in size. As output comes to be measured by purely quantitative and superficial criteria, concern for quality declines.

Front-line teachers have nothing to gain from an expansion of their numbers beyond what is needed for the job, and may even lose a good deal if a fixed amount of money has to be divided among more recipients. In contrast, growth almost always offers many allurements to the ambitious administrator because it normally entails an increase in the number of hierarchic levels and, therefore, more power and money for those who get to the top. Exempt from the need to deal with pupils, administrators are sheltered from any untoward effects of numerical growth such as discontent and indiscipline bred by impersonality. The raising of the school-leaving age to 16, for example, was not favoured by the majority of teachers who, rightly, feared an aggravation of the difficulty of maintaining order. This reform was pushed through by bureaucrats, educationalists (that is, people who teach teachers and, therefore, have a particularly direct stake in growth) and politicians who, in addition to the motives discussed earlier, found in it a method of concealing unemployment. None of them has to suffer from the consequences of a situation where young ruffians are compelled to stay within the school walls but allowed to rampage around. There are comprehensive schools in Britain where the Heads wrap themselves up in paperwork, do not want to know what is going on in their schools and have abdicated from their responsibility for maintaining order, or preventing vandalism and littering. Instead of protecting the teachers from insults and assaults, they put pressure on them (often backed by veiled threats to career prospects) to hush up the scandals.

Although they protect the teachers well enough in matters of pay and hours of work, and too well in matters of security of tenure, the unions have made few protests against demeaning conditions of work in many secondary schools, which have made teaching there into the most degraded of all occupations in Britain today (as it has become even earlier in the United States) – in no other job is the worker expected to endure constant insults and catcalls and threats of physical violence. We can understand this turning of a blind eye to such an essential aspect of conditions of work if we bear in mind that the union's functionaries and politicians do not themselves have to suffer. Their own interests are vested only in the size of their membership and the amount of money their members earn, because on that depends how much the union may receive. From this point of view, it is worth while fighting for shorter hours, or higher staff-pupil ratios, as this may entail engaging more people to do the work. In contrast, protests about deterioration of work conditions, which have resulted from stuffing too many unwilling inmates between the school walls, might elicit a response that the total size of the machine ought to be reduced – which would be against the interests of the union bureaucracy. Equally against their interests would be a splitting up of unmanageably large schools (where the difficulty of maintaining order is largely due to size and anonymity) because in smaller units (as is also the case in industry) there is usually more team spirit and harmony between the hierarchic levels, which might reduce the power of the union leaders.

The link between the financial and power-political interests of the union politicians and the quality of education is negative rather than positive, because the less efficient it becomes, the more of it will often be given. For example, the larger the number of children who do not learn to read in primary schools, the ampler must be the provision of remedial teaching – which means a larger number of potential members of the union. This inverse relationship has helped to push security of tenure to absurd lengths. It is clear that rank and file members have an interest in protecting their jobs. Nevertheless, it does not lie in their interest to push this principle so far that even the most negligent and incompetent among them do not have to worry about the danger of dismissal, because such people not only undermine the reputation of the profession but also impose an additional burden on their colleagues. Too little security of tenure in the public services, where the worth of the work is difficult to assess impartially because of the lack of objective criteria like the profit or the volume of sales, leads to cut-throat politicking which distracts everybody from doing their jobs properly. But there ought to be arrangements for removing people whose negligence or incompetence are beyond dispute. This applies especially to people in positions of administrative authority.

The Postponement of Learning

The bluff about a better chance in life automatically flowing from a longer stay in a school together with the deterioration in the efficiency of teaching has led to a curious and massive postponement of learning. This has reached its most extreme forms in the USA and Canada, where not only the secondary schools (as in Britain), but also the universities, provide remedial classes in reading. Many postgraduate students are taught things they ought to have learnt in the early years of a secondary school. American education is much more varied than the British, and on every level there are institutions ranging from excellent to abysmal, but a very large part of the population learns next to nothing between the elementary school, where they learn to read, write and count, and the graduate school where they have to start studying seriously. Only a very rich country can survive such colossal waste. When Britain catches up with America in this respect, we shall be well on the way to bankruptcy.

The postponement of learning serves the short-term interests of the bureaucratic educational complex because it prompts the growth of the "throughput" and of the input of money and personnel, especially in administration. More time in total has to be spent on teaching because there are many skills which a 10-year-old can learn much more quickly than a 20-year-old. Expenditure per hour is also higher in consequence of the tradition of paying teachers in the tertiary institutions more than in the primary.

One of the most serious consequences of the postponement of learning is a massive shift of personnel to the level of incompetence; large numbers of people who would be very useful as straight teachers – transmitters of existing knowledge – are put into positions where they are expected to make contributions to knowledge, which is beyond their ability, while the tasks which they could fitly discharge are handed over mostly to deadbeats who cannot teach well (especially the abler adolescents) because they don't know enough, and whose boring teaching aggravates the existing impudence of the pupils. Meanwhile, most of those who are given so much time to do research cannot think of anything new but, being obliged to write and publish for the sake of keeping their jobs or a promotion, pollute literature with inept scribbles. Realizing that they know little more than their students, many teachers go in for a backslapping, first-names palliness and (especially in the soft subjects) assume the role of entertainers. The most extreme manifestations of these phenomena can, of course, be found in America, but in Britain we were catching up fast until the lack of money put a stop to the denuding of schools of talent by the universities.

The subordination of educational policy to the vested interests of the bureaucratic-educational complex explains the paradox of the eagerness of the apostles of permissiveness to enlist the help of the police in bringing unwilling pupils to school. One can hardly blame adolescents for being obstreperous when they are taught subjects which they find not only difficult and uninteresting but also of no use. Teaching a foreign language to people who can hardly read their own amounts to using them to provide employment for teachers and educational administrators. Adolescents at the lower end of the range of intelligence, who will be doing unskilled and repetitive jobs, cannot be expected to be keen on learning subjects unrelated to their life and work without any of the prospective rewards which spur candidates for more interesting and lucrative occupations. There has never been a time when the majority of pupils or students studied abstruse subjects for the fun of it. Furthermore, many of the subjects which people preparing for the more interesting professions have to study are unrelated to their future work, and function as mere endurance tests or hurdles. In the past they also served the purpose of excluding from competition people who could not afford the time or the tuition fees; the requirement of Latin, for example, kept the civil service and the older universities out of the reach of the offspring of the lower classes. Schools would have to offer young candidates for unintellectual jobs something they would find useful in order to persuade them to stay at school voluntarily. This would require effort, some imagination, willingness to break with the old routine and a retraining in more practical subjects of some teachers. There would also be the risk that customers would not want what was on offer. It is easier to cover up inertia by empty phrases about equality.

One of the indications that recent extensions of schooling in Britain were due more to the expansionism of the bureaucratic-educational complex than a genuine quest for equality of classes, is the step-motherly treatment of students of practical subjects in technical colleges in comparison with those who study for a degree. Why should a degree student of fine art, sociology, English literature or history be entitled (subject to the parental means test) to a grant which covers maintenance as well as the fees, books and even the subscription to the union, while one who studies agriculture, engineering or catering for a Higher National Diploma can only get a partial grant if the parents are very poor? Although this discrimination against work-oriented courses fits very well under the heading of class injustice, none of the ardent preachers of equality has protested against it.

Many features of higher education can also be explained as stemming from indifference to the quality of the output and the exclusive concern with a smooth flow of throughput. One of them is the allocation of funds on the basis of the criterion of demand for places. This may appear sound economic sense so long as one does not ask what "demand" means. This concept has an economic meaning when goods or services are produced for a market, and consumers pay for them. Students at British universities do not pay for teaching, but are paid for consuming it. In subjects which are not needed for any particular type of work but, at most, constitute a very vague preparation for entering the bureaucracy, the students have no economic incentive for wishing to learn much, and are only interested in getting a degree with least work, though preferably with good grades. As the latter depend on the examiners, students – especially during the euphoric early 1970s – put pressure on them to lower the requirements. This is perfectly rational behaviour given that the value of a degree as a passport to bureaucratic employment depends only on its class and is unrelated to the amount of knowledge acquired.

In view of the shortage of candidates who are able as well as keen, numerical growth (and lately even the sheer maintenance of numbers) called for a lowering of standards. To overcome the resistance of a few unworldly academics, various universities have set up special procedures for revising the verdicts of examiners and deterring them from marking too harshly. In some places there are appeal procedures which amount to putting the chairman of the examiners in the dock where he can be cross-examined by the complaining examinee and has to justify his and his colleagues' decision to a committee which may consist of people who know nothing about the subject but, nonetheless, have the power to overrule examiners and raise marks. You will notice how different this procedure is from an appeal in a court of law, where there is no question of putting the judge of the lower instance in the dock, where the entire evidence is examined anew and the appellant must take the risk of an even more unfavourable outcome.

Red Tape and Dud Certificates

Novelties of the kind described could not perhaps have been introduced without

previous changes in the internal balance of power in favour of full time administrators and academics who are such in fact and intellectuals only nominally – that is,
people who are concerned mainly with the smoothness of throughput and
oriented towards purely quantitative criteria – and at the expense of the authority
of those who have a personal stake in the state of their subject. An important factor
in this change is the self-reinforcing momentum of bureaucratization; as
forms, formalities, committee meetings and procedures multiply, it becomes
increasingly difficult to combine an administrative function with intellectual
productivity. The growth in size of universities and departments is an important
factor here.

The effects of pseudo-democratization have also played an important part in this
process. In the name of wider participation in governing universities, senates and
faculty boards were so enlarged that constructive discussion became almost
impossible and they sunk to the role of mere rubber-stamping machines while real
decision-making necessarily fell into even fewer hands. From being communities
of scholars governed by professiorial oligarchies, British universities moved
towards a flaccid managerial structure where a (usually rather mild) autocracy or
narrow oligarchy at the top is combined with anarchic democracy at the bottom.
Important aspects of this trend towards a combination of bureaucracy with (partly
genuine and anarchic but partly pseudo) democracy are new arrangements about
the headships of the departments in the redbrick universities; under the old system
these remained in the hands of the academically most senior member, which
meant that authority went with presumed eminence in the subject. Now the
principle has been adopted in most places that to lead or chair a department, one
needs no distinction in the subject. Various systems have been adopted; in some
places there is a rotation, either general or restricted to senior members, in others
heads or chairmen are elected by the teaching staff or appointed through a rather
occult procedure of consultations with the vice-chancellor. In some places these
arrangements do not work badly because everybody involved is reasonable. In
others bickering and intrigues consume much of the time which ought to be
devoted to teaching or research. On the whole, however, there is a steady trend
towards an increasingly bureaucratized system where more and more time is
spent on formalities, procedures and internal politics at the expense of the
functions which are invoked to justify the intake of the taxpayers' money.

The transition from professorial oligarchy to bureaucratized semi-democracy
was prepared by the new method of fixing salaries of professors and chief administrative officers introduced in the middle 1960s. Previously their salaries were fixed
and published. Now they are surrounded by secrecy, fixed by a tiny committee
without any publicly declared objective criteria. It is astonishing that this arrange-
ment was foisted upon the universities against the wishes of most professors,
although it can hardly fail to foster unsavoury practices and is clearly contrary to
the time-honoured principle of constitutional government that (with the inevitable
exception of espionage and counter-espionage) no payments from public funds
should be made in secret. No reasons for the present system were ever given, and
it is difficult to think of any except two. One is that the present method enables some
people to pay themselves more than they would dare if it were publicly known; the
other that it might have been conceived by somebody in the ministry as the means

for muzzling the professors and stifling their opposition to the bureaucratizaton of universities and the lowering of standards.

There are many problems of educational policy where better solutions are difficult to conceive, very costly and exceedingly difficult to implement. The aforementioned abuse, however, could be remedied by a stroke of the pen without any cost to speak of. Another easy to remedy abuse is the subsidizing of the young politicians of the National Union of Students, and providing them with money to spend in political activities, none of which has anything to do with education or student welfare, while many are clearly anti-educational. Not everybody knows that with the connivance of pusillanimous administrators and academics, a *de facto* censorship on the spoken word exists in British universities, not to speak of polytechnics; certain topics are avoided, certain speakers will not be invited or will not dare to come out of fear of disruption, verbal abuse or even violence, by gangs of militants. Since only a minority of students favours these antics, they could be stopped, or at least made more difficult, by the simple expedient of adding to what each student receives the amount which is credited on his behalf to the union, and leaving him to decide whether he wants to pass it on to the union or not. This would force the union organizers to pay more attention to what ordinary students want. The fact that both these nasty, but easily removable, warts have been left untouched, does not inspire much optimism about the prospects of wise solutions of more difficult problems.

Among the harmful applications of misconceptions about democracy, mention must be made of the practice – almost universal in the United States and Canada but, fortunately, less common here – of inviting students to write reports on their lecturers. This might be a good idea in courses where the students are prepared for examinations conducted by an external body, and where they might be seriously concerned about how much they are learning. But where a teacher is also the examiner, the practice in question creates ground for crude barter: you give me good marks and I'll write nice things about you. The disappearance of the distance between the students and the lecturers provides grounds for distrusting examination results. The situation is much worse in the United States and Canada, where usually the same individual who teaches the course is the sole examiner, which gives a wide scope to favouritism, intimidation of the examiners, and bribery with, or semi-extortion of, sexual gratifications: Outside the very "progressive" universities this is still rare in Britain because collective marking and the use of external examiners impede the grossest abuses. Nonetheless, there is too much friendliness between examiners and examinees for the results to be entirely trustworthy. For this reason, I would advocate the handing over of marking entirely to external examiners, accompanied by a rule which would prevent people from examining in the departments whence their own externals come; so that there could be no barter on the lines of 'I'll pass your students if you pass mine'. An objection might be that it would be too expensive to employ so many external examiners. But what of the cost to the country when somebody gets a job on the strength of a phoney degree?

It requires no great imagination to realize that if driving schools also conducted tests, they could easily guarantee the results of their teaching. Yet this kind of criterion has been officially adopted for grading universities and departments. The low failure rate is supposed to indicate efficiency. At post graduate level the Social

Science Research Council also adopts this criterion in judging "excellence". It would seem that there are always enough people who shun strict markers and flock to places where they can get an equivalent degree with less work or ability, and that no official encouragement is needed for this tendency. This is a perfect example of the bureaucratic machine mindlessly grinding on.

Devised as an economy measure, the policy of making the continuation of academic posts depend on the number of students causes more waste as dons try to safeguard their livelihood by recruiting more and more unsuitable students and lowering standards. Whereas an academic who has no students costs the country only what he earns, one who succeeds in filling his class with unsuitable students, or entices young people to study a subject which prepares them only for the dole, causes wasteful expenditure on their grants as well, so that the total will be many times larger, given that in the absence of any cost to the demander, the demand is often not for learning or training but for free places in a holiday camp and, in consequence, it favours soft options, while competition for students on these terms stimulates a softening all round. For example, the teaching of Russian is to be reduced while French is flourishing... not because a degree in French offers better prospects of a career or because the country needs so many specialists in French and even fewer in Russian. The explanation is that Russian is much more difficult for English students. Given that the terms of academic appointments include the duty to conduct research, it would be better to switch academics who have few students entirely to research, than to create the incentive to cause great waste by softening up their courses.

The vested interests of the bureaucratic educational complex also account for the excessive weight given to paper qualifications in the staffing of schools. If we look at the entire range of education, we can see an inverse relationship between the importance of the extent of knowledge of the subject taught and the importance of teaching skill. With students writing doctoral dissertations there is no need to worry about their motivation: those who are not keen should be sent away. It does not matter very much if a supervisor is unlikable or ridiculously eccentric but he must be in the forefront of knowledge if he is to be able to help or judge clever people in their mid-20s who have already spent several years studying the subject.

At the opposite end of the spectrum stands the infants' school where the knowledge to be imparted is so limited that any normal adult possesses it, but learning depends above all on the teacher's personal touch. The specialist knowledge lies not in *what* is taught but in *how* it is taught. Like other practical skills – from salesmanship to piloting an aeroplane – teaching can only be learnt by practice, coupled with good advice in practical situations and the example of good practitioners in action. As so much depends on personality and intuitive ability to establish a good rapport, it is impossible to learn to teach by reading books or listening to lectures, although some bookish knowledge is useful. For this reason policy makers would be well advised to turn a deaf ear to repeated calls for even longer training of teachers of young children. The main motive is the desire of the educationalists to expand their business. An additional reason for thrift in this field is that those who train teachers are not always good at teaching, and there is a consensus among practicing teachers that much of what they learnt at college is of little value in the classroom.

The Ideology of a Flat Earth

Everyday observation as well as systematic psychological studies show striking differences between individuals which cannot be explained by the influence of the environment. Many people doing jobs requiring great knowledge and skill were born and grew up in an environment which in no way prepared them for their later careers. Some of today's most eminent scientists, for instance, are sons of unskilled labourers and spent their childhood in homes without books. Equally common are examples of affluent parents in highly intellectual jobs spending vast sums on private schools and special tutors for their children who, despite willingness and effort, cannot get through secondary education. Even more conclusive evidence of the powerlessness of the environment is provided by the mentally defective children of outstandingly intelligent or even gifted parents. People unacquainted with genetics might imagine that such cases prove the powerlessness of biological heredity, but this is not so. The nature of genetic transmission is such that the re-combination of genes produces great variability despite the fact that, when we take large numbers into account, offspring resemble their parents more than anyone else. This is most obvious with physical traits. Yet there are pundits who deny the inheritance of mental characteristics – which might be excusable if they believed in Divine intervention in this matter, but is completely illogical for people who proclaim their "materialist" outlook. As physiology is continuously discovering more connections between mental states and the processes in the brain, one would have to assume an intervention of a Divine Leveller to imagine that genetic mechanisms which determine the formation of all other organs would leave the brain as a structureless void.

The discoveries of physiology and genetics fit in with the findings of psychologists and psychiatrists. The latter have found genetic factors in a number of diseases of the mind, while the former (concentrating mainly on the ability to think logically, known as general intelligence) have found strong correlations between the scores on intelligence tests of close relatives, depending on the closeness of the relationship. Thus, the correlation is higher for full siblings than for half-siblings; and higher still for identical twins, while for non-identical twins (who genetically are no different from ordinary siblings) it is no higher than for the latter. The correlation is higher between the scores of the children and the average for both parents than with the score of each parent taken separately. The most conclusive evidence of the genetic transmission of ability comes from the studies of cases where personal influence and biological parenthood are clearly separated. Thus scores on intelligence tests of adopted children correlate more highly with the scores of their natural parents (whom they do not know) than with those of their adoptive parents who have brought them up from birth. Likewise, the correlation between the scores of natural siblings separated by adoption is higher than between adoptive siblings brought up together. Even more striking is the much higher correlation between the scores of identical twins separated by adoption and brought up in contrasting environments. Such evidence proves conclusively the genetic transmission of ability, as the only alternative interpretation would be to postulate a constant occurrence of miracles.

It does not follow, of course, that environment is unimportant. Physical as well as mental abilities can be developed by training, or atrophy because of the lack of motivation. They can be diminished or even destroyed by disease, severe undernourishment or absorption of noxious substances; or left dormant because of the lack of opportunity to use them. The complicated interaction of genetic potential with environmental factors makes it very difficult to measure their relative importance. The matter is further complicated by the question of how large is the common factor in different kinds of ability. The general consensus is that musical and artistic abilities must be put apart, but that there is a general ability to draw logical inferences (called "general intelligence") which limits the capacity to learn any skill which involves the performance of logical operations. The ability to reason must be distinguished from the amount of information. The former is fully developed by the time adulthood is reached whereas knowledge can grow with age and experience. It is very difficult, however, to disentangle the two determinants of actual performance. For this reason existing intelligence tests are very imperfect, and must be used with circumspection as rough and fallible indicators. Nonetheless, the evidence gathered with their aid proves beyond doubt the existence of the genetic transmission of the potential for learning skills involving logical reasoning.

After this brief summary (necessary only because of constant attempts to conceal these well established findings) we can consider their implications for the questions of social equality and educational policy. As denials of the genetic transmission of abilities are often coupled with proclamations of concern for justice, let me point out that this coupling is unwarranted. Most of us agree that the healthy ought to pay for the care of the sick, and that the muscular must not push around the lame, regardless of whether the differences between them are due to biological heredity or the environment. Likewise, the existence of genetically determined differences in ability does not entail the right of the clever to outwit the less intelligent and to exploit them. Indeed, the recognition of the part played by biological inheritance ought to lead us to the opposite conclusion: namely the duty of the clever to help the less gifted – having inherited a powerful brain can in no way be represented as a result of personal merit! Neither ethical nor pragmatic arguments can be found for paying people for having a good brain, although it might be sensible to pay more for greater skill, in order to encourage the effort needed for acquiring it. Furthermore, all known cases of exploitation and ill treatment of one group by another have been or are rooted in power and property, and connected with membership of an ethnic unit, class, party or lineage. There is no record of a society where the chasm between the exploiters and the exploited corresponded to the differences in innate intelligence. The spreading of wilful ignorance on the subject of inheritance of abilities cannot, therefore, be due to an honest concern for justice.

A sheer intellectual error would not persist in the face of plain evidence were it not propped by its serviceability for the vested interests of the bureaucratic educational complex. Once you recognize the genetic transmission of ability, you have to admit that there are limits to what education can achieve and that many people cannot profit from protracted schooling. But such an admission destroys a major justification for expanding the educational establishments indefinitely. In contrast, if you recognize no bounds to what education can achieve and blame all human shortcomings on the lack of schooling, you can advocate a limitless growth of educational institutions and claim ever more money for the educators and the ancillary services.

Ignorance of genetics also aids the refusal to recognize another limit to educational expansionism, namely, the scarcity of the talent needed for good teaching. In reality, great care should be taken about the deployment of this scarce resource. But if you accept the myth that good teachers can be manufactured in any required quantity, the sky is the limit for educational expansion. The unfortunate truth is that beyond a point more means worse

The data of genetics in no way entail an approval of the way in which selection was done before "comprehensivization". The old system had several faults: in the first place, eleven is too early for an almost irreversible decision. The age was picked out through a series of coincidences and no good arguments were offered for the choice. The natural dividing line is the onset of adolescence, and for this reason it would be better to keep the children in primary schools until thirteen, perhaps with some internal and provisional streaming. The second, and much graver, fault was the finality of selection: once in a secondary modern school it was almost impossible to be sent to a grammar school later, and difficult to proceed to higher education. The third fault was the low status of the technical courses and their dead end character, which made it very difficult to move from a technical secondary course to a university. Instead of trying to remedy these shortcomings by devising a better system, the reformers abolished selection altogether.

As some of the leading figures among the promoters of comprehensive education were sociologists, it is strange that they have disregarded two of the oldest sociological ideas, already known to Aristotle: one is that growth in size makes the maintenance of order more difficult; and the second that a change in the numerical proportions of the components may alter the entire character of the group. Thus, when the percentage of delinquents rises from five to ten per cent, it may be a gross underestimate to say that is becomes twice as difficult to maintain order. The difference may be between something that is still a school which teaches something and a bedlam. The effects of the abolition of selective secondary schools would not have been so bad had traditional discipline been maintained, because an unselective school where there is fairly good order is an entirely different institution from one where rowdies cannot be restrained. However, in combination with the advent of permissiveness, "comprehensivization" has turned many schools into playgrounds for delinquents.

Even more curious on the part of people who call themselves sociologists was the disregard of the fundamental function of education and the exclusive focussing on one of its by-products – the allocation of differential advantages to individuals. If the latter were its sole important function, we could get rid of any "divisiveness" by abolishing all education: there would then be perfect equality .... at least in education though not in health, strength or looks. We cannot do that because without schools to transmit the vast capital of knowledge, civilization would collapse, and the few survivors would lead the nasty brutish and short lives of cave men. So, whatever else they do, schools must transmit knowledge.

Although the abolition of selection was dressed up as a fight for the rights of the working class, it was more a sop to parents in the educated class who could not afford to pay for private education of their children of average or below ability who were in danger of being sent to secondary moderns. Not that the abolition of the 11+ examination has permanently freed such parents from their quandary: now they don't have to face reality until the children are eighteen.

It is one of the proofs of their hypocrisy that people who spout egalitarian phraseology are terrified at the prospect that their children might have to enter the working class which they profess to love and admire. Honest levellers would do something to remove the stigma and disadvantage still attached to working with one's hands, and would be glad that their children might become honest workers rather than superfluous (and therefore parasitic) bureaucrats or educators.

We can also see a rare display of cant in the trendy sociologists' treatment of what they call "social mobility" – that is the movement of individuals up or down the ladder of wealth and status – which used to be called vertical mobility, to distinguish it from movement between groups of similar income and status. It boils down to a "pie in the sky" demagoguery. There cannot be a society in which everybody is a manager, professor or barrister; the conditions of life and work of blue collar workers will not necessarily be improved by turning as many of their offspring as possible into pen pushers, whose work is often more frustrating than most kinds of simple manual labour. From the standpoint of justice, or by the utilitarian criterion of the greatest happiness of the greatest number, we must condemn a situation where people who have a strong vocation and talent for intellectual work are debarred from education by their parents' poverty; but it is an entirely different matter when people are prodded into uninteresting clerical occupations by making them ashamed of getting their hands dirty.

The Trendy Intellectuals' Contempt for the Workers

Well-heeled trendy lefties tend to talk about the working class in the abstract but do not like to have much to do with blue collar workers in the flesh. One of the most preposterous of their prejudices – which leads them to demand that every fairly intelligent child ought to be educated into "the middle class" – is that manual work requires no brains. Whilst this is true only of the simplest unskilled work, the ability to repair a complicated machine needs much more knowledge and brains than do most office jobs. A good illustration of this snobbery can be found in the writings of Basil Bernstein – a professor of education at the University of London – which are revered as the Gospel by progressive educationists. According to Bernstein, people from "the working class" families cannot say anything complicated or subtle: they speak in what he calls 'a restricted code', whereas "middle class" people speak in 'an elaborated code', which means that they can express many complicated ideas. This is a travesty of the reality and a gratuitous insult to blue collar workers. No doubt people who have gone through long formal education can, on the whole, discuss abstract questions better than those who have left school early, but this is only a statistical generalization. Furthermore, there are people who have inherited or married into money and connections, who speak "posh" and are clearly accepted as belonging to the middle, or even upper, class, but who are not very educated and whose conversation consists entirely of drearily stereotyped small talk – 'a restricted code' if there is one. On the other hand, there are people who work with their hands but can discuss very well all kinds of abstract questions, habitually deal with long chains of logical reasoning in their work and are well acquainted with a large technical terminology. It is the height of academic arrogance to proclaim that what they say must be simple or "restricted" just because their pronunciation and certain turns of phrase sound "common".

To prove his contention, Bernstein reproduces conversations which he must have recorded among people of very low intelligence. Now it is true that you can find such people only among those who work with their hands. You don't have to be a genius to be a barrister or a doctor but you cannot be a moron. If you are, you cannot even become a cashier or ledger clerk. In contrast you can collect rubbish bins or carry suitcases or dig holes with a spade even if you are on the border of mental defect. However, even among the least skilled workers can be found highly intelligent individuals who can talk very well about all sorts of things but who, because of bad luck or lack of motivation or persistence, have never learnt a skill. But in no way can a dimwit become a good craftsman. It is absurd to pass a judgement on the linguistic abilities of a very varied class on the basis of examples collected among its least intelligent members. But there is cunning (no doubt unconscious) in this madness. The progressive educationists are nowadays all environmentalists who believe that there are no innate differences in brain power which depends entirely on education. So the poor devils whose utterances are recorded in Bernstein's books could be all taught to speak like the philosopher Isaiah Berlin if only more money were given to the educationists to train more and better teachers.

Even abstracting from any other possible aims of education, and judging solely from the viewpoint of their professed goal of bringing about equality, the promoters of comprehensive education have failed because, by making nearly all secondary schools in the public sector inferior to all except the very worst private schools, they have reinforced the link between parental income and a child's educational opportunity, which the previous reforms have weakened. So they want to complete their reforms by prohibiting private schools. Apart from being a dangerous curtailment of the rights of citizens, this would amount to a dangerous levelling down, as it would mean that because many people have been condemned to ignorance, therefore everybody must be. From the viewpoint of collective welfare there is a fundamental difference between an advantage gained from having an old school tie and being in an old boys' network, and an advantage obtained by acquiring valid and useful knowledge which other people do not have. The country is more likely to survive if only some people possess extensive knowledge (even if they are selected by parental wealth or a lottery) then if nobody has it.

Conclusions

Various schemes have been devised – vouchers, loans and their combinations – to curtail bureaucratic inertia and waste and to introduce some elements of competition and economic calculation into education. Since other authors have discussed them I shall confine myself to a few suggestions for marginal improvements of the system as it exists at present.

Clearly secondary schools are the weakest link, although at the height of the wave of permissiveness many primary schools were also ceasing to teach and turning themselves into mere playgrounds. However, the authors of the Black Papers won and the tide has been turned. In some of the schools the teaching is better than it has ever been and combines insistence on traditional standards with the sounder among the new ideas about how to stimulate and explain. Since there is not much wrong with primary education there is no need to say much about it except that it would be a good idea to keep in it all children under thirteen.

Although universities have deteriorated slightly, they are still good by international standards. The mild lowering of standards could easily be reversed by a more extensive reliance on external examiners and a recasting of the new-fangled appeals procedures (where they exist) on the model of the courts of law, so that the appellant could have his marks either lowered or raised on the basis of a fresh assessment by a new set of external examiners. A minor, though essential, reform would be the elimination of secret salary fixing, establishment of publicly known criteria of their determination and public verifiability of the amounts. If certain functions, subjects or qualifications call for special rewards these could be incorporated in the published scales, as are special payments to medics.

Tenure should be made more difficult to obtain and given only on the basis of a published and substantial contribution to knowledge. The time limit, however, ought to be extended so that people who undertake ambitious research projects would not be faced with the choice of finishing them hurriedly or losing their jobs. An end should be put to the excesses of job protection which maintain on the payroll people who are indisputably incapable of doing (or unwilling to do) any of the work normally expected. There ought to be more grades and less automatic incrementation. Twenty years ago there were six steps to be scaled by promotion; now there are only three. The efficiency bar for lecturers is mostly treated as a mere formality. I know a case of a lecturer who failed a Ph.D. but passed this bar a year or two later without re-taking the examination.

The greatest danger to the quality of the universities comes not so much from budgetary cuts as such as from these being made on the basis of mindless bureaucratic criteria like "the demand" discussed earlier. It would be better if academics felt that they could safeguard their jobs more effectively by maintaining good standards and doing more and better research than by filling their classes by offers of a good time on the campus.

Tinkering with higher education, however, will not stave off decline without a drastic reform of secondary education. Postponing transfer from primary schools until the age of thirteen would help, as children would live under some order and go on learning two years longer. To judge by existing examples, it would be useful to have the proposed sixth form colleges at the other end because, having power to expel and with no forced inmates between their walls, they could undertake serious teaching and attract staff who would not put up with being insulted, which applies especially to scientists and people with practical skills who have better alternative opportunities. Good schools could retain their sixth forms while the bad have too few candidates for them anyway. Even such reforms would leave the irreducible core of three or four years from thirteen to sixteen.

Only a reintroduction of selective education (preferably with more rational and flexible methods of selection than in the past) can restore to the talented and academically inclined youngsters from poor or uneducated families the educational opportunities which people of this type had when grammar schools still existed.

Whilst there was full employment, good arguments existed for lowering the leaving age to fourteen. In the present circumstances, however, it might be argued that it would be better for even unteachables to stay at school than to roam around towns doing mischief. The trouble is that one thing does not exclude the other. Moreover, the rowdies prevent others from learning anything and contaminate them by bad example. The only solution to the problem of disorder is a much ampler provision of special schools and the extension and more frequent use of the power to expel. Special schools, however, would have to be much more varied and adapted to different kinds of material. Some young recalcitrants respond well to a loving approach by teachers and social workers but others would benefit from firm discipline, backed by short but unpleasant incarcerations and fatigues. Those compelled to stay inside schools must also be compelled to behave properly. On the positive side, however, pupils of below average intelligence ought to have a chance of learning practical skills instead of having thrust upon them high-falutin' stuff which was put on the curricula for their age group when staying at school after fourteen meant travelling on a road to privilege.

Looking at the whole system of education, an essential step is to break the link between the size and remuneration which encourages indiscriminate numerical expansion at the expense of the quality. Heads of large units should not receive higher salaries than those in charge of smaller units of similar kind or level.

It ought not to be beyond human ingenuity to devise, for example, a salary scale for head teachers which would have points for such achievements as raising or maintaining the level of knowledge, curtailing vandalism, reducing delinquency or making the place clean.

For people in charge of routine administration an inverse relationship should be devised between their salaries and the total costs of the operations which they direct; so that they would earn more if they organized the work so as to reduce the costs; whereas as things stand now, the more they spend on their staff and equipment the more they get for themselves.

Another antidote to Parkinsonian macrocephaly would be to fix budgets solely in accordance with the size of the personnel on "the firing line" with a fixed percentage allowed for administration. This might prevent such distortions as the recent reactions to budgetary cuts in education, the health service and the forces, where the personnel engaged in producing the services has been reduced while the number of administrators has remained the same – or even grown.

If we are to continue to have grants for students, the amounts should vary according to the marks obtained. It is indefensible and demoralizing to take away money from the workers to maintain idlers in comfort.

A lot of money is wasted in higher education, though probably less than in the other branches of public employment. However, the waste will be aggravated rather than reduced by bureaucratic centralization which will ensure that more and more time is spent on filling forms, writing reports on what one has done, is doing or intends to do, and less on productive work. One of the crassest examples of counterproductiveness is the attempt to rationalize research at the universities by channelling funds to "centres of excellence". As the criterion of excellence was taken the amount of money which departments and institutes have obtained. No attempt was made to assess the value of what they have produced – admittedly a very difficult task. It would sound incredible were it not true that anyone could have thought that one could economize or improve the effectiveness of the use of money, by rewarding those who have spent most and penalizing those who have spent least. In fact, in humanistic and social studies the value of the product tends to be inversely rather than positively related to the costs of research.

An incredibly misguided attempt to save money is the plan to spend more on making people redundant than it would cost to keep them in employment. This could only be justified in cases where the value of the work is less than zero, so that the individual in question contributes to the country's welfare by doing nothing rather than by working. No attempt has been made to ensure that the plan would apply only to such cases. A more rational way of reducing expenditure could be devised with a little imagination whereas thoughtlessly aggravated bureaucratization will stifle initiative and destroy inventiveness on which the future of the country depends. There is also the political danger (which is very serious in its long-term consequences) of alienating the entire intellectual class by exposing them to random chopping which is related neither to a rational plan of reform nor to individual merit.

In financing the universities a clear distinction ought to be made between preparing young people for work, and other functions which come under the headings of research and diffusion of knowledge. Training must be adapted to the labour market and not to the other functions of the universities; but just as they are paying for museums, parks and historical monuments, taxpayers can maintain a few scholars devoted to such unmarketable pursuits as Greek philology, Byzantine music or philosophy of mathematics. There is no way in which specialists in such subjects could make a living by selling their services. The same is true of theoretical economics, comparative sociology and even many branches of pure science and mathematics. The benefits of such studies can be great but they are so indirect and diffuse that no private company would pay for them. So, if civilization needs them, they must be subsidized from public funds. However, people engaged in such pursuits should not have to justify their existence by luring crowds into studying their unmarketable specialities. On the other hand, it makes no sense to make the students pay (whether from their own pockets or from their grants) towards support of activities which have nothing to do with teaching them.

All these proposals do not amount to much but they would be the first steps towards reversing the recent trends towards general slackness and lethargy covered up by pseudo-egalitarian nonsense. But why should we worry so much about the standards? Why not relax instead of trying to push peoples' noses to the grindstone? The answer is simple. One does not have to be a growth maniac to realize that without a great deal of wealth no civilized and humane way of life can be maintained. An overpopulated island with few natural resources, heavily dependent on imported raw materials and food, cannot avoid catastrophic impoverishment if it does not remain in the forefront of progress, which requires making the utmost use of the available brainpower. If Britain fails in this, it will quickly sink to the level of a cold Haiti when the oil runs out – which is likely to happen within the life expectancy of people who are no longer young.

Evaluating and Monitoring Change in Education: the Role of Research

XI
Educational Myths and Research

Fred Naylor

*Research in the human sciences presents special difficulties;
both on account of its greater complexity and also because its
authors may be 'committed'. The 'committed' need to exercise
extra vigilance if their work is to be unbiased and free from
fallacies. Those whose commitment leads them to deny the
possibility of presenting unbiased findings pose the greatest
threat. Against this background five pieces of educational
research, all directly or indirectly connected with streaming,
are examined. They all contain serious flaws or defects, and it
is shown how – with much help from the communicators – they
have played a major part in creating educational myths.*

Educational Research

It is not to be expected that research in the human sciences can be as precise as that in the physical sciences, or its results so clear cut and unambiguous. Not only is the number of variables so immeasurably greater, but for obvious reasons it is not usually possible – as it is in the physical sciences – to control the conditions experimentally in order to isolate the effects of single variables.

Some uncertainty can be removed by making observations of very large numbers of instances where the effects of extraneous factors can be assumed to be cancelled out. Handling such data calls for skill in the use of statistics, and we all know that many pitfalls lurk here.

Another important difference between research in the two areas is that researchers in education often have clear ideas about how the objects of their investigation – pupils, teachers or systems – *should* behave under more ideal conditions. Researchers in the physical sciences, on the contrary, rarely have occasion to consider the behaviour being observed in any ethical sense. Astronomers, for example, are not in the habit of joining political parties to bring about, or hasten, their scientific predictions; yet this is a real option for social scientists. Whilst there is no reason at all why researchers in education should not also have firm ideas about the need to change the educational system, the dangers of allowing such views to influence their research or colour their findings sometimes prove too great.

It is not surprising, given these methodological and other uncertainties, that the fallacies to which the human mind has always been prone are very generously represented in the interpretation of educational findings. The commonest fallacy of all is probably the *post hoc ergo propter hoc* fallacy which is particularly well illustrated below in case study (c).

One of the most persistent fallacies found in all the social sciences is that proceeding from the failure to distinguish a *correlation* from a *cause*. To illustrate this, consider the geographical distribution of the blood group B phenotype. It is a matter of observation that the proportion of individuals in the total population whose blood group is of the B type gradually increases as one moves eastwards from Western Europe to Central Asia. There is, thus, a correlation between the distribution of blood group B genes and longitude. It would, however, be fatuous to suggest that the longitude at which an individual was born, or lived, *caused* his blood group type.

Yet some sociologists seem guilty of fatuities of this order all the time. They note the correlation between, say, the membership of a group or class, which they define in much the same way as a geographer draws his lines of longitude to delineate areas of the globe, and some quality like IQ in which they are interested and, hey presto, the quality is "caused" by membership of the class. Remove the distinctions – income, status, etc – on which class (the cause) is based and you are bound, they say, to eliminate all the differences of IQ (the effect) currently to be found. All would be born with equal brain power in a classless society! The argument is totally invalid if the causal relationship cannot be established and, of course, it cannot. Moreover, they do this however low the correlation happens to be. Instead of using the correlation as a possible guide to their search for causes, they mistake the shadow for the substance. The cause/correlation fallacy will be encountered in several of the case studies that follow, but may be seen in its purest form in *Social Relations in a Secondary School* by David Hargreaves – see case study (b).

The special difficulties that "committed" researchers face have already been referred to. This leads us on to the "radical" sociologists (or psychologists) who actually see the aim of their craft as being not to understand society, but to change it. For them, the purpose of a scientific concept is not to order the data in such a way as to obtain intellectual clarification and understanding, validated by a demonstrated power of prediction, but to change the attitudes of members of society in a direction that they, the radicals, consider desirable. Most radical sociologists and psychologists are Marxists whose declared aim is to overthrow capitalism by means of their subject and the ideas it generates.[1]

Although I do not suggest that more than a small fraction of educational research is politically motivated, Marxist influence on educational thinking and writing is widespread. There are a large number of semi-Marxists who, while denying being Marxist, admit to some admiration for parts of the creed. In such a climate, the notions of objective truth and value-freedom in the social sciences are weakened. This provides a congenial climate for myth-making.

Despite all the difficulties associated with educational research, it remains an important element in the decision-making process that is essential to education – whether the decisions are those of the administrator dealing with finance and manpower distribution, the school management trying to agree on aims and objectives, or a teacher constructing his teaching syllabus and defining his attitudes to his pupils. Communication of information plays a vital role here.

Teachers – who are usually far too busy to study original research projects in detail – have to rely on educational journalists to communicate the results of new research. Alas, even with the best will in the world, some distortion is inevitable and can have a profound effect in the making of educational myths. This places a particularly heavy responsibility on editors and, unfortunately, accuracy is too often sacrificed for effect. A classic example of headline myth-making is provided by the National Union of Teachers' journal, *The Teacher*, in its issue of 1 February 1974 – see case study (c).

Teachers in training have more time than they ever will have again to familiarize themselves with educational research. Yet, in my experience, the average student who emerges with a B.Ed. degree has a lamentably crude perception of the findings of educational research. In part, this arises from the vast amount of research and the almost bewildering complexity of its findings. But it is also the result of his lack of training in handling the data of education. Training in statistics, logic and scientific method, and philosophy needed for a modicum of understanding of the contribution of educational research to the body of educational ideas is noticeable by its absence. Students are not able to check for themselves the inaccuracies, oversimplified accounts and biased presentations that are to be found in many text books and are, perforce, reduced to the regurgitation of a lot of second hand mumbo jumbo. They are particularly vulnerable to radical sociologists and psychologists who take advantage of the situation by refusing to give credit to those of their students who are acute enough – or bold enough – to recognize that alternative viewpoints might exist. The Marxist influence is so strong in some Open University departments that, had they operated in the USSR in the 1920s they would have been among the first to qualify for inclusion in the "Institute of Red Professorship". This is even more sombre when it is recognized that these same students are often the means by which ideas find their way into schools.

It is because of my conviction that few educationalists – let alone students – find the time to read and examine critically the results of educational research in the original that this article looks closely at a few pieces of research that have played a major part in educational myth-making in teacher training and in the wider world of education. I hope that this will stimulate a more critical examination of many currently accepted ideas in education. All the case studies are connected, directly or indirectly, with streaming.

Case Studies

(a) Pygmalion in the Classroom

Consider two statements:
A.   'It is now an established fact that children will perform to the level expected of them – "the self-fulfilling prophecy". Even more startling perhaps is the fact that children are obliging creatures. Teachers also teach to the expectations of their group and available research has shown that if a teacher thinks he is teaching an "elite" group he will often produce elite results.'
B.   'And research has produced the ideas that children will live up to their teachers' expectations, that is the self-concept. If the child is designated a C or D child then they (*sic*) will live up to the attainment levels that such children exhibit. Should children be streamed they will find in their classes more or less stimulation depending where they are placed. A child who may be wrongly placed in an A stream will – as I have found – live up to the attainment ability of the A stream (but only when they are marginally an A child or conversely a B child).'

These are typical statements on streaming by teachers on B.Ed. in-service training courses. They are usually produced in arguments against streaming, for although the argument on "self-fulfilling prophecy" is really an even-handed one – as the author of B clearly recognized in his last sentence – it is usually considered in this age of rampant egalitarianism to be morally right to put the interests of the less bright before those of the bright child.

It is worth admitting at the outset of any discussion on expectancy and the self-concept the truth that all good teachers, officers, parents and leaders of every other sort have always recognized – without the benefit of any sociological study – that there is always an "England Expects" effect which they can exploit. Many, perhaps most, of us do tend to try to live up or down to others' expectations of us, although it has to be recognized that with some people the effect is sometimes reversed, and the subject's efforts are directed at falsifying the other's expectations. What is wrong with most of the researchers on this effect, and with most of those who have taken up with their alleged findings, is that they so grotesquely exaggerate its scope and force. They pretend, against all sense and knowledge, that children are limitlessly plastic and totally mouldable by the expectations of their elders – even where such expectations barely enter consciousness.

How easy education would be if only the performances of children followed the expectations of teachers – as the authors of these statements seem to believe!

Does the author of statement A realize that the content of his first sentence, although used by him in an argument against streaming, must in logic lead him to reject the idea of forming any expectation of the performance of any child in his class – whether streamed or not – with all the consequences that this implies for planning a suitable programme of work for the child? It is time to ask for the source of such delusions and about the nature of the research on which they are allegedly based.

The main source is the book *Pygmalion in the Classroom* by Rosenthal and Jacobson (Holt, Rinehart and Winston, 1968). In it the authors described some work they had carried out in a 6 grade elementary school – anonymously termed "Oak School" – in California, which streamed its pupils throughout (three streams per grade). The experimenters deceived the teachers into thinking that they had devised a test which could identify the pupils who were "bloomers" – that is at a stage of development where they, whatever their IQ level – could be expected to be undergoing a spurt. It was, in fact, a fairly unfamiliar IQ test in two parts (verbal and reasoning) which gave the experimenters the opportunity of surreptitiously measuring the IQ of the children. They then chose some 20 per cent of them, completely at random, and designated them as "bloomers". They passed this misinformation on to the teachers, but asked them not to divulge it to parents or pupils. A year later they tested the children again with the same, or a similar type of, test in the hope of establishing that the children in the experimental group ("bloomers") had made greater gains in IQ than those in the control group, thereby establishing that the view a teacher has of a child can affect his or her progress, even if it is erroneous – an erroneously favourable view of the child leading to a better performance, and an erroneously unfavourable view leading to a worse performance. They were interested in the relative performances of the experimental and control groups in respect not only of IQ but also of progress in each of the school subjects taken (ten for lower grade children and eleven for upper grade children) measured by the school in its usual way.

In conception the research design was good, although it has been criticized methodologically mainly on account of the smallness of the experimental group.[2] The concern in this study, however, is more with the results obtained, the interpretation of the results and the way the authors presented their findings than with a criticism of the technical faults.

In terms of presentation, the authors assumed from the start the result they were ultimately to arrive at – a real example of the self-fulfilling prophecy. The first five chapters of the book contain no mention of Oak School. They do contain much about the self-fulfilling prophecy – 'it is the preparation for war which leads to war' etc. etc. There is no recognition of the existence of contrary views, for example, in the case of war the view that it was the lack of preparedness by Britain and France that led to the Second World War.

It is not until the seventh chapter, engagingly and romantically entitled "The Magic Children of Galatea" that any evidence is produced at all. By this time the trusting reader has been thoroughly conditioned into an acceptance of the infallibility and ubiquitousness of the self-fulfilling prophecy so that he can, with the authors, pick and choose his way through the evidence. It is strongly reminiscent of the way that Mgr R.A. Knox (in one of his satires) proved that Queen Victoria was the real author of Tennyson's "In Memoriam".

What then were the results of the Oak School experiment? Taking IQ first, we find that overall the control group children gained an average 8.42 IQ points, whereas the experimental children ("bloomers") gained 12.22 points. When the results were broken down by school grade it was found that the so-called advantage of the "magical" children was due largely to the performances of the children in the first two grades. The "magical" children in the fifth and sixth grades were in fact those in the control group – the children whose teachers had been led to expect that they would not bloom - although the effect was very slight. In the third grade the performances of the two groups were absolutely equal, and to complicate the pattern, the "magical" fourth grade pupils were back in the experimental group. The twelve members of this group gained an average of 5.6 IQ points, whereas the 49 members of the control group averaged a 2.2 IQ points gain. It is, perhaps, worth noting that because of the smallness of the sample, a difference of this order (3.4) could be fully accounted for by a freak increase of 40.8 points in the score of one "bloomer". That such freak increases cannot be ruled out can be seen from the case study of the pupil, Mario, who is supposed to have increased his IQ from 133 to 202 (*sic*)!

Even if we interpret these results on the hypotheses that the authors want us to – that pupils whose teachers have an erroneously favourable expectation of their performance do better than the others and that the results found at Oak School obtain generally – we are by the same token bound to conclude that the evidence shows that this effect does not operate for pupils above the fourth grade – i.e. above the age of ten.

The authors broke down the overall results for total IQ gain into gains for Verbal IQ and Reasoning IQ, and also by sex. They found that, in respect of Reasoning IQ, advantages possessed by the experimental group were slightly greater than those obtaining in respect of total IQ but, of course, the "advantages" possessed by the same group in respect of Verbal IQ were correspondingly reduced, and had even become negative ones for grades three to six. By looking at the sexes separately it was observed that in respect of girls and Reasoning IQ, the experimental group was highly advantaged. Conversely, it emerged that in respect of Reasoning IQ the "magical" boys in the experimental group did worse than their counterparts in the control group. It also appeared that the truly "magical" girls for Verbal IQ were those in the control group, not those in the experimental group as expected! The authors tried to adduce ingenious reasons to try to explain away these complex findings. Even when the evidence was against them – in respect of the Reasoning IQ of boys and the Verbal IQ of girls – they turned it to their advantage by the use of such phrases as 'we may say most simply that girls bloomed more in the reasoning sphere of intellectual functioning and boys bloomed more in the verbal sphere of intellectual functioning' (p. 81). The ambiguity in the word "more" is used to conceal the fact that boys did *not* bloom in the Reasoning IQ and girls did *not* bloom in the Verbal IQ. Frequent reference to "blooming" even when the "bloomers" failed to bloom was an essential part of the authors' technique.

It should be noted that whenever a sample is sub-divided it becomes more liable to chance effects as it becomes smaller. The original very small sample of "bloomers" chosen by the authors becomes minute when broken down by sex, track, type of IQ etc. The more this is done the more likely are differences to emerge, but the less likely are they to have any meaning. The authors do invite us to consider chance as a likely explanation for all their findings. They themselves mention odds of 49 to 1 against chance as a likely explanation for all their findings. They also refer to the fact that similar studies in two other schools did not show the effects they found in Oak School, which would, of course, shorten the odds very considerably in favour of the Oak School results being a statistical freak.

The reader familiar with the IQ concept may well ask how it came about that the 255 Oak School pupils in the control group showed an average gain per pupil of 8.42 points IQ over the course of one year, when one would expect no change to occur. Whilst it is true that some of the pupils took the same test, and there is thus a possibility of improvement through practice, there was a whole year interval between the testing. In such circumstances the gains are remarkable. It is surprising, to say the least, that the authors nowhere comment on this – a point that will be taken up later.

The authors, very rightly, point out that a gain in IQ points profits a pupil nothing unless there are accompanying gains in the subjects on the school curriculum. How then did the "bloomers" fare in relation to their fellows when it came to achievement levels in the subjects they took? The short answer is that when the entire school was considered the only one of the eleven subjects in which there was a significant advantage for the 62 "bloomers" was reading. The magnitude of the effect can be gauged from the fact that the "bloomers" averaged only a 0.08 increase in grade point in reading in one year, which is equivalent to two pupils showing respectively an improvement from grade four to two and an improvement from grade four to grade one (on a five-point scale), the other 60 showing no change. It should be noted, however, that children in the control group actually lost an average 0.09 grade points.

I mentioned earlier that the authors nowhere made any comment on the quite remarkable fact that the bulk of pupils tested (the control group) averaged an increase of 8.42 IQ points over a year. This is all the more surprising since they did say in another connection that it was extremely difficult for a child to increase his IQ score by practice on tests. Another remarkable omission in relation to IQ was the failure of the authors to use their data to test the hypothesis that children in lower streams make lower IQ gains than those in higher streams. This is truly astonishing in view of the fact that one of the authors' declared reasons for being in Oak School was that the school administrators were questioning the advisability of ability grouping. Many have since tried to translate the investigation of "blooming" made by Rosenthal and Jacobson into an investigation of the effects of streaming which, of course, is not legitimate. The authors, however, had all the data available to examine the relationship between IQ gains and streaming, but they failed to do so. Why? Could it be that when this was done pupils' IQ gains were seen to be unrelated to streaming, and that this finding could not be accommodated to the thesis that formed the basis of the book? The relationship between IQ gains and streaming, as determined by an examination of data from Oak School obtained by Rosenthal and Jacobson, is shown in the Appendix. It must, however, be remembered that the technical faults that render the authors' main conclusions invalid also invalidate any other conclusions that might be drawn from their data.

We may fairly conclude our examination of this most unfortunate episode in educational research by quoting the opinion of Professor P.E. Vernon:

On the other hand there is no justification whatever for the teacher expectancy effects alleged by Rosenthal and Jacobson (1968). Their experiment purporting to show that children who are reported to teachers as being bright obtain significant IQ gains over the next few months was full of technical faults. And numerous attempts at replication have led to completely negative results (see Elashoff and Snow, 1971).[3]

To the question *Pygmalion in the Classroom?* we must, therefore, follow Shaw's Eliza Doolittle and retort unequivocally, 'Not blooming likely'.

(b) Social Relations in a Secondary School

This piece of research by David H. Hargreaves (Routledge & Kegan Paul, 1967) tops the list of those deployed in educational studies to attack streaming. It is peddled *ad nauseam* and in a mindless way by many educational sociologists. Its subtle blend of observation and ideology proves too much for most students.

The study is merely of one school – "Lumley School", a boys' secondary modern school in the north of England – and is confined to some one hundred boys in four streams in Year 4. Rather curiously the lowest stream – E – of the year group is omitted. Even more curious is one of the reasons given for this omission: 'they tended to form a separate group in terms of friendship choices and the special teachers assigned to them' – just the material one would have thought promising for an investigation of social relations in a streamed school.

Hargreaves fully recognized that the qualities of education and the social relationships found in a school are due to a multiplicity of factors and that the examination of a single school cannot possibly uncover the causes of the conditions found in it. As he puts it: '... and many sociological variables receive scant attention. The study does not intend to test specific hypotheses derived from current theories. Rather, the research is exploratory in nature and focusses broadly on the structure of the informal groups of pupils and the influence of such groups on the educative process... To what extent the work has produced useful results and insights can be judged only from further research' (Introduction).

Social Relations in a Secondary School is not, however, purely a piece of educational research. Hargreaves holds very strong views about society and the state of education in it. Whilst there can be no objection to educational researchers holding strong political beliefs, there is every reason why they should not intrude them into the research itself. Hargreaves used this work to propound his own educational and political beliefs, and in the chapter "Some Implications" suggests changes in the organization of Lumley School and 'other similar schools'. This is a thin disguise for the advocacy of the abolition of streaming generally and cannot possibly be justified by any evidence from Lumley School that Hargreaves presents.

In his view 'the [educational] *status quo* is based on an elitist view of education, whereby children are educated and socialized to fit into certain preconceived social strata of life in the modern world' (p.192). Hargreaves makes no distinction between open elites, where entry is on merit, and closed elites or castes, and appears to hold the very naive view that a society devoid of all professions, with their accompanying status rankings, is a realistic possibility. This is the kind of naivety that Bernard Shaw felt came from 'political five-year-olds' and attacked in the following terms:

I reminded him [...a lad who quite seriously believed that professions would cease to exist in England after the Socialist revolution] that in the most perfect socialist state people would occasionally break their bones and need surgeons to set them, that houses could not be built without craftsmen and master builders nor babies born without midwives: in short, that under Socialism there would be as many crafts, professions, and callings as ever, if not several more.[4]

Hargreaves sees a streamed school as a reflection of a society stratified occupationally and, therefore, abominates it.

It is no surprise to find someone with political views of this nature attempting to explain his findings at Lumley by positing *two* opposed sub-cultures. Conflict models are particularly congenial to those interested in the class war, as witness the Basil Bernstein model of *two* languages among children – the formal code of the middle classes and the restricted code of the working classes. That the class struggle is uppermost in Hargreaves' educational thinking may be deduced from his statement (p. 187) 'It may be true that the working class boy is deprived in our middle-class dominated Grammar Schools, but it is clear that an analogous class warfare is at work in this working class Secondary Modern School'.[5]

Hargreaves' work contains much interesting material on peer-group pressures and the attitudes of teachers. There have always been pressures exerted by the non-academic on the academic, as the history of the term "swot" will testify. But with the gradual breakdown of teacher authority the peer group pressures have intensified to fill the authority vacuum thus created. The widely made observation that the difference between the USA and the USSR is that the peer group pressures in the latter are strongly under the control of adults, whereas in the USA they are not, has relevance to the growing indiscipline problems in our schools.

There is also little doubt that the attitudes of teachers towards low-achieving pupils is of considerable importance. Pupils should be encouraged as much as possible and praised where praise is due. The teacher should expect neither too much, nor too little, and his expectations need to be based on a realistic assessment of the pupil's potential. We can all agree on this, but we need to remember that the existence of peer group pressures directed against school work and the need for teachers to deal with low-achieving pupils have no necessary relationship to streaming. They are found in all schools, whatever the organization adopted, and the low-achievers are always going to present the greater problems.

Hargreaves recognized this himself when he said: 'It is, of course, impossible to assess the extent to which sub-cultural formation is the direct result of streaming' (p. 192), and again, 'the association between low stream and delinquency at Lumley may be as much the result of school and peer group influence on personality development as of the fact that the school tends to select certain personality types into different streams' (p. 184). Since, however, he was not carrying out a comparative study, but simply describing the conditions in one school which happened to be streamed, he was forced to use continually such phrases as 'the low-stream delinquent group', 'the low-stream failures' etc. The effect on the reader is to make what is a correlation appear as a cause. It seems to have had the same effect on the author for, at the expense of logic and consistency, he is forced to exclaim (p. 189):

The most radical way in which the formation of the sub-cultures could be suppressed at Lumley is through the complete abolition of the streaming system.

– this despite his very proper insistence elsewhere that it was *impossible* (my italics) to assess the extent to which sub-cultural formation resulted directly from streaming. Need any more be said about the "findings" of this particular piece of research?

(c) Organization in the Comprehensive School

This dissertation by D. Thompson (University of Leicester, 1974) has all the hall-marks of a myth-making classic; a mass of carefully assembled data, a false interpretation of the data by means of the cause/correlation fallacy – compounded by *post hoc ergo propter hoc*; and distortion by journalists, including a prime example of the myth-making headline.

In 1962, Dr. D. Thompson was appointed headmaster of the Woodlands School, Coventry – a school (the evidence for this will be presented later) that was apparently in the academic doldrums. Dr Thompson seems to have been an outstanding head, who set about transforming the school; by all accounts he was a firm disciplinarian. As a result of – or in the interests of accuracy it is better to say "following" – these changes, the school's external examination results began to show significant improvements.

There are a number of very reasonable hypotheses which could be advanced concerning the upturn in the school's academic fortunes:
(i) the strong direction from the new headmaster in terms of leadership and discipline;
(ii) the change from streaming to mixed ability teaching which he introduced;
(iii) a substantial switch in GCE examination entries from what was commonly supposed to be a "difficult" Examination Board to one that was commonly supposed to be "easy";
(iv) other factors;
or a combination of any of these.

Dr Thompson made no attempt to find the cause of the improvement in the school's examination results, nor was it possible for him to have so done from the evidence he presented. What he demonstrated was that the school's GCE O-level results were significantly better in the years following the changes he introduced – which included the introduction of mixed ability teaching – than they were before. He seems to have assumed that the cause was the introduction of mixed ability teaching – a classic example of the *post hoc ergo propter hoc* fallacy. No doubt modesty forbade him to give due consideration to (i) above as a relevant factor.

Part of the trouble was the difficulty over the use of language the researcher faced in commenting on the data and the correlation he had observed. In the course of his very lenghty commentary, Dr Thompson had, for the sake of variety, to avoid the repetitive use of the phrase 'following the introduction of mixed ability teaching'. He, therefore, introduced such variants as: 'with the introduction of mixed-ability teaching'; 'as a result of introducing mixed ability teaching', 'the abandonment of streaming was accompanied by', 'the adoption of mixed ability teaching led to', 'unstreaming led to', 'the abandonment of streaming produced a significant change' etc. In no time at all the reader is rendered insensitive to the distinction between a temporal connection and a causal one. After meeting scores of such phrases, randomly interwoven, he becomes convinced that the connection is, indeed, a causal one.[6] This, of course, does not excuse the researcher, who should either use more exact language or warn the reader of the danger.

One person who successfully presented the correlation established at Woodlands School as a cause was the Editor of the NUT journal, *The Teacher*, who implied that what he thought had been established at Woodlands obtained everywhere else. In trying to communicate the results of Dr Thompson's research to the busy teachers who were his readers, the Editor was emboldened to proclaim in a single headline: 'Proved: Exam Results are Better without Streaming' (1 February 1974). In fact, all it proved was that the NUT was once again prominent in educational myth-making, in furtherance of its declared political commitment to total, compulsory, unstreamed comprehensivization.

It can properly be argued that all that has been demonstrated so far is that Dr Thompson's research failed to show that the introduction of mixed ability teaching brought about the academic improvement in the school. But is there any evidence to suggest that one or more of the other factors was really responsible?

Evidence to this effect is available, and it comes from the City of Bath Technical School, of which I was headmaster around the time of Dr Thompson's work at the Woodlands School. Comparable figures were available for this school which made it possible to compare the examination performance of the Woodlands School over the ability ranges represented against an external yardstick. (See "A Tale of Two Schools", *Times Educational Supplement*, 24 October 1975.) This comparison showed that the chances of a pupil in this streamed technical school obtaining five or more GCE O-level passes were between two and three times greater than they were for a pupil of comparable VRQ score in the Woodlands School, *after* the examination results had been raised to their highest level.

Whilst wariness is needed in drawing general conclusions from the results of two schools, it is certainly safer than forming judgments on the basis of results from one school. By subjecting the Woodlands examination results to the check of an external yardstick, it would appear that the results were not very special and that they had everything to do with remedying what must have been a very poor position indeed initially, and nothing to do with the organization of pupils for teaching purposes.

It is interesting that no less a personage than Professor J. Eggleston, in his article "Research and the Comprehensives" (*Times Educational Supplement*, 24 January 1975), felt obliged on the evidence of this piece of research to single out the high rate of examination successes of the Woodlands School as a striking variation, in the comprehensive field, deserving special mention. He, therefore, played no small part in creating a mythology around both comprehensive schools and mixed ability teaching.

(d) Streaming in the Primary School

Those who wish to learn about the complexity of educational research should read this book by Joan C. Barker Lunn (NFER Publications, 1970). The author is fully aware of all the pitfalls and, for the most part, has avoided them. It may, therefore, appear churlish to be critical, but in view of the book's widespread influence and the certain fact that the average student is unacquainted with its detailed findings, something needs to be said about it.

It is usually maintained that this research establishes two propositions, first that as far as academic success of primary schools is concerned it does not matter whether schools stream their pupils or adopt non-streaming techniques; secondly, that in the matter of pupil attitudes, non-streaming is better. These propositions need to be carefully examined.

In her comparative study of academic success, J.C. Barker Lunn carried out her researches on two samples of pupils – A and B. Each contained streamed and non-streamed schools carefully matched and, in effect – as she acknowledges – this was equivalent to carrying out two studies simultaneously, since schools were assigned to one or other of the samples on a random basis, matched pairs of schools from the total sample being allocated alternatively to become A or B. This is a common device amongst researchers in the social sciences. Consistent results from both samples provide reassurance about the sampling procedure.

The results obtained with the two samples were startingly different. In sample A, pupils in non-streamed schools made better progress than those in streamed schools; 44 of the comparisons favoured non-streamed schools and only six favoured streamed ones. But, in sample B, it was the pupils in the streamed schools who made the better progress – by 52 to 9 in the number of favourable comparisons made. The author was unable to suggest any reason for this difference, beyond saying that it was due to some unknown factor concerned with the sampling. There seems little doubt that on the basis of the evidence in sample A (or sample B) alone, a researcher would have claimed that a strong case for the superiority of non-streaming – or streaming – had been made, something that should alert us to the difficulties in this field.It seems much more accurate to say that J.C. Barker Lunn's study on the effect of school organization on academic success was totally inconclusive, rather than to say that it demonstrated that school organization makes no difference. It is true, as she herself says, that the latter would have been the conclusion reached if the total sample (A+B) had not been subdivided. But it was, and the startling anomaly obtained revealed the existence of a completely unknown and mysterious factor. In such circumstances it would appear to be wiser to suspend all judgment.

On the question of pupil attitudes, the researcher constructed ten new tests to measure the following attitudes: (i) academic self-image; (ii) anxiety; (iii) social adjustment; (iv) relationship with teacher; (v) importance of doing well; (vi) attitude to school; (vii) interest in school work; (viii) conforming *v.* non-conforming; (ix) attitude to class; (x) other image of class. She concluded that, in general, neither school organization nor teacher type had much effect on the social, emotional or attitudinal development of children of above average ability, but that with children of average and below average ability some differences were observed. With regard to attitudes (v), (ix) and (x), children of average and below average ability held more favourable attitudes in non-streamed schools than in streamed schools. On the other hand, in respect of attitude (i), *boys* of below average ability did better in streamed schools. One other difference relating to school policy on streaming was discovered. This concerned attitude (iv), where it was found that below average ability *boys* did better in non-streamed schools, but only with Type 1 teachers.[7] With Type 2 teachers, they did worse in the non-streamed schools.

The author brings out very clearly the rather patchy nature of the findings on the question of differences in attitudes. Where differences exist they are found in special cases only. There is also little said about the magnitude of the effects found, beyond an indication of the level of statistical significance attaching to the observed differences.

A serious criticism of the researcher – that she introduces value judgments into the reporting and interpretation of the results – can be made in respect of the findings on attitudes. This occurs whenever advantages or disadvantages are claimed. For example, there can be little hope of agreement on what constitutes a reasonable degree of "anxiety in the classroom". Nor is it altogether surprising that pupils become less anxious when taught by "permissive" Type 1 teachers. J.C. Barker Lunn seems to regard this decrease of anxiety as good, but many would not be satisfied with the low level of anxiety found in the classroom of Type 1 teachers. The truth is that the educational world is divided on what pupil attitudes are desirable – as the whole streaming debate shows. Whilst disagreement exists about aims and objectives in education, there can be no objectivity on the subject of the desirability of attitudes. It is possible that the author was reduced to a simplistic terminology – with terms like "good" and "bad", "favourable" and "unfavourable", "advantage" and "disadvantage" – in the face of the desperately difficult task of converting very complex numerical data into generalized statements.

A more serious criticism of the research is that the ten attitudes studied are only a tiny fraction of the attitudes that are normally considered important in education. J.C. Barker Lunn is right to remind us that academic progress is not the only thing that matters in education, but in pointing to the importance of some pupil attitudes she omits a host of others such as honesty, self-discipline, responsibility and the like. Many of these are probably related to school organization and teacher type, but have received no consideration in this study. They would be important factors in making educational decisions about schools.

For all these reasons it can be seen why the two propositions, mentioned at the beginning of this section and which are popularly regarded as the conclusions of the Barker Lunn study, are either false or misleading, or both.

(e) The Heritability of IQ

On no other subject are education students more deserving of sympathy, for on no other subject is the conflict between the two notions of truth – the scientific objectivist and the Marxist – more stark. The poor student hardly knows where to turn when bombarded with the contradictory views of the "experts" on the subject of the heritability of IQ.

Two misconceptions need to be dispelled at the outset. Well-meaning people who try to resolve the heredity/environment issue by claiming that the argument is an artificial one, since the truth is that heredity and environment interact, simply add to the confusion. It is of crucial importance to distinguish between the contributions heredity and environment make in the formation of an individual, and the contributions they make towards the observed differences between individuals in a population. For example, the difference between a blue-eyed and a brown-eyed adult is accounted for entirely by genetic endowment. Yet, in the formation of the blue (or brown)-eyed adult both heredity and environment are at work. The gene for blue (or brown) eyes in an individual's germplasm will never be transformed into a blue (or brown) eye, except by being placed in a favourable environment.

Secondly, one must learn to treat each case on its merits. It is no use coming to the evidence as a committed hereditarian or a committed environmentalist. In some cases, as with eye colour, the heritability works out at 100 per cent. In other cases, such as the native language that an individual adopts, the heritability is 0.0 per cent. Between these two extremes lies a range. Proficiency in one's native language would, in most advanced societies, probably lie near the middle. The essential point is that estimates of heritability can only be made on the basis of the empirical evidence available in each case. They cannot be determined ideologically. Another important fact is that the heritability measure is valid only for the population examined at the time of analysis. For example, the heritability measure for proficiency in the English language amongst the population of this country would depend partly on the nature of the education currently being given. The same is true of the heritability of IQ.

The scientist will stress the necessity of estimating the heritability of IQ by looking at the evidence. He will appreciate that his personal feelings on the matter are totally irrelevant. He may strongly desire, for reasons of his own, that the figure be 100 per cent or 0.0 per cent, but being a good scientist he will strive to ensure that his judgment is not coloured. The Marxist, on the other hand, if he allows his training in dialectical materialism to dictate his position, will not judge the matter solely on the evidence but will recognize that his values and feelings will be directed towards the realization of a Marxist society. He will judge the heritability of IQ, which is bound to have political implications, not objectively, but morally. He will interpret what evidence there is in this direction and ignore any to the contrary. It would be inconceivable to him that the findings of any particular science might be contrary to what could be deduced from a conception of nature that is both dialectical and material. His actions may be conscious, but if he is well practised it is more likely that they would be done without knowing.

To illustrate the point, Madan Sarup, Lecturer in Sociology at Goldsmith's College, London University, defines in his book *Marxism and Education* a very progressive teacher as one who believes, among other things, that intelligence is not determined by heredity (differential educational performance being due to differences in motivation).[8] It is clear that "very progressive teacher" is a label attached by Sarup to those with a particular philosophy and not to those who have closely examined any evidence on the subject (or any other subject for that matter).

Again, Professor Steven Rose of the Open University claimed in a joint article[9] with Professor H.J. Eysenck in the *New Scientist* (they advanced opposing views) that the question 'how much does genetics (*sic*)[10] and how much does environment contribute to differences in intelligence between ethnic or social groups?' is on a par with 'How much does Camembert and how much does Stilton contribute to the composition of the moon?' Having said that science can have nothing to say on this question, he goes on to consider the differences in IQ measures between different social groups. He has no hesitation in answering what he has just described as a meaningless question, and categorically states that the reasons for the IQ differences must be sought in environmental differences – 'discrepant cultures, languages and social experiences within *xenophobic* societies' (my italics).

The New Scientist article arose out of a pamphlet on Race by Rose and Richardson for the NUT. (See also the article on the NUT on page 119 for more on this.) It claimed to be a teacher's 'guide to the facts and issues' and was subsequently criticized by Professor Eysenck as being biased and factually incorrect. The authors quoted from a 1950 UNESCO statement on Race which was based on the thinking of a group of scientists who had examined the scientific evidence for the existence of innate differences between races – despite the fact that Professor Rose says he does not think this and similar questions are meaningful. My correspondence with Professor Rose revealed that he and Richardson were unaware that the 1950 statement had been withdrawn by UNESCO and replaced by a new statement in 1951.[11] This new statement spoke of the cultural factor being the major factor accounting for differences between people or groups, the genetic factor, by implication, being a minor one. All the scientists evidently thought the question a meaningful one and tried to answer it by considering the scientific evidence. They did not try to link the question of differences between races with that of differences between socio-economic groups. Rose and Richardson did just that for the NUT, evidently not considering that there were two distinct issues and, apparently, making up their minds before looking at any evidence, that differences of IQ between races and between socio-economic groups are to be accounted for wholly by environmental factors.

The great difficulty in doing controlled experiments with human populations makes determining the heritability of IQ a daunting task. But it is possible, through the study of identical twins, siblings, foster children and the like, to isolate the genetic and environmental factors in turn and so determine the relative contributions of each to IQ differences. The problem is capable of scientific solution, although the statistical techniques required are very sophisticated.

Professor Philip Vernon, who has a very high reputation in the field of intelligence studies, recently reviewed all the evidence on this subject in an article in the *British Journal of Educational Psychology*.[12] From his examination of a large number of independent investigations he concluded that there was a fairly close convergence on a genetic percentage of around 65, environmental 23 and covariance 12. The (Genetic-Environmental) covariance is a term that refers to the interaction between heredity and environment, in the sense that intelligent parents, who pass on superior genes to their offspring, are also likely to provide them with a more stimulating environment. So long as we continue to live in a society where children are not taken away from their parents at birth, such covariance factors can for all practical purposes be counted as part of heredity. What it all amounts to is that there is a large genetic component to differences in IQ – the so-called Intelligence A of Hebb. No intelligence test so far devised, however, has been capable of eliminating environmental influences and thereby providing a direct measure of Intelligence A. No doubt the search for tests which more closely approach this ideal will continue.

Why is the heredity/environment issue so important in education? If it were true that differences of IQ (and differences in all the personal qualities, too, that make for success in education) were determined solely by the environment, then it would be possible to move gradually towards a greater equality of educational results (outcome) by gradually eliminating inequalities in the environment. It should be noted, however, that complete equality of outcome could not be attained without complete equality of the environment, with all that this would entail.

If, on the other hand, differences of IQ and of other factors leading to educational success are due in some measure to genetic endowment then, given the genetic variety we know to exist, it would be impossible to achieve equality of educational outcome except by the introduction of a handicapping system. The severity of the handicapping needed would depend on the extent to which differences of IQ etc are determined genetically. Such a system would interfere with the right each individual possesses to have an equal opportunity for self-development. Those who think along these lines stop short of embracing the ideal of equality of result and prefer, instead, equality of opportunity.

The conflict between those who believe in the educational goal of equality of opportunity, and those who believe in equality of educational results, is no academic one. It is a real struggle to determine the whole purpose and direction of education.[13] The educational battle is a battle over the kind of society we wish Britain to be. The tragedy that results from basing "progressive" or Utopian plans on a false view of nature can be seen around us in the totalitarian Marxist states where – far from withering away – the state has had to extend its grip in every sphere of life. This is why it is so important that educational research on the heritability of IQ should be objective, and why those who are concerned with decision-making should have a good understanding of the issues involved.

Appendix

The data from Rosenthal and Jacobson's *Pygmalion in the Classroom*, examined for the effects of streaming on IQ.

GAINS IN TOTAL IQ's WITHIN EIGHTEEN CLASSROOMS (CONTROL AND EXPERIMENTAL GROUPS COMBINED) – derived from Tables A-7 and A-4

Class	N	Mean Gain	% Gain[a]	Class	N	Mean Gain	% Gain	Class	N	Mean Gain	% Gain
1A	18	7.39	7.11	3A	20	12.55	12.35	5A	21	18.81	17.09
1B	19	15.42	17.33	3B	16	0.44	0.43	5B	0[b]	–	–
1C	18	19.00	25.60	3C	18	0.72	0.74	5C	14	15.43	18.30
2A	25	8.64	8.03	4A	23	7.18	5.79	6A	24	14.33	13.17
2B	17	9.35	10.23	4B	19	(–0.47	–0.46)	6B	17	8.59	8.76
2C	17	8.94	11.22	4C	19	0.89	0.98	6C	15	6.73	8.08

a Figures in this column are the gains in total IQ, expressed as a percentage of the mean IQ of the pupils tested in each class. The actual gains are shown in the preceding column. Since a gain of ten points is a more significant gain for a pupil of low IQ than it is for a pupil of high IQ it is the percentage gains in this column which are used in the comparisons of the A, B and C streams.

b Through examiner error only the verbal subtest was administered.

THE STREAMS COMPARED: MAGNITUDE OF ADVANTAGES

YEAR 1   C > B > A
YEAR 2   C > B > A

YEAR 3   A > C > B
YEAR 4   A > C > B
YEAR 5   C > A
YEAR 6   A > B > C

Without knowing the reliability of the IQ test used it is not possible to specify the significance of these differences in any detail. In a general way it is clear that if significant advantages accrue to A streams in certain year groups, then they also accrue to C streams in other year groups.

THE STREAMS COMPARED OVERALL

THE AVERAGE % GAIN FOR ALL A STREAM PUPILS 10.6
THE AVERAGE % GAIN FOR ALL B STREAM PUPILS 7.4
THE AVERAGE % GAIN FOR ALL C STREAM PUPILS 10.5

If these figures show anything, they suggest that A stream and C stream pupils are advantaged to the same extent. Certainly C stream pupils are not disadvantaged with respect to B stream pupils – a conclusion which is also reached if actual gains, and not percentage gains, are used in the comparison.

Notes

1. Colfax, J.D. and Roach, J.L., *Radical Sociology* (Basic Books, New York, London, 1971).
2. Only one or two pupils were in the experimental group in some classes.
3. Vernon, P.E., "Intelligence Testing, and the Nature/Nurture Debate, 1928-78: What Next?", *British Journal of Educational Psychology* 49, pp. 1-14 (1979), invited address: Scottish Council for Research in Education.
4. Shaw, G.B., "The Proposed Abolition of Classes", *Everybody's Political What's What?* (Constable, 1944).
5. The extraordinary notion that the working class boy is disadvantaged by the state grammar school is used by leftwingers in their attack on grammar schools. The author recalls a visit by a team of investigators from the BBC to a northern grammar school in which he taught in the 1960s to seek evidence to support this theory. Discovering that the evidence supported the contrary position, the BBC team decided to have no programme rather than one which pointed to an ideologically uncongenial truth.

    The belief that grammar schools are middle-class-dominated was exposed as absurd by hard evidence in the Crowther report, *15 to 18* (1959), in which the results of four independent surveys showed that the percentage of *academic* sixth formers in direct grant and maintained grammar schools coming from the lower three (of five) socio-economic groups was somewhere between 41 per cent and 57 per cent (the latter in Yorkshire grammar schools) (Vol. I, p. 230).
6. This happens in most research of this kind, and explains the ease with which the *post hoc ergo propter hoc* trap is sprung.
7. Type 1 teachers, amongst other things, believed in non-streaming, were

"permissive", tolerant of noise and talking in the classroom (p. 52). Type 2 teachers were the opposite.

8. In view of the other case studies, Sarup's second criterion for identifying the very progressive teacher is interesting: '[a belief that] Streaming maintains social divisions as it favours middle-class children. It fixes the expectations of teachers and pupils and is likely to lower motivation. (Besides, the criteria of stream allocation have been discredited anyway.)'

9. *New Scientist*, "Race, intelligence and education", 15 March 1979.

10. Surely he means "genes" not "genetics".

11. There were so many reservations even about the 1951 agreed statement that UNESCO published a book, *The Race Concept; Results of an Inquiry* (Paris, 1952), setting out the background to the statement and detailing the reservations. This book should be obligatory reading for all interested in the race question.

12. See (3) above.

13. See Torsten Husén, *Social Influences on Educational Attainment* (OECD, 1975), for an account of this struggle.

XII

Cause for Concern: Research on Progress in Secondary Schools

Caroline Cox and John Marks

The National Children's Bureau (NCB) report Progress in Secondary Schools, *published in July 1980, was hailed by the press and by Labour politicans as a success story for the comprehensives. It is nothing of the kind. The report is full of dubious data – for example, reading attainment at 16 was measured using the same test as had been used at 11 – and the data are consistently interpreted in a partisan pro-comprehensive way. What the results actually show is that on attainment in reading and maths, truancy, behaviour in school and parental satisfaction, the comprehensives do badly in comparison with the grammar and secondary modern schools which they replaced. Even more worrying, the longer the schools have been comprehensive, the worse they are.*

In July 1980 a Report[1] by the National Children's Bureau (NCB) hit the headlines: "*Clever Children Do As Well In Comprehensives As In Grammar Schools*"; "*Full Marks! Comprehensive Schools Come Out Top Of The Class For Bright Youngsters*"; "*Report Explodes Comprehensive Myth*".

These claims are misleading. In September 1980 we published a report *Real Concern*[2] which sought, as we saw it, to put the record straight. Our report showed, we thought, that (a) the research produced by the NCB was "*No Vindication Of Comprehensive Schooling. Rather, The Findings Are An Indictment Of The Comprehensive System*" and (b) the research presented no significant evidence about the academic attainments of clever children.

The report by the NCB seemed to us to be full of data of whose value we were sceptical and to have drawn misleading conclusions. Yet it has already been widely quoted (see, for example, *Woman's Own*, 9 August 1980). So it is desirable to expose its flaws.

What is Wrong with the Research?

a) *Data of which we are sceptical*
    The report does not give the original results of its survey. All the published data are "adjusted" yet no information is given to show how or by how much; the statistical appendix merely provides formulae empty of content. When asked whether the data would be made available, a spokesman of the NCB said that it would not be, since to publish the actual figures would be 'so misleading as to be dangerous'. This paternalism is surely an insult to the public. Publicly funded researchers should be required to publish data of public interest (with appropriate explanation).

(b) *The Tests of Educational Attainment*
    These seemed to us to be seriously inadequate, especially for bright children. 'Reading attainment at 16 was measured using the same reading test as had been used to measure attainment at age 11'. Miss Jane Steedman admitted to a "ceiling effect" on this test but only mentioned this in her main report and not in the summary report *Concern*, the publication which was intended for general reading. *Concern* indeed contains *no information of any kind* about the reading and mathematics tests. Nor did the main report discuss the problems which the "ceiling effect" must have caused, particularly in assessing the progress of the more able pupils. This seemed a curious omission since "ceiling effects" in this type of reading test are well known. A study by the National Foundation for Educational Research,[3] published in 1972, used a parallel reading test and found it too easy for the 'brighter *15-year-olds*, with a consequence that their test scores do not adequately reflect their reading comprehension ability'. How much worse must this "ceiling effect" be for the 16-year-olds in the research of the NCB? Also, the mathematics test was originally designed for comprehensive school leavers aged 15 and yet was used for 16-year-olds from all types of school with no adjustment for the extra year's schooling. This test too must have limited value for able 16-year-olds.

    So both the reading and mathematics tests are 'totally unsuitable for measuring the academic progress of the more able pupils. The reading test is virtually useless for this purpose and the mathematics tests is unsatisfactory'. Yet these tests – and the reading test in particular – were the sole basis of the alleged "success story" for the comprehensives – that bright children do as ✳ well in comprehensives as in grammar schools. ✳ NOT TRUE

(c) *Interpretation of Data*

The Report by the NCB seemed consistently partisan: no credit was ever given to the achievements of secondary modern and grammar schools. The findings which reflected adversely on comprehensives were explained away. For example, parental dissatisfaction is highest for comprehensives – so the report made a virtue of parental dissatisfaction. (Cold comfort for parents who may be acutely anxious about their children's schooling!)

What is Wrong with our Secondary Schools?

We are not "anti-comprehensive" and we recognize that there are many good comprehensive schools. Yet the data in the Report by the NCB 'should be seen as *deeply worrying* for everyone concerned with comprehensive schools'. We summarize some of these data. Remember that all these results have been "adjusted" to allow for differences in intake and in social class.

(a) The educational results for comprehensives are worse than for pupils in the system which they replaced: the combination of grammar and secondary modern schools. In reading there was little difference between grammar and comprehensive schools for pupils in the top fifth ability group. The "ceiling effect" at work, perhaps? For the next three-fifths – 60 per cent of the sample – the results in grammar schools were better than those in comprehensives. This was particularly disturbing because, by definition, the middle three-fifths represent the "average" children who will be the majority – and, clearly, they under achieve in comprehensive schools. But there was little difference between the performance of the vast majority of pupils in secondary modern and comprehensive schools.

In mathematics, grammar school pupils had much the highest score in all the top four ability groups, even after the scores have been "adjusted", while there was little difference between pupils from secondary modern and comprehensive schools.

(b) On such matters as truancy, school behaviour and parental satisfaction, comprehensives consistently have the worst records – consistently worse than secondary modern schools, although the intakes of the secondary modern schools were more "disadvantaged" than their counterparts in the comprehensives. Given this, and the fact that their educational performance was scarcely very different from that of the comprehensives, the report by the NCB could have been interpreted as a success story for the secondary modern schools. But neither the researcher nor the press chose to highlight this.

Truancy: pupils in the top ability group in comprehensives were six times more likely to play truant than those in the grammar and secondary modern schools together.

Behaviour: 'The behaviour of pupils in comprehensive schools was significantly worse that that of pupils in grammar and secondary moderns taken together'.

Parental satisfaction: parents with pupils in comprehensives were nearly twice as likely to be dissatisfied with their children's schooling as were parents of grammar and secondary modern pupils. In the words of the report itself, 'for those in the top fifth of ability test score at eleven, the ones in grammar schools were more than three times as likely to have "satisfied" parents'.

(c) Early=Worst: a particularly worrying trend is that those comprehensives which had been in existence longest (pre-1966, that is), came out worst on educational attainment, truancy, behaviour and parental satisfaction. On behaviour, in the words of the report of the NCB: 'Those in grammar and secondary moderns seemed to be rated more favourably; the average for them after allowing for other factors was the lowest, ... and well below that for those in 1965-or-earlier comprehensives, for whom the highest "disturbed behaviour" score appeared ... Whatever the source of these behaviour ratings, teachers in the older comprehensives were most critical of the behaviour of their charges, and the combination of teachers in the secondary moderns and grammars seemed least likely to regard their pupils as having signs of disturbance, maladjustment or distress. This is in accord with the findings for truancy and staying away from school, in that those in the grammar-modern combination appear, as a group, "better" behaved, or "better" adjusted to school'.

There is thus a consistent pattern of "Early = Worst" even after the results have been adjusted to allow for differences in intake. So Miss Jane Steedman's 'message to the 85 per cent of children who now go to comprehensive schools ... that there is no reason to be downhearted' (*Daily Telegraph*, 15 July 1980) would not seem to follow logically from her own data.

Conclusions

(a) This NCB Report has already been used by Mrs Shirley Williams and others to vindicate the policy of comprehensivization which had led to 85 per cent of the nation's children now being in comprehensive schools;

(b) There is, however, no *justification* for this policy in the findings of the NCB Report;

(c) The pattern of "Early = Worst" raises serious questions: could more recent schools still be benefiting from the legacy of pre-comprehensive traditions and practices? Is there perhaps a tendency towards a deterioration in educational standards, truancy and behaviour which is reflected in parental dissatisfaction? If so, the prospects for the children in our comprehensive schools are bleak.

Recommendations

(a) The full facts (i.e. the original data) should be published so that the public can judge for themselves and not have them filtered through a statistical smokescreen. It is also essential that future research reports should contain concise and comprehensible summaries of original data. Since the current research by the NCB was so inadequate in this respect, the Department of Education and Science should insist on such summaries in the continuation study now being carried out (also by the NCB) of the public examination results for the same cohort of children as were studied in *Progress in Secondary Schools*.[4]

(b) Further plans to impose a monolithic system of comprehensive schooling should be resisted.

(c) Encouragement should also be given to policies which promote diversity of types of school; more parental choice; and more information about schools on which to base that choice.

(d) Future educational research, particularly when it is funded by public bodies such as the DES, should be better planned, executed, presented and supervised. We think it little less than a disgrace that this research by the NCB has been condoned and commended by no less than Professor A. Halsey (Chairman of the Advisory Group to the Secretary of State for Education and Science which supervised the NCB research): 'The bureau team has given us evidence which far surpasses the quality of that on which policy debate over comprehensives has hitherto been conducted.'

(e) The record must be put straight if the myths created by the Report by the NCB are not to become received truth and used as the basis for education policy for years to come. To build policy on such foundations of sand would be most unwise.

Presentation to the Media and the Public Debate

Educational research can have important implications for public policy. Indeed, according to Mrs Shirley Williams, the research by the NCB was funded for this reason. So it is important for research findings to be presented to the media, to the public and to policy makers as clearly and as openly as possible. In this case, the media had already given wide publicity to a leak[5] about the findings of the NCB which were claimed to show that 'bright children do just as well in comprehensives as in grammar schools'. So it was rather unfortunate that the NCB's own summary of their research in their journal *Concern* – all that was sent to the NCB's own members and on which most of the subsequent media comment was based – gave no information about the tests of reading and mathematics and no quantitative information about the test results at sixteen – save for two graphs with no scales along their vertical axes.

The overwhelming impression created by the coverage in the media was that comprehensives were doing very well and that bright children did just as well academically in them as in grammar schools. This coverage led to the research being widely quoted as a reassuring vindication of comprehensives. This was also the line taken by politicians such as Mr Neil Kinnock, Labour spokesman on education, by Mrs Shirley Williams and by at least one Conservative Education Committee chairman, who all used these "findings" to advocate the establishment of more comprehensive schools.

The report of the NCB is the only evidence cited in Mrs Shirley Williams' recent book *Politics is for People*[6] concerning academic standards in comprehensives. The research was commissioned by the DES in 1977 when Mrs Shirley Williams was Education Secretary. She has subsequently claimed some of the credit for initiating this study:

> Because of the sensitivity of the subject of the research it was a matter for ministerial decision … The findings of such research would be invaluable to those making policy decisions, so I personally authorized it… I had a hunch that comprehensive schools had been unfairly attacked in many quarters and that facts would counter prejudices.[7]

In her public comments Mrs Shirley Williams has hitherto ignored the limitations of the research. Even before the report was published, she wrote:[8]

> …I am quite convinced that on social and academic grounds comprehensive schools have a great deal to contribute to the country, and I am strengthened in that belief by the recent research on behalf of the National Children's Bureau, research which I myself authorized, although it is yet to see the light of day. That research indicates that boys and girls in comprehensive schools do just as well as they do in the selective schools taken together…

Even now that the report has appeared and been publicy criticized, Mrs Williams continues to quote the NCB research to justify a policy of wholesale comprehensivization. In *Politics is for People* she calls the report 'the most significant single piece of research in Britain' on children's progress in secondary schools, and claims that 'contrary to popular belief' it shows that 'children who were above average at eleven were doing at least as well in comprehensive schools at the age of sixteen as they would have been doing in grammar schools.' The research, she says, '…does not prove that children do *decisively* better in comprehensive schools, but it shows *convincingly* that they do as well as they would in segregated schools' (our emphases). Since the research did not show the comprehensives as *decisively better* at anything and actually showed them *worse* in certain important respects, and since, as we have shown, there is nothing *convincing* about the NCB's own claims, Mrs Williams' hyperbole reveals a positive disrespect for the critical evaluation of evidence which is surely disturbing.

On this issue, as on other educational issues, there is little difference between Mrs Williams' position and that of her former Labour party colleagues, who, in their recent discussion document *Private Schools*, state that: '…the National Children's Bureau report proves that such pupils of high ability would not on average have a higher attainment by attending a school practising selection than by attending a comprehensive school'. One can scarcely believe that these confident statements both by Mrs Williams and the Labour Party are made on the basis of results from two tests of reading and mathematics, both of which had serious limitations.

The Aftermath

Following the publication of *Real Concern*, various comments have been publicly made by the NCB[9] and other writers, and a seminar was held at the University of Exeter Institute of Education to discuss the issues raised both by the report and our own criticisms of the study.[10] We wish to comment briefly on some of the points raised in these discussions:

1. *Accessibility of data.* It has been claimed that the NCB did not need to publish their unadjusted findings since the raw data for the original survey by the NCDS* are in the Social Science Research Council archive. This misses the point of our criticism. It takes time and money to analyse data concerning 16,000 children

---

* National Child Development Study.

and to extract the many different kinds of information used by the NCB in their sub-sample. At our own expense, we obtained the appropriate codebooks from the SSRC and we estimate that a major research project, which would involve access to computing facilities, would be needed to extract the information which was omitted from the NCB report. Whilst it is desirable for the raw data to be available in the archive, that is not a substitute for a concise and comprehensible summary in the report itself for the benefit both of other researchers and also of the public, who do not have research facilities.

2. *Reworking of data.* We have been criticized for not reworking the original data before commenting on the research of the NCB. It would be even more expensive in time and money to repeat all the NCB's regression analyses. Making such a reworking a precondition for criticizing research findings would be an effective way of stifling the kind of public criticism and debate in which researchers should be prepared to engage.

3. *Political affiliations.* Repeated public attention has been drawn to our political affiliations. These affiliations, which we openly acknowledge, are irrelevant to much of the debate. That our work is published by the Centre for Policy Studies has *no* bearing on the accuracy or validity of what we write.

4. *Statistical naiveté.* It has been asserted that our criticisms are invalid because, it is said, we do not understand the statistical techniques used by the NCB. In fact statistical techniques are important, in very different ways, in our professional work. We are aware of many of the complexities and limitations of multiple regression and other forms of multi-variate analysis. It is well known that such techniques need to be used and interpreted with care if misleading conclusions are to be avoided. We therefore argue that it is the NCB who are statistically naive when they claim that such methods are not matters of current debate and controversy even among statisticians.

5. *The tests of attainment.* The NCB continue to claim that the tests used, including the reading test, did not underestimate the progress of able children, and that their conclusions about such children were justified. But their original report concedes a ceiling effect in the reading test. Miss Jane Steedman is also reported[11] to have said that 'no attempt had been made to assess the top 5 per cent'. In the light of the evidence and of what was said at the seminar at Exeter, we argue that, while the tests used are useful measures of some aspects of *basic* attainment, they do not adequately measure the full attainment of sixteen-year-olds at the top of the ability range. If this had been made clear in the NCB report and their summary *Concern*, much of the subsequent misunderstanding could have been avoided.

Many of our criticisms were supported by other contributors to the seminar at Exeter. Our discussion of the reliability and validity of the tests of reading and mathematics is confirmed by Mr D. Evans[12] who comments that the reading test

... is said to be "parallel to" the Watts-Vernon test of "reading ability" which was devised in 1947 as a "silent reading" test. One has to agree with the comment in the Bullock Report (1975, p.16) that this test cannot be regarded as an adequate measure of "reading ability", but that what it measures is a "narrow aspect of silent reading comprehension". There is no information available which would tell us about the validity of the test as derived from a comparison with other reading tests; nor is the predictive validity, i.e. the degree to which it might predict success at "reading", known.

Of the mathematics test Mr Evans writes:

No validity co-efficients are available. So, again, one is left to decide on the basis of inspection what exactly the test is measuring.

A major contribution to the seminar was made by Professor J. Wrigley.[13] Under the heading *Misrepresentation of Results*, Professor Wrigley states that:

> ...the NCB report is long and complicated and the process of simplification and possible distortion began with the publication of the more popular account given in the NCB's journal *Concern*. This simplification was then continued in the various press reports. In the process the qualifications made by the authors of the original report with regard to the narrowness of the cognitive measures or the necessity to adjust the scores are either forgotten or ignored. For example, the test used to measure pupil's achievement in schools at age 16 in the field of their native language, English, is a reading comprehension test which had already been used with the same pupils at age 11. It is a simple test of vocabulary of the kind severely criticized in the Bullock report *Language for Life*. Yet results from this test are reported as if it were a valid measure of achievement in the secondary school in the field of English.

On the controversy arising from statistical analyses, Professor Wrigley writes that:

> it would have been more satisfactory if the original mean scores for groups A and B had been quoted unadjusted for IQ, mathematical or reading attainment or social class. Such unadjusted mean scores, potentially misleading as they may be, have a reality and a meaning beyond that of the adjusted scores. Most people would be capable of realizing why the average scores of groups A and B differ but would prefer to have as much of the data as possible presented to them in an easily available form. The most disturbing aspect of the whole seminar for me was the NCB intention of publishing the results derived from public examinations in the same fashion – that is to present adjusted examination results rather than actual grade averages. I hope wiser thoughts will prevail. When I attended my own local municipal high school years ago it was clear that my immediate fellow pupils and I belonged, on average, to a lower social class than our contemporaries at the nearby direct grant school. We know now (and we had a slight inkling then) that we were handicapped in our studies by our lower social class. We also knew that our examination grades would not be adjusted. The same truth has to be faced now. Let us, as Cox and Marks have suggested, have access to the original grade and test average, and more information on the statistical procedures used to produce adjusted grades. Furthermore, let us recognize the considerable difficulties encountered when these statistical adjustments are made, whatever method is used. These difficulties are two-fold – first the technicalities concerned with linear regression techniques, and second the problem of what exactly the original matching variable is. We may partial out, or adjust for, rather more, or sometimes rather less, than we imagine.

And on the presentation of data, Professor Wrigley comments that:

> In view of the difficulty of gaining access to the original data and the further difficulty of actually carrying out the re-analysis, it seems certain that few researchers will bother, and I therefore reinforce Cox and Marks and suggest that in this particular case more facts could have been given so that such a re-analysis would not be necessary.

Finally, Professor Pring concluded[14] that '...the NCB enquiry has led, on the basis of rather slender evidence ... to a rather tentative hypothesis that bright children in comprehensive schools do as well in a limited number of tests as do bright children in grammar schools'. And he states that 'this hypothesis' is 'by no means proven...'. We can think of no better way of summarizing the findings of the NCB on attainment. If these findings had been presented to the public in this tentative way in the first place, one of our main causes for concern would never have arisen.

So, we argue that our major criticisms of the original study have been shown, in subsequent debate, to be legitimate. Therefore, we suggest that they still stand.

A Forward Look: Some Implications for Future Educational Research

In any kind of research, it is desirable that the primary data should be set out clearly. This is important both for practical purposes – so that the data are open to critical scrutiny and checking – and to try to minimize the dangers of value-bias. In reporting complex research projects in the social sciences, it is vital to give sufficient information to allow alternative analyses to be made, for the same data may be capable of diverse interpretations and inferences. Such considerations are particularly important when the issues concerned are of considerable political significance and could be used as the basis for policy decisions. So we regret the repeated defence by the NCB of their original decision not to publish any unadjusted data for the outcome measures of progress in secondary schools. We regret even more their decision to refuse to provide the unadjusted results of their forthcoming survey of GCE and CSE examinations.

We think that decisions like this are likely to jeopardize the reputation of educational research. Such research is not an esoteric activity of interest only to a few academics. Like much research in the social sciences, it can interact with, and change, its subject matter – in this case, the educational system. Educational research is educational policy in the making. So it is vital for researchers to ensure that their work is presented to policy makers, to politicians and – through the media – to the public in ways which are as informative as possible. They must recognize that any research data, in the process of being publicized, will inevitably need to be simplified; they must therefore strive to ensure that simplification does not become distortion.

More generally, researchers in areas of public policy must work with humility, recognizing that they are dealing with a complicated reality which can probably never be known in all its detail. Therefore it is necessary that findings of research should be presented as clearly as possible in order to avoid pre-empting alternative interpretations. Research, if it be sensitive, open and humble, will then be able to fulful its vital role as honest broker in the educational system.

Notes

1. Jane Steedman, *Progress in Secondary Schools,* National Children's Bureau, 1980.
2. Caroline Cox and John Marks, *Real Concern* – an appraisal of the National Children's Bureau report *Progress in Secondary Schools* by Jane Steedman – (Centre for Policy Studies, 1980).
3. Start and Wells, *The Trend of Reading Standards*, NFER, 1972.
4. The NCB received £36,000 of public money from the DES for this piece of research and also had another £36,000 for research into the GCE O and A level and CSE examination results for the same group of children. It is essential that this next piece of research should be of better quality. We cannot afford another £36,000 of mystification from the NCB and the |DES when what is at stake is vital information about the education of the nation's children.
5. *Sunday Times*, 18 March 1980.
6. S. Williams, *Politics is for People* (Penguin, 1981).
7. Letter in the *Guardian*, 25 March 1980.

8. *The Observer*, 30 March 1980.

9. National Children's Bureau, *Real Research*, October 1980, and comments in the press.

10. A report of this seminar, which was held in December 1980, has been published (*Children's Progress in Secondary School, Perspectives 6,* School of Education, University of Exeter, June 1981). The Exeter professors initially refused to invite us to contribute to this issue of *Perspectives,* despite our having been major invited speakers at the Exeter seminar and although we had been assured earlier that our contribution would form part of any publication resulting from the seminar. It was only after we heard, quite by chance, that publication was imminent, that we put considerable pressure on the Exeter professors and induced them to change their minds and include our contribution *Real Concern: The Continuing Debate* (*Perspective 6*, pp. 54-60).

11. *The Guardian*, 17 October 1980.

12. D. Evans, *The Use of Tests in National Surveys, Perspectives 6*, op cit.

13. Professor Wrigley is Professor of Education at the University of Reading and a member of the Social Science Research Council; his contribution to *Perspectives 6* is entitled *The NCB Report – Some Problems*.

14. In *Objectivity and the Reconciliation of Differences, Perspectives 6*, op. cit.; Professor Pring is Professor of Education at Exeter University.

Education, Society and Culture

XIII
What's the Free New World doing to the Children?

Patricia Morgan

Born in East London, she attended the local grammar school and college of technology. She has contributed numerous articles to newspapers and magazines on topics in the fields of criminology and social psychology. Her publications include Child Care: Sense and Fable *(an exploraion of the empirical and theoretical status of maternal deprivation and other psychoanalytical doctrines on human development),* and Delinquent Fantasies *(a critique of present policy and influential theories on delinquency).*

Child-centredness has been represented as both scientific and caring. Its essence is that there are somehow natural 'needs' in the child which direct his development and how he ought to be reared.

Yet, indications are that the application of 'modern' child rearing is nothing if not detrimental to the intellectual and social development of the young. At the very least, it is associated with a general abandonment of upbringing and a withdrawal of adults from children's lives, which is difficult to distinguish from old-fashioned neglect. This, it is argued, is inherent in ideas which deny the cultural nature of mankind; the centrality of learning to human development; and the way in which the human world is an artificial place of rules and values, not instincts and impulses.

This human world has to be passed on to children: they cannot make or find it for themselves. And such transmission is directly dependent upon adult control and participation in children's lives. It is time, therefore, that we were more aware of those attitudes, policies and social developments which make it difficult for adults to carry out their age-old responsibilities.

Follow that Child – Child-Centredness as a Breakthrough in Civilization?

It has often been said that this age can pride itself – if nothing else – on being the Century of the Child. With the history of childhood described as a 'nightmare from which we have only recently begun to awake',[1] the past is cast as more or less misunderstanding, maltreating and warping its young; squandering vast human resources on the way.

Far from being a potential adult or immature, inexperienced member of society, The Child is different, separate and complete. Adults can no longer take it much for granted that children will, or should, live up to their expectations; learn the purpose and meaning of things as they see them; share their goals, tasks and sentiments and be judged by their standards.

The Child has not just become accepted as an end in himself – but the first principle. The result is that the world seems to have been turned upside down, with human development tacitly ceasing to be held as critically dependent on cultural transmission. Instead, its course has been characteristically represented as dictated and determined by the "needs" born in the child itself (where it seems to "know" what is best in a quasi-instinctual way), and the outcome a result of how much these "needs" are satisfied and thwarted. It is debatable what is the more extraordinary – the tenet of non cultural Man, or the way in which it has been so widely accepted as if it were the most unremarkable fact in the world.

Child rearing literature has been apt to represent The Child as being almost unequipped to deal with the world that Man has made – almost as if he were a being from a far planet. If we are not careful, his personality will be involved in damaging clashes with adult demands and expectations. Putting him through a process of cultural induction has been cast as tantamount to declaring war on his sensibilities and, hence, a "price" will be paid in distortion and sorrow. As much, or more, than the hardships and tragedies of life before the demographic and industrial revolutions, or the age-old tyrannies of the strong over the weak, it is the presumption that children will acquire and carry a heritage which appears to make the *History of Childhood* that nightmare to the book's editor.

Nature's Child ousts Culture's Man

Clearly, the errors of child rearing are not what they were even in the relatively recent past; being the very opposite of a lack of vigour in education and training. This outlook acknowledged learning as the vital process in human development and success, where adult intervention made sure that children acquired many lessons and were prevented from finding others rewarding. In contrast, the *raison d'être* of permissive and much child-centred theory and advice appears to lie in notions that the child contains both autonomous growth processes and constantly replenished reservoirs of energies or forces which have to work their ways out unimpeded. Such an almost demonological view of motivation calls for the lifting, rather than the imposition, of social pressures, in order to prevent dangerous internal and external reactions.

Such inner forces owe themselves largely to Freudian psychoanalysis: various Rousseauesque notions of spontaneous development received a substantial

boost from its accounts of the stages through which they progress. Also und
influence, little attention has been paid to the long years between depend
infancy and full maturity that life provides for human learning compared with all th
sound and fury over the First Five Years. And here, any survey of post-war child
rearing literature demonstrates how the interest has been as much, or more, in
sensory or biological matters like breast-feeding or toileting, than factors such as
the sensitivity of the only symbol-using creature to speech. After five, the guru
Piaget, among many, declared – and with particular reference to moral education –
that the influence of adults naturally waned, so that matters had to be left to the
child's peers. At the same time, there has been a down-grading, or dismissal, of
relationships for the child outside his most immediate family, or with anybody but
mother. With his traditional disciplinary and educative role presented as reprehensible, dispensable or simply moribund, it seems that father has only been able
to hang on to the family with his fingertips as a second-rate Mum. Of course,
sociologists have spoken of the modern father's *greater care* for his children –
measured in terms of nappies changed and prams pushed. Father has been part of
the baggage thrown out with learning. Nature favouring the female, the child-
rearing shelves bulge with the biological miracles she might work. Hence, social
harmony can be assured with the "right" form of childbirth or osmotically acquired
via bodily contact in the early months.

When the human cultural breakthrough harnessed language to learning, it freed
people from the constraints of their own experience. Knowledge could be
accumulated and disseminated across time and space, making instruction or
teaching the crucial cultural function. However, if the child is to discover the world
anew each time, then all of this is wholly, or largely, redundant. 'The curriculum is to
be thought of in terms of activity and experience rather than knowledge to be
gained and facts to be stored', claimed the 1967 Plowden Report *Children and
their Primary Schools*. With official backing for its distillation of child-centredness
for the classroom, no other document this century has had such an effect on British
primary education. But, when it said that 'Any practice which predetermines the
pattern and imposes it on all is to be discouraged', did it envisage the child's raw
experience adding up to a viable picture of the world without any need for
correction, interpretation or agreement with anybody else's "pattern"? Or were
they, as free play, simple dead ends to be enjoyed for their own sake and, by the
same token, directed to no goals and constrained by no rules? The aims and skills
which distinguish more purposive human activity – including those of social
cooperation – have to come from the better informed. But such adult direction
appears to be precluded by definitions of child-centredness in terms of parents, for
example, taking trouble over things in which they personally have no interest.[2] By
this, parenting becomes socially irrelevant. It is largely just a means for amusing
children.

However, whatever tangent taken by arguments over children's true "needs"
and whatever fashion may push to the fore, questions about child rearing in recent
history have essentially been cast in terms of how Nature intends us to rear
children. A universal blueprint is assumed to lie within the newborn. Child-rearing,
therefore, ceases to differ according to human custom on how the young are
handled and what they are taught. Instead, like medicine, there is but one healthy,
"scientific" way to further all the underlying potential and avoid "mistakes". It is as if

nto choice, control and consciousness were not now its only
adillo from which we could easily jump back into the arms of

ssion to a Sick Society

has witnessed the usurpation of parental authority by medical or psychiatric "experts". As so well described by Christopher Lasch in *Haven in a Heartless World*,[3] we have experienced a therapeutic revolution or "medicalization" of society, which made its biggest gains in America in the 1940s and 1950s, and in Britain in the 1960s. If Harry Stack Sullivan called for a 'world wide mobilization of psychiatry' against everything from war to personal anxiety, less brash but equally grandiose was the World Health Organization's definition of good health as 'complete physical, mental and social well-being', thereby extending the province of the helping and healing professions into home, school, workplace, courtroom and community. But, far from these places furnishing the ideal, it seemed that all produced personal and social pathology at a rate vaster and faster than anyone could ever hope to cure. So, in the service of prevention, the social scientists invaded the realm of values as physicians to a sick society and gatekeepers to Utopia. They sought, and often succeeded, in occupying the provinces of education, law, religion and morality – as much as the family – in their drive against "damaging" beliefs and practices. Only when freed from the crippling burden of constraints and strictures about right and wrong, good and bad; and only when all the categories, hierarchies and boundaries which throttled our "growth" had been broken down, could our child rearing and our personalities become tolerant, authentic and "whole". This meant that much of what had hitherto encompassed human life was cast by the therapists as inimical to it.

In Britain, the 1969 Children and Young Persons Act handed over much of the juvenile justice system to social workers. No longer catering for delinquents as such, it was to be an ambitious vehicle set to tackle all '...the problems of children and families ... without being inhibited by distinctions which are not relevant to the diagnosis of Needs'. Any perusal of literature on "treatment" programmes for meeting the "needs" of "damaged" children – institutionally or otherwise – will find that both the means and purpose consist in the creation of an inchoate, normless, formless and goalless world, where everybody therapeutically "expresses" and "relates" like lost souls in a new Hades. Less a "cure" for law-breaking, such ventures are seen more in the nature of pioneer colonies of the future good society.

Nothing Comes Free in this World – the Price of Child-Centredness

Advice, of course, does not have to be taken by laymen; "experts" – however many and strident – can be ignored. The utter failure of the century-long campaign against contraception by the Churches and the medical profession bears eloquent testimony to that. Nevertheless, a survey of child-rearing in the United States[4] over a 25-year period showed parental behaviour to be undergoing widespread and dramatic changes in the mid twentieth century. Data analysed from some thirty studies indicated a universal trend towards permissiveness (particularly in the years following the Second World War) which applied to everything from speech to sex, aggressiveness to cleanliness and movement outside the home.

Parallel developments which were also manifest on both sides of the Atlantic by the 1960s included much elevated and escalating levels of crime and violence in all spheres of life. At present, New York's suburbs are in the grip of a soaring crime rate, whose killers, robbers and rapists – and their victims – are increasingly the children of a city where even middle-class boys now spend most of their lives with peers. And, if widespread gang violence used to be confined to Eastern city slums, about 350 gangs with a membership of between 20,000 and 30,000 now operate in Los Angeles district alone. With 192 youth gang murders in Los Angeles in 1980, 60 per cent of those who die in the violence are bystanders; and families in the more run-down districts live on the floor because of guns fired through windows for fun. Attitudes are exemplified in the reactions of the youth who splashed another's brains around a telephone box: 'Bang, bang, bang. I've got the fool. I'm kind of happy' (*Sunday Times*, 13 September 1981). Britain's violence and delinquency has now entered a second, more vicious, pervasive and mass phase, and represents a microcosm of what has reached truly horrifying dimensions in America. (We can be thankful that, at least, we have been able to control the spread of guns, if not of more home-made weapons.)

Particularly in America, many other indicators appeared to be showing falling levels in basic social and intellectual skills over the past couple of decades. A report to the President of the United States from the White House Conference on Children asserted that 'America's families and their children are in trouble, trouble so deep as to threaten the future of the Nation.' Social psychologist Urie Bronfenbrenner, who served on that committee, spoke of the 'unmaking of the American child' and claimed that:

> In some segments of American society, notably among the economically disadvantaged, the social disorganization has been so extreme as to impair psychological functioning and development to a point that counter-measures have had to be introduced on a national scale. Among the well-to-do, the effects are not so extreme, but are nevertheless perceptible primarily in the spheres of motivation and social behaviour.[5]

In Britain, the number classified as ESN increased by 78 per cent between 1960 and 1976 (from 0.6 to 0.77 per cent of the school population), and those ascertained as maladjusted by over 500 per cent (from 0.023 to 0.141 of the school population). The latter is based on well established symptom scales which record behaviour which obviously distresses the child or those around him, markedly, and for long periods. (Maladjustment is typically characterized either by fearful withdrawal or aggressive and distractible behaviour.) It is suggested that the lower figures for earlier years reflect the shortage of special school places, so that children were not previously formally identified unless there was accommodation available. There is truth in this, especially in respect of the ESN. (There was a special school building programme in the 1960s, following the Underwood Report.) But it is also the fact that 83 per cent of the English LEAs' special unit places (providing accommodation within school hours for the 'serious behavioural problems' of truants and disruptive pupils) in existence in 1977 had been established only since 1973. Their growth has continued apace, as has that of 'sanctuaries' or 'sin-bins' to deal with day-to-day disciplinary problems that cannot be resolved or contained in the classroom. If the need for all this special provision always existed in fixed proportion in the school population, how is it that all indicators show that schools were more peaceable at a time when they *could not* get rid of their more troublesome charges – whether the very maladjusted or the greater numbers of disruptive pupils? The possibility may also be that there has been an actual increase in very difficult children. Moreover, part of the cause of both this and the continual demand for specialist provisions, may be that schools are less able, or willing, to tackle and reduce deviant behaviour than they were.

'It is as though our society had bred a new genetic strain,' commented a *New York Times* reporter in the early 1970s, on the arrival of the 'child murderer who feels no remorse and is scarcely conscious of his acts'. We hadn't. And neither, as a friend of mine speculated, had anybody dumped anything in the water supply to cause a plague of hard, hateful brats. On both sides of the Atlantic society had become a laboratory for a catastrophic social experiment. Cross-cultural studies comparing children in different societies or ethnic groups and research literature on child-rearing patterns in this country suggest that it is permissive, child-centred – rather than adult-orientated – child rearing which is associated with problems. One of the most dramatic illustrations of the differences alternative child-rearing styles make to children's development was provided by a study of families in semi-derelict inner city environments, characterized by large numbers of children, bad housing and the lowest incomes.[6]

The factor which the researchers found so significant, distinguishing entire families of delinquent from non-delinquent children, was described as chaperonage. This involved the making and enforcing of rules; restricting the child's movements, or both. Chaperoning parents shared a strong sense of obligation that their children needed protection from certain aspects of the environment, both for their own good and that of others.

Such a conclusive finding prompted the researchers to make more detailed examinations of any other possible relationships between a strictness/permissive dimension of parenting and children's behaviour. Permissive parents who did not rebuke children who refused to help or who did not seek to limit their sex-play or impose any restrictions on their play generally, were also those who allowed children to roam at will. Such unregulated children were more poorly adjusted in the classroom and more maladjusted generally. The researchers concluded that '...delinquency is not a product of personality disturbance or maladjustment, but both delinquency and poor adjustment are the results of lax methods of parenting. The findings merit more research'. They do, in fact, receive some support from the large-scale, long-term study of delinquent and early adult criminal behaviour being undertaken by the Cambridge Institute of Criminology,[7] which found that low supervision was the only aspect of poor parental behaviour which remained associated with law-breaking which continued into adult life. The inner city study had itself observed how supervision patterns were not only related to the children's current behaviour, but seemed to continue influencing the teenager's conduct several years later.

A similar story emerged from a comparison of English and Asian children in Leicester.[8] Matched for age, sex and class, the English children were rated three time more maladjusted than their Indian counterparts. Family size, social class and mother's employment were not involved with the difference. On the other hand

40 per cent of English families had only one parent or were exposed to severely strained relationships at home. (This still meant, of course, that 60 per cent came from apparently reasonably stable backgrounds.) In comparison, no seriously disrupted homes were reported for the Indian sample. But, overall, the English children were far more free and independent with less supervision and discipline than their Indian counterparts – whatever the state of their homes. In the Indian sample, where there was '...close supervision of children and firm discipline', the parent-child relationships were also characterized as '...warm and loving and, despite strictness, reasonably harmonious'. There was, however, a tendency towards higher rates of maladjustment in Indian children the longer a family had stayed in this country.

Such results may be compared with the observations made by a delegation studying the development of young children in China[9] – a country still much wedded to traditional practices and largely oblivious of any "child psychology". Finding children at home, in kindergarten and school 'extraordinarily poised and well behaved' and 'very respectful and courteous' towards their elders, the team was to ask the inevitable question 'whether or not the children were paying a psychological price for the relatively high levels of discipline, academic demands and pressure to conformity' that prevailed. But they failed to find much in the way of 'disorders of behaviour we have come to expect... in American schools... hyperactivity, impulsiveness, isolated withdrawal and neurotic symptoms'. Other assumptions that any conformity with adult demands meant apathetic surrender and was incompatible with '...spontaneous laughing, smiling' and individual initiative, were also falsified. Moreover, relationships between children and adults appeared to be friendly, with youngsters 'emotionally expressive, socially gracious and adept'.

A recent study of 120 families and their children was designed to put the association of parental supervision and delinquency in high crime areas to further test. The findings, in both suburbia and inner city, confirmed the close association between supervision and delinquency or other anti-social behaviour, official as well as self-reported. The increase in delinquency with increasing parental laxness was highly significant, and far more important than measures of the families' level of "social handicap" in determining misbehaviour. The delinquency rate in the lax families was over seven times that in the strict families; while the rate in severely handicapped families was only under three times that in families with low social handicap.

Redundant Parent = Abandoned Child

Bronfenbrenner has himself suggested that his data indicating a universal trend towards parental permissiveness, could equally be interpreted as indicating a progressive decline in contact between parents and children amounting to neglect and, in many cases, virtual abandonment of the next generation. (He identified the ultimate in neglect as the American rumpus room – which might equally be described as many a child-centred or progressive educationalist's dream. Here, freed from restricting hazards, surrounded by stimuli and insulated from any need for adult intervention, children work out their destinies undisturbed.) It must be remembered that however much the motives behind permissiveness and "traditional" neglect may differ and, indeed, be polar opposites of each other – the effect on children may be identical. This is perhaps illustrated in the kind of finding showing that low levels of punishment by parents have the same outcome for the child's behaviour as rejection and harshness.[10]

Cross-cultural studies certainly seem to be revealing a sharp decline in parent-child contact with the adoption of "modern ideas".[11] In the early 1960s, compared with Americans, German parents gave their children more help and affection, as well as more discipline, and engaged in more joint activities with them. This was particularly the case with fathers, despite the fact that Americans were more likely to see themselves as "a pal" to "the kids". Yet, a few years later, German parents had moved substantially closer to the American (and English) pattern of low parent-child interaction, even though the Americans were still moving in the same direction. Germany has, of course, recently experienced one of the most sudden and steep leaps in violence and delinquency in the post-war world.

Social historians have used the term child-centredness to characterize changes in family life and child-rearing patterns which spread with urbanization and industrialization. In pre-industrial society, children grew up in the public world under the influence of a number of adults (often from different social strata), be they craft-masters, tutors, employers, servants etc., whose role in their development was as great, or greater, than the parents'. Later, children and child-rearing were to assume more importance in the family unit to become focal concerns of privatized, nuclear households. Associated particularly with the urban Victorian middle classes, this form of socialization made the shaping of the child's intellect, personality and morality an intensive endeavour which cultivated and used the dependencies created by strong, emotional ties.[12] Inextricably bound up with this development was that nineteenth century reforming alliance of science and Non-conformism – busily defining and solving social problems as it set itself to the general betterment of society. Almost inevitably, this was going to say a lot about child-rearing, and its heirs intensified the search for an "objective" basis to it.

It would be interesting to know what the reformers and philanthropists would have made of the Freudian metamorphosis of the traditions of the Enlightenment and the Reformation, since the gospel the social therapists have pushed is one which, ironically, nullified upbringing itself. The equation of child-centredness with the primacy of child "need" succeeds in negating *any* intensive *and* protective educative process.

At the same time parenthood or, rather, motherhood, is constantly presented as such a skilled job that it must only be undertaken by those fully committed to its responsibilites. Yet it is difficult to discern what aims it is permitted and what means have not been denied. As she anxiously follows the child, the passive, insecure and largely superfluous parent receives constant reminders of the daunting sacrifice and the plethora of pitfalls involved in the "most important job in the world".

Modern Parenthood – Perils Unlimited with no Rewards

Where the environment is adult orientated – for all that it has been condemned as bad for children – the adult as a deliberate educator must involve himself actively and closely with the child. Moreover, however much the *responding*, rather than initiating and controlling, adult tries to make himself a source to be drawn upon "on demand", his anxious endeavours have been directed largely to avoiding directing and affecting the child. The concept of the child as a most impressionable creature no longer presents the adult with a glowing opportunity to mould such sensitivity, but comes to warn him off making any impact at all. Trauma, neurosis, complex – by the mid-twentieth century, parents began to be almost frightened to breathe on their offspring in case psyches snapped. They have acquired total liability at the same time as children – and people generally – have been able to blame their sins and omissions on their backgrounds. There has been an infinitely expanding catalogue of ways for the interfering, self-interested or un-giving parent to go wrong. With child care advice be-spattered with "irreparable damage" and "untold consequences", a thousand perils lie in anything which could be construed as frustration, upset or deprivation. Where it is apparently the child who knows best, by conviction or in confusion, the parent comes to feel that it is wise to give him what he seems to want and otherwise leave well alone.

And, for all that child psychology has talked of the overriding importance of emotional life, it appears to have been to the achievement of bland, low-key relationships, purged of "disturbing" demands, loyalities, conflicts and passions. From these – when *they are ready* – the young will effortlessly detach themselves. As small children, the automatically satisfying world they are supposed to inhabit is calculated, by the same token, to make no mark upon them at all. (Logically, a world smoothly geared to "needs" in the child, would leave him largely oblivious to an external world. It would hardly be capable of developing the complex reciprocity inherent in human social life!)

In fact, a number of commentators have now drawn attention to what they feel has been a recent and gross deterioration in the quality of human relationships. Interaction, particularly as it involves the young, is defensive and predatory, where it is not indifferent and callous. Jeremy Seabrook, in his *What Went Wrong?*, blames the impoverishment on a frenetic pursuit of living standards, where the consumption of goods has become the only goal, the only measure of success, the only source of worth, fulfilment and identity.[13] In such an atmosphere, a parent's '...caring is vested solely in granting her children access to all the things that the economy holds out as guarantees of compliance, control and satisfaction'. In one case:

> The older children come home and criticize their mother; this is deeply hurtful to her. She is anxious to propitiate them all the time, to forestall their resentment at what she feels is her own inability to provide all the things they want... She feels humiliated and guilty. If she had been able to give the older ones what they wanted, she believes that they would not have done wrong... They had demanded money from an Indian youth in a train; and it was as as result of this that Spencer is in Borstal. Mrs Hellence has a deep sense of failure, and a feeling that if she could provide more things for the children, everything would come right. If they had beautiful clothes, records, bikes, holidays, tape recorders, transistors, skateboards, money, there would be no problems. She watches the younger ones grow... she feels them slipping from her control; and the only way she can gain their obedience is by promising increasingly lavish rewards.

Where money *is itself* a primary source of status which does not have to be legitimized by achievement, effort or excellence, this may indeed mean untoward changes and problems for society, the implications of which go far beyond this paper. Insofar as consumer materialism is held to adversely affect *parental* behaviour, such an argument might appear to support those advocates of child-centredness who put the blame for the results of much that has been done in its name on lazy, inadequate or ignorant parents who think that they can replace the "right kind of love" with presents. But, very many children have been reared in prosperous conditions without adverse consequences either for their own behaviour, or that of their parents. The difference is that the latter's confidence in laying down standards and making demands has not been undermined to the extent that they see themselves only as '...humble, self-effacing servitors of their own progeny, [who] can only monitor their needs and wants'. Once the parents' role in cultural transmission has been cut away little is left but the provision of treats, toys and thrills. "Wants" are the most obvious candidate for that nebulous category "needs" and meeting them represents to the confused parent an *unobtrusive, yet potent* way of demonstrating his goodwill. What Seabrook says of the forces of commercialism and consumerism applies equally to the "expert" and "helping" professions and it is clear that he is well aware of this:

> Parents soon learn that they are helpless: merely enabling agents for all the beneficent industries and professions devoted solely to the process of coaxing children into their natural growth and development. It is through this that the old transmission of identity has been broken. Parental caring is secondary in providing things indispensable to the child. Instead of learning by imitation and absorption from the past, childhood has become virgin territory. The real human fear about the vulnerability of young children through the early stages of life is exploited by all the industries and manufactures which alone claim the power to guarantee children a safe passage through the conquered domain of childhood: they are the occupying colonising power, to which parents have no choice but to defer.

It is sad but true that people, being what they are, usually put more effort into enterprises where there is the prospect of some return. It is not just that children return the attentions of those whom they are involved with and whose ways they are used to sharing. In other ages and societies, adults have regarded children as their investment in the future, whether this is cast in terms of insurance for old age, status, a carrier for religion, trade or learning, and so forth. While, in one sense, this may all militate against that valuation of the child in and for Himself Alone and bring down accusations of "living through children", who 'didn't ask to be born' etc., it does serve to keep adults interested and concerned enough to stay close to children and equip them with the skills required in society. And, to a greater or lesser extent, people do have and rear children because they want to share and perpetuate their lives and ways. Given this, suggestions that what adults possess is somehow unworthy to bequeath or presumptuous to impart, simply leads to dis-association. In the last analysis, if upbringing goes because it is oppressive to children, or because our society is not good enough for them, then there is little need for children themselves. In more ways than one, the generation that the children's liberationists would completely free from adult domination would be the last.

The Shares of Pretty Images and the Mine of Good Intent

The evidence no more suggests that more adult-centred child-rearing regimes produce a crop of mental ills, than it shows that they necessarily produce fearful resentment in children and a lack of contact and sympathy between generations. Child-centredness is now a very loaded term which trades heavily on a good image of true devotion at the cradle, and enables doubters to be dismissed as punitive, frigid and anti-child. With its complement – permissiveness – it is common to find both automatically equated with 'doing good to children' and in an age very ready to measure outcome in terms of input and intentions, with being good *for* children. That advice is sought because children are important, is something which sanctifies the content of advice and convicts critics of denying the fact. The manners of the past may sometimes have been rough and heedless, but that adult ascendancy is not a licence for the callous disregard of the young is illustrated by the generous, warm and kindly attention they receive in numerous more traditional communities throughout the world today. Indeed, some members of these might have cause to ponder what "care" means in a society lucky to live without grinding poverty or high mortality, when children are free to throw away their lives at glue-sniffing parties.

Children without Adults

If the impact of permissive child-centredness on parent/child relationships can look remarkably like neglect, its effects on children are not easily distinguishable from those of the child rearing practices of the "classic slum", described in so many sub-cultural studies of delinquency.[14] (In recent decades one has probably served to exacerbate the other.) Both seem to work against the integration of youth into society and their commitment to its norms. This attachment to society is fostered by involvement with people who transmit and uphold its ways and values, with the amount of time spent in shared acitivites – in family, community, school and work relationships – and the degree to which these relationships overlap and support each other. As intimacy declines within relationships and across them all, so children and young people become less socially integrated and more likely to be involved in anti-social, delinquent and violent acts. They are left to the company of their own peers, with evidence suggesting that here *is the one category of relationship which actively encourages, rather than constrains or diminishes, delinquency.*

The children's peer group is a world aligned to the pursuit of thrills, where the attractions of excitement and immediate gain are constrained by little or nothing in the way of moral considerations. Moreover, adults who are only marginally involved in children's lives are not in a position to use the potent range of social pressures which make people conform anywhere. If the child is allowed to become independent of their interests, company and favour, they lose their position as a source of support and control. Bearing out many other studies, when one researcher looked at the peer group in which middle-class New York boys spent so much of their time he found that – in most cases – once the attitudes of peers were taken into account, those of parents made no difference. This was particularly true for anti-social behaviour, where the influence of the peer group was all-determining. On both sides of the Atlantic, children from all classes are becoming extensively – and often almost exclusively – involved in peer group relationships at an ever earlier age.

Parental nervousness and disinclination to play an active, demanding role in their children's lives has occurred in the midst of a more general undermining of the social integration of the young, often in the name of policies and reforms supposedly aimed at their welfare and future. Employment has been restricted and schooling – often of a most doubtful quality and use – continually extended.

Concern for the young has been generally and sloppily conveyed by removing tasks and responsibilities from the child's shoulders and by insuring that he occupies a universe of idle leisure. Delinquency is thus planned into the system where

> ...if the institutions of our society continue to remove parents, other adults, and other youth from active participation in the lives of children, and if the existing vacuum is filled by the age-segregated peer group, we can anticipate increased alienation, indifference, antagonism, and violence on the part of the younger generation in all segments of our society...[15]

For a number of years before the major eruptions of summer 1981, Britain has been subject to increasing juvenile rioting and group warfare – as well as the now familiar manifestations of child society, such as football hooliganism. And, as many have cashed in on the parental insecurities engendered by the experts, so the more unscrupulous among the media and the entrepreneurs have fed and fuelled the juvenile thirst for thrills and supplied the fads and tokens in which a crude, collective identity is sought. Just as dunghills breed maggots, the combination of trash and nihilism have, in turn, spawned whole schools and institutes of Marxist sociologists, creating professorships and publishing careers out of interpreting skinheads, punks, teds and other assorted toughs as noble waves of resistance to capitalism.

Many children will, of course, desist from law-breaking once they move away from peer group influence into the constraint imposed by adult responsibilities. However, early and continued relinquishment of the child to the peer group can have serious repercussions for the acquisition of basic intellectual and social skills. The study published as *Growing Up to be Violent*,[16] traced a large group of youngsters over the course of their development. This pin-pointed both the very poor levels of interpersonal competence shown by anti-social and violent adults and how social adequacy depended upon parental tuition. Where might is right, a child adapts and survives in the peer group only with aggression or withdrawal. As it can only ingrain such a narrow repertoire of behaviour, by the same token it is not the place where a child can learn other, more sophisticated, moves to solve the problems he might otherwise confront with violence. Simple adult arbitration in children's disputes itself helps to impart an understanding of justice and of principles to which conduct and choices can be referred. A recent review of all the observations and experiments pertinent to Piaget's claim that moral education had to be more or less relinquished to the child's peer group as he grew up, because adults could exert so little influence whatever they might wish, demonstrated that all evidence lay to the contrary. Adults were found to be more effective than peers in shaping moral judgements at *any* age and – furthermore – this potential influence increased, not declined, as children grew up.[17]

The dismal results of growing up with peers are described for one Liverpool estate in *View from the Boys*.[18] Disappearing "out" much of the time, its children have very free, unrestricted and exploratory childhoods. Infants quickly become involved in thieving, "cheeking" and vandalism and are well into gross acts of arson – and carry weapons – by the age of ten. As young men, they expect immediate, intense and continual gratification and cannot countenance anything requiring the slightest effort or concentration. Lack of excitement means rage against "boredom". All strangers are regarded with hostility and "the boys" are ever ready to launch into gross assaults at the least provocation – real or imagined. Attitudes to women and sex are exploitative and brutalized; any difficulties or differences are settled with beatings. The exigencies of pregnancy, the penalties of the adult court, and a dearth of easy criminal pickings gradually manoeuvre some into a minimal compliance with the conventional adult world. The more vicious males, who cannot meet the most elementary demands of any work or home, continue to inhabit the street corners where they egg the next generation on to greater degrees of much vaunted "hardness".

Adults and the Necessity for Upbringing

Observations of adults with children suggest that verbal skills and the subtleties of social cooperation are particularly developed when they are involved together in the pursuit of a goal, or task – however simple – where the rules of all are imparted together. Human evolutionary survival and success have depended upon joint action to attain goals, and it is in this context that language to pass on information, plan and co-ordinate activities is at its greatest premium. That a child of any age is involved with others in common objectives helps him to identify with them and their fortunes. When the system goes on to give him his own duties and jobs, it also hands him a stake to protect and preserve. Those given functions to perform are commonly found to take on the values associated with these – with Professor Michael Rutter finding, for example, that schools which gave children responsibilities along with high standards tended to have the better behaved and more highly motivated pupils.[19]

The peer group child may appear to "manage for himself". But it is a mistake to confuse his independence with the skilled assurance of children in societies where they share a working life with other age-groups. Instead, he largely knocks around the streets without a purpose, for children are scarcely able to envisage positive goals unless they are first taught them. Even if they could, they are hardly capable of reaching them on their own initiative. While the child is learning, he is open to all manner of distractions and false leads, which makes the adult educational role partly one of filtering stimuli and preventing the child chasing after them. If stimulation is not restricted, the child's attention and grasp of skills have no chance to extend and establish themselves. In trying to account for the relaxed and socially attentive quality of Chinese children in contrast to the edgy, distractible nature of so many American ones, the research I mentioned earlier pointed to the fact that in the more traditional eastern environments all child activity is adult-initiated, maintained and terminated. Here adults are quick to intervene with calmer, more co-ordinated alternatives when children's behaviour starts becoming aggressive and chaotic. If anything, we have been encouraged to abandon such practices for the maximization of stimulation, as the child's "need" for unfettered play has become a fetish.

Also, from the earliest age, the adult has a continuously interpretative – as much as guiding and shielding – function to perform *vis-à-vis* the child. This does not involve him in developing all the flickerings of attention from stimulus, but picking out the tiny number of moves that have a meaning, or significance, in his culture. These are named and encouraged or discouraged. Communication can be established only by some items being deliberately selected as stable tokens and others, which surround them, being suppressed. If every item of every experience was equally "meaningful", nothing could occupy the unchanging role which carries the same meaning from one situation to the next. Such a selective, interpretative process is necessary for the formation of stable concepts and advances the child's understanding and awareness of himself, other people and his environment generally. It opens up deliberate choice and self-control: the child is no longer mindlessly knocking about, but accumulating moves he can use intentionally. It is in this way that *freedom* is attained – not by being abandoned uncomprehendingly to chaos.

The intellectual results of poor contact with adults were perhaps illustrated in an article on a scheme for giving long-standing truants the rudiments of very basic domestic skills (*The Guardian*, 20 June 1980). The claim was made that these teenagers would probably never make paid employment – not necessarily because of a lack of jobs, but due to their inability to follow through tasks or resist for the shortest periods the urge to aimless wandering. What was as, or more, sad was the lack of questioning of child rearing practices which are resulting in such pitifully handicapped people.

No More of the Same!

The problems of "maladjustment" are essentially those of the Great Untaught. No better – if not worse – than the uncritical acceptance of harmful methods, are the prescriptions for cure which amount to another dose of the medicine which struck the patient down.

The vast crop of behavioural units or "sin bins" which have sprung up in our schools are partly an indication that many teachers no longer accept that socialization is a normal part of their role to the degree that they used to. If the child is thought to be "damaged", then adults must withdraw even further to prevent aggravating the "disturbance". He may be held in need of "compensation", which often unfortunately means a tolerant cosseting of his ignorant confusion and a prohibition on adult demands. Alternatively, he may be thought to be making an inarticulate political protest. Peter Newell,[20] of the Advisory Centre for Education, for example, accuses schools of provoking the soaring rates of maladjustment with their rules and regulations. It is a recent twist to the old story about "authoritarian structures and hierarchies"[21] playing havoc with the human mind and messing up that naturally wholesome, spontaneous development process. However, the paradox of human development is that no child could take advantage of Newell's free expression, self-governing and relevant schooling, unless adults had first imposed upon him the apparatus with which to do so. It is ironic that shortly after Newell said his piece, we should have heard about the success of the fee-paying John Loughborough (Seventh Day Adventist) School, already over-subscribed by West Indian parents anxious about the behaviour and attainments of children in the more *laissez faire* comprehensives.

It is quite clear by now that much which had been advocated under the heading of child-centred rearing is at variance with basic humanization processes. The human social world is based in values and composed of symbols, rules and goals; it cannot emerge from the satisfaction of quasi-biological or instinctual "needs", however much we may wish Nature to take away our choice of what we are and what we want to become. Children cannot enter it when they are regarded as creatures apart, trapped in that void epitomized in the slogan "Play is Children's Work". Logically, a child-centred society must presuppose a cultureless society. For human beings this is a contradiction in terms, a way for society to negate its worth and very existence. Child "need" and the whole search for a scientific "way" to rear children is inherently and unavoidably nihilistic since society is – and can be no other than – a moral order.

The human world has to be passed on to the child. He cannot re-make it, suggest it or find it himself. He is entirely dependent upon the initiative and capacities of the adults in his life. Anything which undermines their motivation, gnaws away their confidence or reduces their standing in the eyes of the child is of no help to him or anybody else. If this has implications for all manner of policy makers and professionals, then so too does the falling number of adults that are actually involved with children *at all* and the continuing trend to greater segregation of age groups. These developments are often the unrecognized by-product of a very large number of social processes and decisions – sometimes taken for the most benevolent of motives and constructive of reasons. The banning of the cane in some educational areas, for example, has been said to have led to teachers withdrawing generally from disciplinary matters and a greater confining of children in "sin-bins". What can begin as the kindliest of measures can clearly have the most detrimental of unintended results, so that whatever one thinks of the cane – and I have no particular brief for it – the risks to children's welfare should make one think twice about abolishing it elsewhere. The children's rights lobby is now pressing for the Swedish law – making it an offence for a parent to smack a child – to be introduced in this country. Given the present state of many a parent's morale and motivation, it is just the sort of measure calculated to do nothing but harm to parent/child relationships.

Putting Adults back into Children's Lives

If seemingly small and discrete changes can have a dramatic impact on adult behaviour, how much more pervasive and devious can be the ways in which housing or educational policies, trends in leisure or changes in family structure, affect the willingness, availability and capacity of adults to undertake the upbringing role. I noted earlier how an overlap of significant ties aids the child's social integration. As the two most important centres for socialization in the industrial world are the family and the school, it is clearly detrimental to children's development to do anything which decreases parental satisfaction and participation in their education. If choice increases the confidence of parents and involves them more closely with schools, then choice needs to be preserved and extended for these very reasons. If the price of some nebulous political or social engineering goal is disgruntled and alienated parents then it simply isn't worth the price. (In teaching itself we need to take a long, hard look at the pervasive drift away from *in loco parentis* towards the nine-to-four employee.) Social integration of the young would also be better served by a relaxation on employment. If the adolescent can find work, and has attained a certain standard in the basics of literacy and numeracy, then it is better that he make a useful contribution to the outside world than be retained at school at no small expense and often greater trouble. Provision in further education can always be made should he wish to return at a later date when he has a better idea of where his interests and aptitudes lie. As employment has become unionized, bureaucratized and swathed in regulations, the economic aspects of a job have been emphasized to the exclusion of all else. One consequence is that – unless numerous laws are broken – simple jobs which enabled the young to gain experience of life and pick up elementary skills have been driven off the market; often because relatively unproductive labour has been made prohibitively expensive.

As far as the family is concerned, there has been little thought given, for example, to the social consequences which tend to result when large numbers of males are uninvolved in any child-rearing or family responsibilities. In turn, the only models of male behaviour available for many boys growing up in one-parent "families" are the vicious stereotypes of the media, which have such an attraction for the thrill-seeking, peer group boy. Not in contact with somebody who demonstrates socially acceptable standards of masculinity, he acts out a brutalized caricature. It is as if there were a global conspiracy to get rid of father. Those who want to tie women to the home have not minded too much about kicking him out of it as they have emphasized the child's exclusive need for mother. The women's liberation movement has become another branch of anarchic individualism. Since all family structures involving more than one person must impose some obligations and restrictions on the other, it has repudiated any in favour of free-floating personal "growth" and "exploration". Whenever father is discussed, it is invariably in terms of whether the child needs him. The answer, if any, is usually "not really". But, as fatherhood is a social role *and* if the question is put that way, then – when it comes to it – the child does not *really* "need" a schoolteacher, aunt, grandmother, social worker or, indeed, a mother. It is – again – more a question of what we want people to do and be. This simply re-emphasizes my point that if we persist in framing questions about upbringing in terms of what children "need", the answer is apt to be – nothing.

Notes

1. Lloyd de Maure (ed), *History of Childhood* (Condor Books, 1974).
2. J. Newson and E. Newson, *Four Years Old in an Urban Community* (George Allen and Unwin, 1968).
3. C. Lasch, *Haven in a Heartless World* (Basic Books, 1977).
4. Urie Bronfenbrenner "Socialization and Social Class Through Time and Space" in Eleanor E. Maccoby, Theodore M. Newcomb and Eugene L. Hartley (eds), *Readings in Social Psychology* (Methuen and Holt, Rinehart and Winston, 1958).
5. Urie Bronfenbrenner, "Children, Families and Social Policy: An American Perspective" in *The Family in Society: Dimensions of Parenthood* (DHSS/ HMSO, 1973).
6. Harriette Wilson and G.W. Herbert, *Parents and Children in the Inner City* (Routledge & Kegan Paul, 1978), also "Parents can cut the crime rate", *New Society*, 4 December 1980.

7. D.J. West and D.P. Farrington, *The Delinquent Way of Life* (Routledge & Kegan Paul, 1977).
8. A.M. Kallarackal and Martin Herbert, "The Happiness of Indian Immigrant Children", *New Society*, 28 February 1976.
9. William Kessen (ed), *Childhood in China* (Yale, 1975).
10. Monroe M. Lefkowitz, Leonard D. Eron, Leopold O. Walder and L. Rowell Huesmann, *Growing Up to be Violent* (Pergamon, 1977).
11. E.C. Devereux, U. Bronfenbrenner and G.J. Suci, "Patterns of parent behaviour in America and West Germany: A cross-national comparison", *International Social Science Journal*, 14, 1962, pp. 488-506; and E.C. Devereux, U. Bronfenbrenner and R.R. Rodgers, "Child Rearing in England and the United States", *Journal of Marriage and the Family*, 31, 1969, pp. 257-270.
12. Philippe Ariès, *Centuries of Childhood* (Jonathan Cape, 1962); and Edward Shorter, *The Making of the Modern Family* (Fontana, 1977).
13. Jeremy Seabrook, *What Went Wrong? – working people and the ideals of the Labour movement* (Gollancz, 1978).
14. Paul C. Friday and John Halsey, "Patterns of social relationships and youth crime: social integration and prevention", in *Youth Crime and Juvenile Justice*, Paul C. Friday and Lorne Steward (eds) (Praeger, 1977); and Michael J. Hindelang, "Causes of Delinquency: A Partial Replication and Extension", *Social Problems* 20, 1973, pp. 471-87.
15. Urie Bronfenbrenner, *Two Worlds of Childhood* (Allen and Unwin, 1971).
16. See note 10.
17. M. Siegal and M.C. Boyes, *British Journal of Educational Psychology*, 1981, vol. 50, p. 105.
18. Howard J. Parker, *View from the Boys* (David and Charles, 1974).
19. Michael Rutter, Barbara Maughan, Peter Mortimore and Janet Ouston, *Fifteen Thousand Hours* (Open Books, 1979).
20. Peter Newell, "Sin Bins: the integration argument", *Where*, July/August 1980.
21. Ibid.

XIV
Conservatives, Culture and Education

Arthur Pollard

Professor of English at the University of Hull (since 1967), he was educated at the Universities of Leeds (B.A.) and Oxford (B. Litt). He has worked as Lecturer and Senior Lecturer at Manchester University, and was Director of General Studies, Faculty of Arts, from 1964 to 1967. His publications include Let Wisdom Judge (*Simeon's sermons),* New Poems of Crabbe, English Hymns, English Sermons, Mrs Gaskell: Novelist and Biographer, Anthony Trollope's Satire, *and he edited* Webster's New World Companion to English and American Literature.

This chapter is concerned to show that education is neither a thing nor an end in itself, but arises from and should seek to sustain the tradition and culture within which it is set.

It should not, however, be an instrument of "social engineering". It shows how radical change, in disowning the past, is likely to destroy the very future that it seeks to create. It suggests that education in Britain has developed within the framework of an organic tradition of Christian humanism which respects the dignity and integrity of the individual, by which alone a free society, tolerant and possessing both quality and opportunity, may be attained and sustained.

The conservative, whether spelt with a capital or lower case letter, values three things in education over all else – its setting within a vigorous and healthy culture, the experience of the past, and the supreme importance of the individual.

It is not easy, perhaps in the end quite impossible, to define culture, as anyone who has read T.S. Eliot's brave and persuasive attempt in *Notes towards the Definition of Culture* will recognize. For one thing, culture is always changing. When it ceases to change, it is dead. For another, it must not change too much too fast; if it does, its whole character will have gone. In the present, culture may well be, as Eliot suggested, 'simply that which makes life worth living'[1]; from the past it is in Arnold's phrase, 'the best which has been taught and said in the world'; for the future it must be, as he called it, a 'pursuit of our total perfection'.[2] Culture is not something that can be created or even improved by deliberate intent. It is organic; part of the essential life of the nation. Indeed, as Eliot pointed out, such well-meaning attempts to alter it can produce the very opposite effect: 'There is no doubt that in our headlong rush to educate everybody, we are lowering our standards, and more and more abandoning the study of those subjects by which the essentials of our culture ... are transmitted'.[3] The wrong sort of education at the wrong place can be the enemy of culture.

What, then, is the right sort of education? To begin at the beginning, 'the real purpose of educating a child is primarily moral and only secondarily secular'.[4] Education is about character and principles before intelligence and ideas. The former are the bedrock of the latter, and without them the latter are likely to produce quick wits and little else. Because this is so, the conservative is always anxious to place a proper value on things other than reason. If tradition provides the objective evidence, instinctual experience often supplies the subjective guarantee for the culture he is concerned to maintain and pass on. Thus it is also that education is more than training. It is concerned with the development of the whole man as man and not just as technician in the widest sense of that word. Such education must also, for the conservative, be set within the disciplined structures of past experience. It must produce the rounded man capable of standing on his own feet, capable of independent thinking, of being able to discern quality when he sees it and to reject the spurious substitute.

At the same time the conservative is careful to recognize the limits of the achievement that education in the formal sense can provide. He does not subscribe to the belief in the unmitigated value and efficacy of education. That is part of the myth that forms the Whig interpretation of history. It embodies the twin heresies of apparently unlimited progress and the perfectibility of man. Such a belief proceeds from excessive self-confidence, from the idea that we in the present know better than all our ancestors in the past. Mannheim put the contrast well when he wrote: 'Revolutionary thought derives its force from the desire to realise a rationally well-defined pattern of perfection of the social and political order. Conservative thought, opposed to the fulfilment of utopia, is forced to consider why the actually existing state of society fails to correspond to such a rational pattern'.[5] The idealist disinherits himself from the past and fails to make the most of the present. Because the actual is not perfect, he rejects it in favour of the untried which may be better but which, equally, may be worse. He is always the victim of hope triumphing over experience.

The conservative is not so optimistic. He is content to accept and, at most, cautiously to modify the actual. This may not be very exciting, but it is usually reliable. The conservative has learnt not to place too high hopes in humanity. Utopias have a habit of degenerating into corruption, revolutions into blood-baths and oppression. He does not find this surprising. Humanity's potentialities are limited; original sin is a powerful and persistent force. But whatever else may be said of him, the conservative is, at least, realistic. For him the attainable possible is better than the unattainable perfect. As Bishop Blougram put it in Browning's poem:

> The common problem, yours, mine, every one's
> Is not to fancy what were fair in life
> Provided it could be – but, finding first
> What may be, then find how to make it fair
> Up to our means – a very different thing!
> No abstract intellectual plan of life
> Quite irrespective of life's plainest laws,
> But one, a man, who is man and nothing more
> May lead within a world which (by your leave)
> Is Rome or London – not Fool's paradise.[6]

Such a limited objective may appear to accord ill with what I have said about culture as the study of perfection. Not at all. For as with the Christian doctrine of sanctification we must at once study the best and yet recognize frankly that, try as hard as we can and must, we shall never attain, only hopefully draw ever nearer.

This condition of moderate expectation is part of conservative realism, which recognizes humanity for what it is. To pursue the theological comparison a little further, this is the awareness of original sin, that man is always less than he might be, and the more so when he is considered in the mass, in society. 'The virtues of western society in modern times were in reality the product of much education, tradition and discipline; they needed centuries of patient cultivation. Even without great criminality in anybody – merely by forgetting certain safeguards – we could lose the tolerance and urbanities, the respect for human life and human personality, which are in reality the late blossoms of a highly developed civilization'.[7] It is a terrifying prospect, and just to confine himself to one area, the conservative recognizes the fragility of human institutions. He sees that they have been built up through long, patient and unceasing struggle, that they can so easily be subverted or overthrown and that to sustain them requires the proverbial eternal vigilance – and much more.

Progress consists in refining the past, not in disowning it. The conservative is therefore suspicious of change and innovation. Michael Oakeshott has put it better than I can: – 'A Conservative is a man particularly disposed towards a certain exactness or frugality in conduct ... He is not worried by the absence of innovation and is not inclined to think that nothing is happening unless great changes are afoot ... He perceives the loss in every change more readily than the gain ... He favours a slow tempo, and is averse from large or sudden changes which he considers to be unnecessarily extravagant. Decay he can often view with equanimity; what grieves him is the wanton dissipation of achievement'.[8] This is not fossilized inaction, it is not resistance against all change, but it is resistance against fundamental change – for several reasons.

First amongst these is, or should be, the religious basis of society. As Lord Hailsham expressed it, 'I can see no hope for secular society unless it be based upon a fundamental recognition of the spiritual nature of man and the providence of God'.[9] Unless man sees his purpose in life as involved in and subsumed under the all-embracing purposes of God, he is going to make himself the judge of all things and determine his attitude towards and relationship with his fellow-men in society without the restraining influences of a wider and a wiser view.

Second among the reasons for resisting fundamental change is the conservative's view of the state. It is an organic view, seeing the state as a body politic and not as some sort of machine. He is concerned not so much with the state as an organization as with the nation as a body of people. He is concerned with national character, with those qualities which have made the people what they are. Writing of Coleridge, J.S. Mill listed three requirements for the establishment and maintenance of human societies, namely, 'a system of *education* ... of which, whatever else it might include, one main and incessant ingredient was *restraining discipline*...; the feeling of allegiance or loyalty .... viz, that there be in the constitution of the State *something* which is settled, something permanent, and not to be called in question...; a strong and active principle of cohesion among the members of the same community or state..... a principle of sympathy, not of hostility; of union, not of separation.... a feeling of common interest'.[10]

Such prerequisites can be attained only by appeal to an accepted body of common belief, and this is the third reason why the conservative resists fundamental change. This explains his regard for tradition. Let me pursue a comparison with Coleridge. Wilfred Ward is writing of Newman: 'The philosophy which underlay his views was the philosophy of Coleridge. Like Coleridge he vindicated the claims of tradition as representing the thoughts of great minds and the revelation of Christ Himself. Tradition thus supplies the human race with knowledge not provable by the individual reason. The mind of the ages was an authority which the individual thinker had no right to set aside because he could not establish by his own demonstration what was really based on the experience and insight of many minds in the past. The corporate conviction which had its roots in past experience, and had stood the test of later experience, was an authoritative basis on which the individual thinker could work'.[11]

We come thus to the fourth reason, to the conservative's humility, to his horror at the presumption of those who believe so much in their own abilities that they would make radical changes. We are back to Mannheim. The revolutionary thinker, confident in his own powers of reason, dismisses what he regards as irrationalities; the conservative may well attribute to such phenomena 'the character of super-rationality'. And because of his humility, because he has so little confidence in the ability or reliability of individuals *per se*, the conservative places faith in tried and tested institutions. Above all, given what is said above, he recognizes the importance of the Church as an essential, perhaps the one essential, part of the establishment. Thus it was that Coleridge argued in *On the Constitution of the Church and State*. If the Church is not maintained and the citizens are not educated, the state will cease to exist. The Church not only symbolizes divinely-appointed authority, it is also the repository and transmitter of the national culture; and thus in this country the central importance of the Church of England. Its ethos and its values have not only penetrated the nation; they have done so because they have, at least until recently, informed the whole of our educational system. The signs of their decreasing influence are not a happy augury for the future.

The conservative looks to the past for wisdom. He does not rely on subjective and untested inspirations, however visionary these may seem. But he must nonetheless face the future like everybody else. With this organic view of society he sees history as a process of growth, decay and renewal. Renewal, be it noted, not innovation or even renovation. To achieve this there is no panacea: we do not move towards any utopia. The process must be pragmatic, finding at best *an* answer for current problems, not *the* answer to all or several. All experience tells us that life is a struggle, now advance and now retreat, and that even the latter can be creative in terms of character and wisdom. In approaching the future, the conservative begins by accepting what he regards as inevitable limitations. One of these is that we should not look to the state always to provide the solution. So often those who do this do so, it appears, either because they do not trust individuals or because they think in their self-appointed superiority that they know better, or because they combine both these views. Parents are not to be allowed to choose the ways and places in which they will educate their children. "Big Brother" knows best. Thus with terrifyingly totalitarian assumptions Professor Musgrove can write 'It is the business of education to eliminate the influence of parents on the life-chances of the young'.[12] The conservative rejects such views with abhorrence.

Another limitation which the conservative has always accepted, and which belatedly some of our latter-day utopians are now discovering, is that education cannot change society. There are, of course, those who would still try – with ever more desperate remedies, with ever more ingenious suggestions for restricting opportunity and restraining intelligence. If they are not grinding all down to some lowest common denominator of comprehensive education, they are, just to quote one of the crazier suggestions – that of Mr Howard Glennester in a Fabian pamphlet – advocating the application of a handicap to midldle-class children in public examinations. Education should not be a means of social engineering. Where it is, it will work less than efficiently and produce some crippling results. But, more important, people are not subjects simply for manipulation, not even if it is for their own good.

Education as social engineering cripples not least the academically brighter child. Conservatives cannot accept such a consequence, and as a result they are content in their realism to accept yet another limitation, namely, that men are not created equal, whatever those who use that word in this context may intend it to signify. We are all different and, whether we like it or not, some are more highly gifted than others. Even if the handicap I spoke of above were effective and even if, at some point, all men were alike, the result would be a temporary dull uniformity. Society would be at a disadvantage, for the best would be restrained; but even if this were so, it would not be so for long, because in the colloquial phrase, you can't hold a good man down. It is far better, then, to expand opportunity and to encourage talent than to hold some children back in the name of an inefficient egalitarianism.

The natural condition of man with his different abilities and inclinations makes equality impossible. It makes, too, for diversity. The health of society requires both hierarchy and variety. As Eliot has commented, 'No true democracy can maintain itself unless it contains these different levels of culture.... Complete equality means universal irresponsibility.... A democracy in which everybody had an equal responsibility in everything would be oppressive for the conscientious and licentious for the rest.'[13] This last phrase tells us much about the welfare-state with its emphasis on rights and provisions at the expense of responsibilities and duties. It also goes far towards explaining an important element in the egalitarian temper – the envious desire to level down. Dr Johnson saw it in the eighteenth century in the lady who wanted such to happen, but was outraged when it was suggested that the condition of her servants should be raised so that they might enjoy her own standard of life. Envy is not a respectable criterion. As Gregory Vlastos has remarked, 'The fact that envious people are made unhappy by an institution is no evidence of its injustice'.[14] Conservative realism confronts the inescapable recognition of class, not that it may try to circumvent the phenomenon but that it may be employed profitably within its social philosophy. To quote Eliot yet again, 'a people should be neither too united nor too divided, if its culture is to flourish. Excess of unity may be due to barbarism and may lead to tyranny; excess of division may be due to decadence and may also lead to tyranny'.[15]

A healthy society will manifest its tensions, but they must be kept within bounds. To this end the conservative prefers to encourage the individual rather than to repress him. He recognizes the limitations of political possibilities, especially as these tend in the main either to uniformity or oppression. Excessive intervention may, moreover, represent an indefensible intrusion upon the independence and integrity of the individual. Sir Isaiah Berlin put it well when he wrote 'To manipulate men, to propel them to goals which you – the social reformer – may see, but they may not, is to deny their human essence, to treat them as objects without wills of their own and therefore to degrade them'.[16]

This point is of especial importance in relation to what the conservative regards as one of the bulwarks of any civilized society – the family. That is why a remark such as that of Professor Musgrove quoted above cannot be other than anathema, not least because 'the primary vehicle for the transmission of culture is the family and ... to ensure the transmission of the culture of different levels there must be groups of families persisting, from generation to generation, each in the same way of life'.[17] It is in this respect, therefore, that the conservative places the highest emphasis upon the rights of parents to educate their children as they wish within the limits of their capacities. It is for this reason also that the conservative believes in the greatest possible variety of educational provision.

Of course, there will be those who say that such freedom is a denial of equality. Perhaps so. You cannot have freedom and equality: it must be one or the other, albeit with appropriate restraints. What is more, you cannot have equality at all for long. And freedom is so much more important. The argument for freedom is not against organization and control, but against exclusive overriding organization and control. It is important therefore that there should be freedom, even if only a minority is in a position to enjoy it. Without liberty there can be no responsibility. We are back to education being about moral beliefs and standards. That is why, as Hayek puts it, 'a successful free society will always in a large measure be a tradition-bound society'.[18] Or, in Tennyson's words, 'Freedom slowly broaden(ing) down from precedent to precedent'.

But there is another reason. Variety expands opportunity and, to quote Hayek again, 'the growth of civilization rests largely on the individuals' making the best use of whatever accidents they encounter, of the essentially unpredictable advantages that one kind of knowledge will in new circumstances confer on one individual over others'.[19] I should have said 'another two reasons', namely, the opportunity for the individual – and the consequent good for society which flows from his seeing and grasping that opportunity. 'In a healthy society this maintenance of a particular level of culture is to the benefit, not merely of the class which maintains it, but of the society as a whole. Awareness of this fact will prevent us from supposing that the culture of a "higher" class is something superfluous to society as a whole, or to the majority, and from supposing that it is something which ought to be shared equally by all other classes.'[20] The stress on individualism, therefore, does not mean, in Arnold's phrase, doing what one likes. As he was careful to emphasize in distinguishing the two conditions named in the title of *Culture and Anarchy*, doing what one likes leads only to the latter. The individual will only make the most of his opportunities when these are developed within the framework and discipline of an inherited culture.

We come therefore to the question of standards and the role of élites. Without élites you cannot have standards. 'You can have equality; you can have culture; but you cannot have both'.[21] But you can have democracy and culture. As Mannheim realized, there can be 'a democratic optimum of the élite-mass relationship which falls far short of the complete disappearance of the élite. An optimum need not be a maximum; if democracy involves an anti-élitist trend, this need not go all the way to a utopian levelling of all distinction between leaders and led'.[22] But try, if you can, to ensure that your élite is a proper one, both in intelligence and character. This, however, cannot be a matter of deliberate legislative enactment which can only produce a bogus élite. Élites belong to culture, to a way of life; and through the accumulated wisdom of the ages they are self-generating and self-perpetuating. But what the politician cannot improve he may yet go a long way towards destroying. That is another reason why the conservative is suspicious of so-called state provision and prefers to encourage the initiative of the individual.

The existence of standards is the opening for opportunity, the opportunity to strive. There is nothing easy about this. If the standards are there, there should also be the encouragement to emulate. This gives scope at once for the response to social expectations and the fulfilment of individual potentialities. Only by such striving and competition shall we be able to maintain the highest standards. This too is a further argument for variety in educational provision. Moreover, the presence of superior quality itself acts as a pace-setter to the rest. The sharpness of competition is a necessary element in any healthy society.

In our own society there are vast and ruthless forces massed against the individual. There are the forces of the state which the conservative believes should be kept to a minimum. He considers that the state exists for the individual, and not the other way round. He thinks, therefore, that education and culture should make for the fullest and freest development of the human personality consistent with life in society. The task of education and culture should be to help men to become self-reliant so that they may enjoy an ordered liberty, fulfil their responsibilities freely and keep themselves safe from the malign influences that beset them. These latter include such forces as those of the mass media with their insistent pressures towards a mindless and materialistic conformity. But men must *be* self-reliant; there are as many dangers in over-protection as in no protection at all. What a man does and what a man thinks, these things he must do and think as a free and consenting member of society. He must be conscious of his moral freedom, acting within a tradition of moral behaviour.

Given what I have said, the conservative believes, in sum, that the culture of a society is what primarily matters and that this is as much moral as intellectual, probably more so. Education in the formal sense is subsidiary to culture, and will only be valuable in proportion as it accommodates itself to, and helps to promote, this culture by an appropriate regard for the inherited traditions of the society which it serves. To this extent the values of the church and the family will be more reliable than any which the state may seek to impose by whatever means. To that end, therefore, the needs of the individual must be paramount over those of the state. A vital culture can survive only through variety of provision, the proper maintenance of standards and the nurture of those groups who are their guardians.

Notes

1. T.S. Eliot, *Notes Towards the Definition of Culture* (Faber, 1948), p. 27.
2. Matthew Arnold, *Culture and Anarchy* (Murray, 1935), p. viii.
3. Eliot, op. cit., p. 108.
4. Q. Hogg, *The Case for Conservatism* (Penguin, 1947), p. 145.
5. Karl Mannheim, *Conservative Thought*, 1927, p. 147.
6. My attention was drawn to this quotation by Angus Maude's use of it as the epigraph to his book, *The Common Problem* (Constable, 1969), to which I owe more than this borrowing.
7. Sir Herbert Butterfield, *Christianity and History* (Bell, 1949), p. 31.
8. Michael Oakeshott, *The Spectator*, 11 October 1954.
9. *The Case for Conservatism*, op. cit., p. 18.
10. *Mill on Bentham and Coleridge*, ed. F.R. Leavis (Chatto, 1950), pp. 121-4.
11. J.H. Newman, *On the Scope and Nature of University Education* (Everyman, 1915), pp. xvii-xviii (introduction by W.P. Ward).
12. Frank Musgrove, *The Family, Education and Society* (Routledge, 1966), p. 135.
13. Eliot, op. cit., p. 48.
14. Gregory Vlastos, "Justice and Equality" in *Social Justice*, ed. R.B. Brandt (Prentice Hall, 1962).
15. Eliot, op. cit., p. 50.
16. Sir Isaiah Berlin, *Four Essays on Liberty* (Oxford University Press, 1969), p. 137.
17. Eliot, op. cit., p. 48.
18. F.A. Hayek, *The Constitution of Liberty* (Routledge, 1960), p. 61.
19. Ibid.
20. Eliot, op. cit., p. 35.
21. T.S. Eliot to G.H. Bantock in G.H. Bantock, *T.S. Eliot and Education* (Faber, 1970), p. 78.
22. Karl Mannheim, *Essays on the Sociology of Culture* (Routledge, 1956), p. 200.